Alan Quirk

Obstacles to Shared Decision-Making in Psychiatric Practice

December 2015

Dear Zoe

Good luck with your

finals!

Alan x

Alan Quirk

Obstacles to Shared Decision-Making in Psychiatric Practice

Findings from three qualitative, observational studies

LAP LAMBERT Academic Publishing

Impressum / Imprint
Bibliografische Information der Deutschen Nationalbibliothek: Die Deutsche Nationalbibliothek verzeichnet diese Publikation in der Deutschen Nationalbibliografie; detaillierte bibliografische Daten sind im Internet über http://dnb.d-nb.de abrufbar.

Bibliographic information published by the Deutsche Nationalbibliothek: The Deutsche Nationalbibliothek lists this publication in the Deutsche Nationalbibliografie; detailed bibliographic data are available in the Internet at http://dnb.d-nb.de.

Coverbild / Cover image: www.ingimage.com

Verlag / Publisher:
LAP LAMBERT Academic Publishing
ist ein Imprint der / is a trademark of
OmniScriptum GmbH & Co. KG
Heinrich-Böcking-Str. 6-8, 66121 Saarbrücken, Deutschland / Germany
Email: info@lap-publishing.com

Herstellung: siehe letzte Seite /
Printed at: see last page
ISBN: 978-3-659-75227-8

Table of contents

Acknowledgements

First and foremost, I would like to express my gratitude to the many hundreds of service users and NHS and local authority staff who made this research possible but who must remain anonymous.

I gratefully acknowledge the support of the funders of the three studies reported in this book: the Department of Health (for the Mental Health Act Study), Eli Lilly (for the Prescribing Decisions Project), and Dr Jim Birley (a former President of the Royal College of Psychiatrists, whose generous personal donation to the College's research unit was used to fund the Acute Ward Ethnography).

I owe an enormous debt of gratitude to my supervisor, Professor Clive Seale, who was inspiring throughout, and whose incisive comments have kept me on track. He offered me just the type of kind encouragement I needed to complete the task. I am also particularly grateful to Dr Paul Lelliott, my director at the Royal College of Psychiatrists' Research and Training Unit. He will know that this book simply would not have been possible without the support, encouragement, and insights he has provided me with over many years.

I have been inspired by other outstanding academics earlier in my research career, particularly Professor Gerry Stimson, director of the Centre for Research on Drugs and Health Behaviour, where I worked between 1991 and 1998, and Professor David Silverman, under whose tutelage I obtained my Masters degree from Goldsmiths' College in 1997. I remain very grateful to both of them. I would also like to thank Professor Lindsay Prior and Dr Timothy Malewa, for their exceptionally helpful comments on an earlier version of this manuscript.

Others have made helpful comments and suggestions that have contributed to the book: Les Back, Rob Chaplin, Chris Fitch, Neil Hamer, Sarah Hamilton, Ian Hutchby, Julia Jones, Sarah Mars, Jim McCambridge, Nikolas Rose and John Witton. Many thanks also to those who helped me with the proof reading, including Cathy Pettinari and others already mentioned.

I owe a very special thank you to my partner, Lizzie, for the love and support she has given me from day one. I am also eternally grateful to my Dad and my late Mum, who would have been so pleased to see me complete this book.

Chapter 1

Introduction

CONTENTS

1.1 Overview

This book presents findings from three discrete research projects, undertaken over a seven-year period while I worked as a Research Fellow at the Royal College of Psychiatrists' Research Unit. The studies are listed below.

(1) Prescribing Decisions Project: A conversation analysis study of how decisions about long-term anti-psychotic prescribing are negotiated in outpatient consultations.

(2) Acute Ward Ethnography: An ethnographic study aimed at understanding what everyday life on an acute psychiatric ward is like, from the patient's point of view.

(3) Mental Health Act (MHA) Study: An ethnographic study aimed at understanding (i) how MHA assessments are conducted, and (ii) the roles and experiences of participants.

Together, the three studies constitute a programme of qualitative, observational research into how decisions are made in psychiatric practice. As a health service researcher and paid employee of the Royal College, my priority was to address social problems and offer recommendations on how to improve service provision. Writing this book has given me the opportunity to rework the materials and refocus the analysis in order to address sociological questions that were not formulated until quite late on in the programme. The resulting account is, I believe, unique in that it compares how the same mental health professionals and service users interact in some of the many psychiatric settings in which they may encounter one another; namely, routine outpatient consultations, acute psychiatric wards (including the ward rounds held on them) and assessments for compulsory admission to hospital. In turn, this allows these one-off encounters to be understood in the context of the longer-term doctor-patient relationship in 'deinstitutionalised' mental healthcare, as practiced in the U.K. at around the turn of the 21st century.

Shared decision-making is characterised by the involvement of at least two participants (doctor and patient), information sharing by both parties, consensus-building about the preferred treatment, and the reaching of an explicit agreement on the treatment to be implemented (Charles *et al*, 1997). Little is known about the use of shared decision-making in everyday psychiatric practice or about the obstacles to its diffusion in this field of medicine. By examining how psychiatric decisions are made in both routine consultations and crisis situations, this book adds knowledge about how shared decision-making is accomplished and the conditions in which it is possible.

1.2 Aims

This book aims to make contributions at three levels. First, the findings from the three qualitative, observational studies are combined to identify obstacles to the use of shared decision-making in modern psychiatric practice. Second, at a methodological level the book aims to produce a coherent, unified research account from two very different versions of qualitative inquiry; namely, conversation analysis (CA) and ethnography. And third, an attempt is made at a theoretical level to combine Erving Goffman's micro-sociology with Michel Foucault's analyses of disciplinary power/knowledge in order to create a sound theoretical base for research. The key content of the chapters is summarised below.

1.3 Chapter summaries

Chapter 2 reviews some key texts by Goffman and Foucault, and argues that observational researchers can draw important lessons from both of them. Goffman's work provides the theoretical base for this book, but it is strengthened in three main ways. First, where available, naturally-occurring data are examined using CA methods, thus revealing a new level of skill in how people conduct themselves in psychiatric interactions. Second, Foucault's concept of disciplinary power/knowledge is used to reveal the subtle form of control through expertise that would be missed in a purely Goffmanian study. And third, Foucauldian thinking is applied to add a historical, 'macro' dimension that Goffman's work so conspicuously lacks.

Chapter 3 reviews relevant research literature, covering the rise of patient-centred medicine in Western healthcare systems, decision-making in medical settings, the nature of contemporary psychiatric practice, and the 'elephant in the room' in psychiatric encounters – the underlying threat of compulsion. Also reviewed is the literature relating to acute inpatient care and compulsory admissions. Both are healthcare contexts in which the whole notion of shared decision-making is problematic because (a) the patient's ability to make rational decisions is often explicitly in question, and (b) the underlying threat of compulsion is typically much harder for participants to 'ignore' than would be in a routine outpatient consultation.

Chapter 4 describes the three studies' methods and settings, and how the data were analysed. The various methods used to enhance the credibility of the findings are discussed. The chapter concludes with a lengthy 'confessional tale' about the anxiety I experienced while undertaking fieldwork on acute psychiatric wards. This has been included to show how some of the central claims in the book emerged and to offer readers further material with which to evaluate the trustworthiness of the account.

Chapters 5 & 6 hold the findings from the Prescribing Decisions Project. The former chapter presents an analysis of how pressure is applied in 'negotiated' decisions about medication, and the latter chapter examines communication about adherence to long-term anti-psychotic prescribing. The next two chapters present findings from the Acute Ward Ethnography, which examined interactions in a healthcare context in which the threat of compulsion is typically much more overt than it is in the outpatient consultation. The study's central claim is made in *Chapter 7*, it being that today's acute psychiatric wards are better understood as permeable institutions rather than closed or 'total' institutions. *Chapter 8* examines an aspect of lay/professional interaction occurring in such 'permeable' institutions – patients' methods of non-cooperation and resistance in ward round decisions. *Chapter 9* presents findings from the MHA Study on how assessments for compulsory admission to psychiatric hospital are made, this being a context in which the ideal of shared decision-making can seem very remote. Throughout the findings chapters, particular attention is paid to how patients' choices about their treatment are facilitated or constrained by the actions of mental health professionals.

Chapter 10 summaries the findings and offers typologies of pressure and non-cooperation, constructed on the basis of detailed empirical evidence from the three studies. Implications of the research for psychiatric practice, research methodology and sociological theory are discussed, as are the limitations of this work.

Chapter 2

Theoretical background

CONTENTS

This chapter attempts to establish an adequate theoretical base for the sociological study of communication in psychiatric settings. Particular attention will be paid to the works of Goffman and Foucault, and it will be argued that observational researchers can draw important lessons from both of them. I also review others' attempts at combining aspects of their work as theoretical background for research. The chapter concludes with an outline and rationale for the theoretical base adopted in this book. The research literature pertaining to shared decision-making in psychiatric practice is reviewed in the following chapter.

2.1 Goffman: the interaction order

2.1.1 Overview

Erving Goffman (1922-1982) announced at the end of his career:

> "My concern over the years has been to promote acceptance of [the] face-to-face domain as an analytically viable one – a domain which might be titled, for want of any happy name, the *interaction order* – a domain whose preferred method is micro-analysis." (Goffman, 1983, p. 2)

Goffman's view was that this domain of activity is something that can be studied *in its own right*, and his primary aim was to begin to unravel the procedures employed by people in their dealings with each other. His principal concern therefore was with social interaction, which he defined as that which uniquely transpires in social situations; that is environments in which two or more individuals are physically in one another's response presence (Goffman, 1983). Goffman's contention is that much of what goes on in face-to-face interaction is relatively independent of the wider social structures within which interaction can be located; that the organisation of interaction arises largely from the interactional circumstances themselves. Most fundamentally, this arises from the fact of people being physically present together in the same place, within range of one another's observation and communication. Hence the view that Goffman was above all the theorist of co-presence, not of small groups (Giddens, 1988), and one who was mostly concerned with the 'grammar and syntax' of social interaction; that is, the numerous and elaborate rules that govern conduct in social interaction and maintain orderliness most of the time.

As Williams (1988) summarises, the key to the interaction order for Goffman is through understanding that it is a *ritual* order. For example, in his first book, *The Presentation of Self in Everyday Life* (Goffman, 1959), the general perspective is that social behaviour is essentially communicative and that individuals are continuously communicating self-impressions. Goffman argues that when an individual enters into the presence of others, he or she commonly seeks to acquire information about that person (e.g. about their competence and trustworthiness), and this can be found in the smallest detail of speech, tone, posture or dress. Such information, and that which is known beforehand about the individual, helps to *define the situation*, enabling others to know in advance what this individual will expect of them (Goffman, 1959). So when a person projects a definition of the situation and therefore makes a claim to be a person of a particular kind within it, a *moral demand* is made of others, obliging them to value and treat him or her in the manner persons of that kind have the right to expect.

According to Goffman we communicate in two radically different ways: through expressions that are given, and expressions that are *given off* (Goffman, 1959). The first is communication in the "traditional and narrow sense"; that is, the use by the individual of verbal symbols or their substitutes for the admitted and sole purpose of conveying the information that the actor and the 'audience' are known to attach to these symbols. The second involves a wide range of action that others can treat as symptomatic of the actor – the non-verbal, presumably unintentional kind. For Goffman it is through our knowledge of the second type of communication that social interaction becomes a 'game' in which people have 'strategies' and make 'moves'.

While Goffman's conceptualisation of interactional conduct may be viewed in instrumental terms (i.e. that our actions are purely a means to the end of achieving favourable self-impressions), it is one in which the notion of ritual is central. Giddens (1988) notes that there is a persistent misunderstanding about the nature of the actors portrayed in Goffman's writings: the view that "actors are mere performers, who constitute an amoral universe through their concern to pander to their own vanities by presenting themselves in a false and manipulative fashion". But, as Giddens rightly points out, this interpretation is far removed from the main thrust in his work, which is to emphasise the fundamental importance of *trust* and *tact* in binding social interaction, wherein *collaboration* between parties (e.g. helping the other to 'save face') is essential. As will be seen, this aspect of interaction is important for understanding how people behave in psychiatric settings.

In the *Presentation of Self in Everyday Life*, Goffman (1959) analysed how people sustain creditable selves in normally-problematic situations of everyday life; that is, while interacting with others who are willing and able to collaborate in sustaining mutually acceptable self-definitions, and in circumstances where the price of failing to do so is perhaps no more than embarrassment. However, in his next book, *Asylums: Essays on the Social Situation of Mental Patients and Other Inmates* (Goffman, 1961), the focus shifts to situations in which the self comes under deliberate and sustained assault.

2.1.2 'Asylums'

In perhaps Goffman's most influential book, *Asylums* (Goffman, 1961), it is argued that U.S. state mental hospitals of that time were examples of a 'total institution'. His aims were to identify the “underlying structural design” of such ‘closed’ institutions (others include the army and prisons), and to describe how inmates adjust to their new life within them. One characteristic of the total institution is a basic split between staff and the managed group (patients/inmates), the distancing between which maintains antagonistic stereotypes. According to Goffman, this distancing means that two social worlds develop, "jogging alongside each other, with points of official contact but little mutual penetration" (ibid).

New inmates are subjected to numerous “assaults on the self” which have a demoralizing effect (Goffman, 1961). Direct assaults which ‘mortify’ or ‘curtail’ the self include ‘role dispossession’ (people lose the social roles they had before admission, such as their occupational status); the stripping of possessions (reinforced by the failure to provide inmates with lockers); the loss of ‘identity equipment’, which prevents the individual from presenting his or her usual self to others (e.g. via clothes, make up, other status symbols); loss of sense of personal safety; and forced interpersonal contact and forced social relationships, characterised by limited control of information about the self. Indirect assaults include the subjection of patient activity to regulations and judgements by staff; the disruption of even the most minor activities due to the obligation to seek permission or supplies from staff; and the loss of bodily comforts, such as quietness at night.

Goffman viewed the mental hospital as being unique among total institutions, because it left inmates with no possibility for distancing themselves from their prescribed institutional role as a mental patient. Inmates are robbed of the "common expressions through which people hold off the embrace of organisations", such as insolence, silence and 'backchat', because the meaning of those acts is transformed from the defiance the inmate wishes to display, albeit cautiously, into mere symptoms of sickness and confirmation of inmate status (Goffman, 1961, p.306; see also Rosenhan, 1973). Nonetheless, Goffman observes, patients managed to 'make out' while in hospital, engaging in activities that constitute the hospital's 'underlife'. These activities include attempts to 'work the system' (e.g. using group therapy sessions to meet patients of the opposite sex), and the development of 'stashes' when private storage areas were not allowed (Goffman, 1961).

Like his contemporary Michel Foucault, whose work will be discussed shortly, Goffman wrote about institutional surveillance, but he did so from a very different perspective.[1] He describes in great detail how inmates actively *avoided surveillance* in total institutions, either to allow them to engage openly in tabooed activities, such as gambling or drinking alcohol, or purely to obtain relief from surveillance and the noise of the place, in a kind of safe haven (Goffman, 1961). He invented the term *surveillance space* to describe where individuals are subject to the usual authority and

[1] Goffman's focus is on external surveillance by others (i.e. staff) and how inmates avoid it, whereas Foucault focuses on self-surveillance (see section 2.2 below).

regulation, and where resistance must be "veiled" or disguised – otherwise the inmate lays him- or herself open to the risk of being punished. He also invented the concept of *free space*, which is defined as space where ordinary levels of surveillance and restriction are markedly reduced, for example in hospital grounds, where individuals can to some extent be the person they were before being admitted to the institution (ibid).

Less dramatic than the process of stripping inmates of all their social roles and privileges but equally stained morally is the process leading to hospitalisation, including detention under mental health legislation. In the moral career of the mental patient (Goffman, 1961), Goffman describes powerfully the "betrayal funnel" pre-patients are drawn through, at the end of which they retrospectively discover that while they were cooperating with others so as to spare them embarrassment or pain, those others were stripping them of their civilian rights. Further, discovering that those with whom they had intimate personal relations could no longer be assumed to be trustworthy means that they have betrayed them (ibid).

The introduction to Chapter 7 provides further discussion of *Asylums*. This short section will have conveyed the continuing relevance of Goffman's analytical concepts in the sociological study of psychiatric practice. The book draws extensively on Goffmanian concepts, albeit modified in their application to a modern setting.

2.1.3 Goffman's dialogue with CA

This book also makes extensive use of methods of conversation analysis (CA). This distinctive approach for analysing communication stands on the bedrock of sequencing (see Chapter 4). Some regard CA as building upon Goffman's work.

> "[Conversation analysis] can be seen, variously, as following [Goffman's] path, or further developing it, or exploring what it might entail and how, or transforming it." (Schegloff, 1988)

Goffman's early work certainly anticipated and helped shape the development of what subsequently came to be called 'conversation analysis' (Giddens, 1988). Goffman argues that if sociology is to have a contribution to make in the analysis of talk, and to "compete in this heretofore literary and psychological area", then sociolinguistics must find a structural means of doing such analysis (Goffman, 1981a). While sharing this concern with CA, Goffman makes his central point; namely that there is more to conversation than its sequential organisation – it is *ritually* organised too.

In *Replies and Responses* (Goffman, 1981) Goffman argues that an account of communication must extend beyond the formal procedures through which we exchange 'messages' – the approach of the "communication sounds engineer" (ibid, p.14). His view is that the model of communication presented by CA is one of *system* requirements and constraints; these referring to the context-free, physical constraints of any communication system, such as concerns with the distribution of turns and with evidence that the messages are getting across (ibid, p.15). As Schegloff acknowledges, many of CA's concerns are included here (Schegloff, 1988).

Goffman characteristically draws attention to, and places emphasis upon, the importance of ritual, his argument being that ritual considerations – such as forms of ritual restoration of 'face' – also have explanatory power in the analysis of conversation. He observes that while system constraints might be conceived of as pan-cultural:

> "… ritual concerns are patently dependent on cultural definition and can vary quite markedly from society to society. Nonetheless, the ritual frame provides [for the analyst] a question that can be asked of anything occurring during talk and a way of accounting for what does occur." (Goffman, 1981, p.17)

In what he terms "ritual interchanges", speakers not only convey information, they also attend to the *"social acceptance"* of what they are saying; that is, whether or not it is compatible with the recipient's view of the speaker and themselves (ibid, p.18). And, once again, Goffman emphasises that the very structure of social contact, such as perfunctory service exchanges at a supermarket checkout, can quite routinely involve physical as opposed to verbal (or gestural) moves, and "such words as do get spoken are fitted into a sequence that follows a non-talk design" (ibid, p.38). Goffman also emphasises that the social setting of talk (e.g. hospital or an outpatient consultation) not only can provide for 'context' it can also penetrate into, and determine, the very structure of interaction (ibid, pp.53-54).

In assessing Goffman's dialogue with CA, Silverman (1985) argues that it is nearly impossible, given the limited systematisation in Goffman's work, to provide a "balance-sheet" of the relative merits of Goffman's emphasis on culturally-defined rituals and CA's concern with formal rules of sequencing talk. However, Schegloff (1988) argues that Goffman's view that ritual should be at the heart of interaction studies, and that the system is somehow pre-sociological, is mistaken. Schegloff's view is that by having "ritual" at the heart of sociology in studying interaction, Goffman is more interested in the individual and his or her psychology that the syntax of actions across individuals (ibid).

For this writer, the question over which should be prioritised in the study of talk – system or ritual – remains open. However, I agree with reservations expressed about Goffman's methodology, specifically those referring to the *status of the data* used in his texts, which include not only materials derived from real-time observation, but also newspaper clippings, vignettes and invented examples. Schegloff rightly notes that Goffman's texts rarely give "puzzling data", actions that have not been solved, and argues that what is required for an account of "how it is in interaction actually" is the capacity, in principle, to analyse *any* spate of talk, not just those which are useful for illustrative purposes (ibid). These methodological issues will be discussed further in Chapter 4. Here, I limit my point to agreeing with Schegloff, who argues that while Goffman's use of materials was highly effective in identifying what must be the central domain for the social sciences (the interaction order), different data may be required to actually find it; that is, detailed transcripts of naturally occurring interaction (ibid, p.132).

I will now briefly consider an exemplary CA study (see Box 2.1) in order to illustrate how a CA approach to doctor-patient interaction differs from Goffman's interactionist approach.

Box 2.1: Sequential organisation of embarrassment in medical examinations

Heath's (1986; 1988) research was concerned with visual and vocal behaviour between the doctor and patient, the analysis of which was based on a substantial number of video recordings of naturally-occurring medical consultations. Heath argues that while Goffman's work on embarrassment is extremely valuable in directing analytic attention to this phenomenon, its focus on ritual aspects and the problems of self and identity and impression management *conceals its sequentially organised nature.* Heath's research is thus a good example of research into communication in medical settings that combines the insights of Goffman with the methodological rigour of CA. Further, it indicates that the thrust of Goffman's argument about the need for understanding of both talk and non-verbal behaviour was well taken by at least some CA researchers (Silverman, 1985; Heritage & Maynard, 2007).

Goffman (1959) had examined embarrassment in relation to the interactional nature of the self and identity within the framework of situations and face-to-face encounters, arguing that embarrassment arises "if expressive facts threaten or discredit the assumptions a participant has projected about his identity": colloquially, when you have been 'found out'. However, Heath argues using such an analytic framework would conceal the actual conduct of participants. Heath's research shows, I believe convincingly, that embarrassment consists of actions and activities that are systematically organised by the participants, and that embarrassment emerges in relation to specific action produced by a co-participant (Heath, 1989, p.154). By investigating the sequential organisation of vocal and non-vocal activities, Heath found that there is a "precarious balance" in the way that participants attend to each other during the physical examination and that this can easily be upset. A prime example of this was where a doctor attempted to retain the patient's involvement as a fully-fledged participant throughout the encounter, rather than as someone who is seemingly disattentive during the breast examination, through adopting a "middle-distance" orientation, accomplished by turning to one side and slightly lowering eyelids.

Heath welcomes the growing interest in training general practitioners in communication skills and, in particular, in encouraging doctors to develop rapport and adopt a more informal approach during the consultation (discussed further in the following chapter). The contribution of his research is to invite consideration of the *local production* of the phenomenon of embarrassment and to show precisely how consultations need to be handled if it is to be avoided. Further, Heath's findings indicate the need to investigate how patient participation is actually *done*, because it may take very different forms and is not always be wanted by the patient.

By focussing on the interaction order, and treating it as analytically distinct, Goffman and his CA successors often seem to exclude the impact of forces and variables beyond the frame of the situation at hand. Goffman was well aware of this point and was ready to pre-empt criticism. For example, in the introduction to *Frame Analysis* (Goffman, 1986), one of his later works, he makes the limits of his endeavour very clear:

> "This book is about the organisation of experience – something that an individual can take into his mind – and not the organisation of society. I make no claim whatsoever to be talking about the core matters of sociology – social organisation and social structure. Those matters have been and can continue to be quite nicely studied without reference to

> frame at all. I am not addressing the structure of social life but the structure of experience individuals have at any moment in their social lives." (Goffman, 1986, p.13)

We can only speculate on whether Goffman's candour was a 'move' to blunt the criticism of his liberal and radical colleagues, whose concern was the way in which the core 'facts' of macro-sociology determines one's access to the resources of interaction (Berger, 1986). But if we are to remove the "brackets" that Goffman put around his own work (Giddens, 1988), how might we proceed?

A fruitful way forward, I believe, is to consider how best to draw upon the work of Michel Foucault. In the following section I begin doing this by presenting some of Foucault's main ideas and then discuss how they compare with those bequeathed by Goffman. It will be argued, in section 2.3, that both sets of concepts, or theories, offer something distinctly valuable to any researcher seeking to undertake an observational study of modern psychiatric practice.

2.2 Foucault: disciplinary power/ knowledge

2.2.1 Overview

At around the time when Goffman commented on his life's work (to promote acceptance of the interaction order as a viable domain of enquiry), Foucault (1926-1984) summarised his own:

> "… the goal of my work during the last twenty years has not been to analyze the phenomena of power, nor to elaborate the foundations of such an analysis. My objective, instead, has been to create a history of the different modes by which, in our culture, human beings are made subjects." (Foucault, 1982, p.208)

Foucault's method for analysing how new kinds of people come to be at particular times, was to analyse 'discourses' of the past, thus revealing taken-for-granted, present-day strategies of power and manipulation. Underlying these analyses was a new conceptualisation of power which, Foucault claims, is unique to modern Western societies. The brilliant originality of the idea can be lost today, but it should be remembered that prior to Foucault power was commonly understood to be a repressive force that imposes a limit on behaviour and reality. Foucault's contribution, in his books on madness (1967), prison (1977) and sexuality (1981), was to show that power it is not simply imposed on people and, in fact, it is more often invited in.

Foucault's thesis is that there has been a shift from the repressive model of power (sovereign power) in pre-modern societies, to a disciplinary, creative form of power in modern societies:

> "We must cease once and for all to describe the effects of power in negative terms: it 'excludes', it 'represses', it 'censors', it 'masks', it 'conceals'. In fact, power produces; it produces reality; it produces domains of objects and rituals of truth." (Foucault, 1977, p.194)

In *Discipline and Punish,* Foucault (1977) famously offers the metaphor of the Panopticon, with an architectural design that induces inmates to act as if surveillance was constant, in order to convey how social control may be achieved automatically, economically, and without the need for direct forms of coercion (Foucault, 1977). Foucault argues that the success of disciplinary power derives from the simultaneous use of three simple instruments or techniques of person production, each of which intensifies the effect of the other two. These techniques are discussed below.

"Hierarchical observation" refers to the sites where individuals can be observed, such as hospitals, schools and factories. They are designed in such a way as to facilitate observation of those within it. The old simple arrangement of confinement and enclosure – thick walls and a heavy gate to prevent people from entering or leaving – began to be replaced by the "calculation of openings, of filled and empty spaces, passages and transparencies" (ibid, p.172). The source of power in the Panopticon lay in the fact that guards had, if they wanted it, total surveillance, which induced inmates to watch over themselves (self surveillance): the effect of the Panopticon was "to induce in the inmate a state of conscious and permanent visibility that ensures the *automatic* functioning of power" (emphasis added, ibid, p.201). It is also a "laboratory of humans" in that it can be used as a machine to carry out experiments, generate scientific knowledge, alter behaviour and train or correct individuals (ibid, p.203). It was thus, as Foucault puts it, "A superb formula: power exercised continuously for what turns out to be minimal cost".

"Normalizing judgement" refers to the fact that the actions and attributes of each individual are compared with the actions of others. Individuals are assessed and measured, which permits a *norm* to be established. There are numerous judges of normality, such as psychiatrists, social workers and nurses.

> "Like surveillance and with it, normalization becomes one of the great instruments of power at the end of the classical age... In a sense the power of normalization imposes homogeneity; but it individualizes by making it possible to measure gaps, to determine levels, to fix specialities and to render the differences useful by fitting them one to another." (ibid, p.184)

Supervision in a factory, for example, is both individual and general – the quality of work and application of individual workers can be *compared* (individual supervision) while the production line can be observed as a whole (general supervision). Discipline creates fixed positions (ranks or grades) and permits circulation between them. A rank is thus the place an individual occupies in a classification (ibid, p.145). Knowledge of bodies is produced within these institutions and this has contributed to medical science (discussed below).

"The examination" is the third instrument of disciplinary power, which combines the other two instruments described above. Through the examination, the individual can be assessed, classified and corrected. Examinations generate epidemiological data, which allow *standards* to be generated against which individuals can be assessed.

Foucault's central insight was to co-implicate the development of modern medical and social sciences, such as psychiatry and sociology, with the development of disciplinary power. The key to his analysis is the demographic upswing of the C18th and C19th. The argument goes that as capitalism matured and new cities rapidly developed, a crisis of urban control emerged which led to the need to regulate the population. New forms of knowledge about people developed - that of people as objects to be counted and monitored, or, to use Foucault's word, *surveyed*. Statistics became a crucially important discipline. The 'body' (of individuals and populations) bore new variables, and within a whole series of institutions – asylums, hospitals, prisons and so on – bodies were examined and information processed about them. This, Foucault points out, is a process that is unique to modern societies.

In various detailed case studies ('genealogies' or 'archaeologies'), Foucault shows how disciplines of knowledge developed with the aims of predicting and controlling the behaviour of individuals and to provide the state with information to control and monitor these individuals. Foucault's term 'disciplinary power' is a play on words. The new academic 'disciplines' such as psychiatry and medicine, were also 'disciplines' in that they prescribed how people should act and behave, and *established norms of behaviour* which they could enforce. The new disciplines established the 'scientific' criteria by which we distinguish categories of people, such as the sane, the insane, the sick, and so on (Foucault, 1967). The critical twist Foucault gave to the Orwellian nightmare of a world in which people are controlled by external technologies of surveillance, was to visualise a world in which social control is achieved through normalisation and *self*-surveillance; that is, control is located in our subjective realities through the internalisation of scientific concepts of 'health' and 'normality'. To convey the idea that the power to define normality is derived from, and is synonymous with, expert knowledge, Foucault invented the concept of 'power/knowledge': the idea being that professional groups have developed whose claim is both to understand human beings (knowledge), and to prescribe to them how to act (power). Foucault thus draws attention to a more subtle, invidious form of power than the repression and associated external surveillance technologies documented by Goffman; namely the *creative* power of the human sciences, derived from their capacity to define what is normal, and thus to outline the borders beyond which deviance occurs.

Disciplinary institutions, such as the old asylums, tended to function by confinement, relying on enclosure and visual (Panoptic) surveillance for their successful operation. According to Cahill, such institutions remain the settings in which technological control of the person production process is today most obvious (Cahill, 1998). Foucault's argument, though, is that the functioning of this new form of power has spread from the laboratories in which its exercise was perfected (the enclosed, disciplinary institutions) to the whole social body, creating the 'disciplinary society' (Foucault, 1977, p.209). For example, there has been what later writers have termed the 'psychiatrisation of everyday life' (Castel *et al*, 1982) in which the growth of 'psy' technologies, especially psychology, has had a key role in reshaping the practices of those who exercise power over others, such as social workers, teachers and nurses (Rose, 1998; 1999).

2.2.2 'Madness and Civilisation'

Madness and Civilisation first appeared in French in 1961,[2] in the year when *Asylums* was published. Foucault's objective was to return to that "zero point in the course of madness" at which madness is an

[2] It was entitled *Histoire de la Folie.*

undifferentiated experience. The book addresses the question of the historical conditions of emergence in the course of C17th of a distinction between reason and unreason, reason and madness. It also examines the conditions of possibility for the emergence and development of the human sciences of psychiatry and psychology and analyses the decline of the old regime of institutional confinement and the birth of the asylum at the end of the C18th (Foucault, 1967). Foucault argues, convincingly, that the nature of observation of inmates changed with the move from classical confinement to the moral treatment given in the asylum. In classical confinement, observation only involved an individual's "monstrous surface and visible animality", while in the asylum the madman became directly involved in observation, and was obliged to objectify himself in the eyes of reason (self-surveillance) (ibid). Mental illness must be understood not as a natural fact but as a cultural construct, sustained by a grid of administrative and medico-psychiatric practices. In line with his bigger project, Foucault's alternative history of madness is an account not of disease and its treatment but of questions of freedom and control, knowledge and power. As Smart (1989) rightly notes, such themes are found throughout Foucault's work.

From Foucault's point of view, it is not until the very late C18th and early C19th that the worst and most thorough expulsion of the mental deviant occurs. Reformers Pinel (in France) and Tukes (in England), in different but parallel ways, replace the fetters and bars of the old madhouses by the closed, sealed order of an asylum system founded on a "gigantic moral imprisonment", that of the medical management and control of insanity. In Tukes' York retreat and Pinel's Bicetre, which were to become the exemplars for the most advanced mental institutions of their time, patients were subjected to panoptic surveillance; that is, the disciplinary techniques of continual scrutiny and normalising judgement of their keepers and doctors. For Foucault, then, the history of psychiatry is anything but the history of the gradual liberation of the insane from cruel, coercive treatment at the hands of their keepers. Rather, the liberation of the mad from their chains was simply a shift to a more subtle form of control based on self-surveillance. Instead of coercion by others (sovereign power) another type of power (disciplinary power) now came into being. For Foucault, the way power is manifest changed, from breaking the body to controlling the mind, but this does not represent an improvement. If anything it means that the workings of power have become more sophisticated and subtle. It is thus a provocative account which, as Porter (2003) puts it, stands the progressive ('Whiggish') history of psychiatry on its head, and turns "heroes into villains".

In light of this, it is not surprising that *Madness and Civilisation* has provoked much criticism. For example, the contention that 'kind' psychiatry is no more impressive and in some ways worse than 'cruel' confinement, is, as Porter (1990) has pointed out, not subject to straightforward empirical confirmation or refutation. Other critics, such as Sedgwick (1981) and Scull (1993), have picked up on Foucault's "cavalier tendency to overgeneralise", for example over the nature and extent of confinement of the 'socially useless' (including the mad and the poor) across Europe during the C17th and C18th. Foucault's argument is that in the "classical age" of bureaucratic rationality (the age of Reason), the main European countries experienced the "Great Confinement" in which the poor and wandering insane were swept up and locked away in special institutions: the *Hopital General* in Paris and 32 provincial cities, and the workhouses of England. Foucault notes that the insane were caught up in a general proscription of idleness and beggary (though largely undifferentiated inside the houses of confinement, they were still rendered into a spectacle for the visiting public). They were caged but not treated or diagnosed, and the rigid, sectarian rules of the institution expressed for Foucault the triumph of Reason over its vanquished, controlled opposite (Foucault, 1967). These central claims have been contested by some English historians. Scull (1993) points out that the mad formed only a tiny fraction of the total swept up and confined in the *hopitaux generaux*, so argues that Foucault's attempt to identify "all forms of social uselessness" with madness, and to see confinement as constituting a grand confrontation between Reason and Unreason, rests on little more than "verbal gymnastics and tricks" (Scull, 1993, p.7). While Foucault's account may portray quite accurately the response in France, it is questionable whether it accurately represents developments elsewhere.

Nevertheless, I agree with Sedgwick's (1981) view that *Madness and Civilisation* helps to reveal the capacity of psychiatric medicine/practice to produce quite different rationalisations for a relatively constant practice over its long history. Many of its innovations have come from developments in technique or in the hardware of technology, rather than in basic method. For example, electro-convulsive therapy may be viewed as providing a modern-day 'plunge' equivalent to the douche of cold water provided in earlier times. And my general position is that regardless of the empirical evidence, Foucault's *idea* of disciplinary power/knowledge is a very useful one.

2.3 Combining Goffmanian and Foucauldian approaches

> "Goffman's 'microsociology' and Foucault's analyses of disciplinary knowledge/power need not be unrelated scholarly projects that they now often are. They can be integrated around the single project of a sociology of the person." (Cahill, 1998, p.145)

> "[Q]ualitative research is a creative process which necessarily involves making choices about methods and data, on the one

hand, and asking analytic questions about the data, on the other." (Miller, 1997, p.35)

2.3.1 Key concepts compared

Goffman and Foucault each offer a useful set of concepts, or theory, for organising thinking about present-day psychiatric practice; ones that the sociological analyst might use to help them ask incisive analytic questions of their data. Here, I briefly recap on some their main ideas (see Figure 2.1), after which I will review what are in my opinion three successful attempts at combining their contrasting analytic approaches.

Figure 2.1: Key analytical concepts for the study of modern psychiatric practice

Goffman	**Foucault**
o Total institution (ideal type)	o Panopticon (metaphor)
o Closed social system	o The C17th 'great confinement'
o Dehumanisation	o Laboratory of humans
o Hidden underlife of institution achieved through inmates avoiding staff surveillance	o Architecture (layout) induces self-surveillance among inmates and staff

o *Side-steps grand theory – focuses on the interaction order*	o Rejects grand theory – destabilises sociological 'truths'
Interactionist sociology – analytic foci	**Archaeology/genealogy – analytic foci**
o Micro/interaction o Situated meanings & doings o Negotiation of medical encounters o Process of psychiatric labelling, and resistance to it	o History of the present o Transformation of medical encounters o Installation of systems of psychiatric classification o Dynamic relationship between human sciences (e.g. psychiatry, sociology) & their respective subjects
Repressive power	**Disciplinary power/knowledge**
o Exercised by the state, its institutions and individual staff o Patients are silenced and communication with staff is blocked	o Medical and social sciences establish behavioural norms o Exercised via normalisation & self-surveillance

○ Social distance between patients and staff ○ Institutionalism among inmates of total institutions	○ Patients are compelled to speak (the 'new medicine')[3] ○ Psychiatrization of everyday life (the 'psychiatric society')

2.3.2 Hacking: dynamic nominalism

The first attempt to combine these contrasting approaches has a Foucauldian analytic 'home base'. Starting from there, Hacking (2002a; 2004) turns to Goffman to offer a general model for understanding better the process through which new kinds of person are made up (Hacking, 2002a; 2004). He starts by critiquing the philosophical tradition of nominalism for ignoring the fact that when the things being labelled are human the persons so labelled can do something about it – unlike, say, a given plant or type of snow. He examines how classification systems open up or close down possibilities for human action; how classifications affect the people classified by them; and how changes to the people who are classified feed back and change the classifications. Hacking's framework for analysing and describing the process through which new kinds of person emerge involves examining labelling from above by a community of experts (e.g. psychiatry) who create a 'reality' (a diagnostic category) that some people make their own ("I'm a

[3] This Foucauldian idea, from Arney & Bergen (1984), is discussed in the following chapter.

schizophrenic/an anorexic/bipolar"), and the autonomous behaviour of the persons so labelled, which every expert must face, and which may lead to modifications to the classification system and even the elimination of certain diagnostic categories (e.g. homosexuality as a psychiatric disorder). Hacking's model thus allows us to understand better how classification systems change over time and, relatedly, the dynamics of the relationship between the human sciences and their respective subjects.

> "Dynamic nominalism remains an intriguing doctrine, arguing that numerous kinds of human beings come into being hand in hand with our invention of the ways to name them." (Hacking, 2002a, pp. 113-4)

Hacking considers the phenomenon of "transient mental illnesses" which come and go, contemporary candidates for which perhaps include anorexia and chronic fatigue syndrome. He argues that it is unlikely a single story can be told about making up people; each category has its own history and requires its own genealogy. An example of this is presented in his book *Mad Travellers* (Hacking, 2002b), which tells the story of a mental illness that was born, flourished and virtually died away within the space of twenty-three years. He tells the tale of the first diagnosed mad traveller who suffered from a strange compulsion that led him to travel compulsively, often without identification, not knowing who he was or why he travelled (ibid).

Hacking's model for combining Foucault's archaeology with Goffman's interpersonal sociology is well suited to investigations of the dynamic relationship between human sciences and their respective subjects. It seems less helpful for studying face-to-face communication in psychiatric settings. Better suited to this, I believe, are the other two approaches to be considered.

2.3.3 Baron: 'Asylum to Anarchy'

Asylum to Anarchy, by Baron (1987), reports findings from a participant observation study of a 'radical' psychiatric day hospital in which formal controls had been removed. This 'anti-institution' aimed at rejecting the control dimension of psychiatry by removing formal rules and clear cut roles, and by promoting patient participation and equality between staff and patients. In short, the hospital was attempting to provide humane treatment in a 'democratic' context. Baron was therefore "very baffled" when, in the early stages of fieldwork, she started to sense the degree to which this libertarian anti-institution exercised power over its members – a far-reaching exercise of power underlying the surface liberality.

In a situation where rules had been consciously rejected, the need for control resulted in the staff using psychoanalytical interpretations to stem deviance and dissention. The desire for democratic treatment started to turn into a "devious search for control and eventually a tyranny over the feelings and actions of day hospital members", with an increasing emphasis on the unconscious dimension (ibid, p.112). Baron describes how patients responded by organising their own counter-groups to run alongside those run by staff, ridiculing the sexualised psychoanalytical interpretations that staff made of *everything* (staff were told they had "one track minds"), and setting up a "resistance movement" that ultimately led to the resignation of the unit's medical director.[4]

Interestingly, Baron's discovery did not cause her to contradict Goffman's findings. Rather it led to the description of an *additional* type of manipulation to those he described. Goffman's analysis of power was limited to overt mechanisms of control – via rules and rigid structures – prompting Baron to turn to Foucault for a more general analysis of power, because his concept of power/knowledge "seemed more relevant to the more subtle forms of control through expertise that were apparent in the day hospital" (ibid, p.5). Baron thus sees herself as using Foucault's concepts to take over from where Goffman left off; that is, to analyse the exercise of power in a type of rule-less psychiatric institution that had *yet to be invented* when Goffman made his observations:

[4] The crisis was triggered by staff issuing a letter to day patients terminating the provision of daily lunches and travelling expenses. Their response was to send a formal letter of complaint and demand an inquiry, a process which culminated in the medical director's resignation.

> "The story of the day hospital… can thus be seen of an illustration of a type of manipulation and resistance against it that goes beyond the scope of Goffman's theory. Indeed, I see my work as taking up where Goffman left off, explaining an area he could not have known about at the time of writing. For history has thrown up from the antithesis of the asylum another form of power, which bears lessons just as Goffman's did." (Baron, 1987, p.7)

To conclude, Baron placed herself in a research setting which she found could not be adequately understood or described using Goffman's theoretical concepts alone. (Intriguingly, Goffman's ideas undoubtedly contributed to the spirit of the time which made it possible for institutions like the one she was studying to be invented.) Baron used Foucauldian concepts to analyse how a different kind of power compelled participants to act, and tells the story of the active role played by day patients to bring about the demise of this ostensibly democratic institution. Baron's account thus helpfully corrects the impression given in Goffman and Foucault's accounts that power either totally crushes or tames individuals. It also serves as a powerful warning of how well-intentioned de-institutionalisation in mental health care can go badly wrong. One may speculate that this could apply to other kinds of psychiatric care that have developed since Goffman. This will be considered in my discussion, in Chapter 7, of the permeability of today's acute psychiatric wards.

2.3.4 Cahill: ceremonial and technological aspects of person production

The third and final attempt at combining Goffmanian and Foucauldian approaches is made by Cahill (1998), who argues that an adequate sociology of the person – which focuses on the publicly visible beings of intersubjective experience – should consider both the ceremonial and technological aspects of person production. Drawing on the works of Goffman and Foucault in roughly equal measure, Cahill considers three interrelated aspects of the person production process. Considering first the ***processes of person production***, he notes that Goffman's study of interaction involves an analysis not of the individual and his or her psychology, but an analysis of the local, collaborative manufacture of the person. Next, he considers the ***relations of person production***, noting that individuals do not play an equal role in the person production process: for example, patients on the back wards of a mental hospital find it to be a social environment in which it is difficult to be a person. Similarly, certain individuals, such as infants and people with severe disabilities like Alzheimer's, contribute much less to the production of their person in a variety of settings. For example, others attribute thinking or grant them 'theoretic' status (the ability to make rational decisions) by reading meaning into their gestures and movements, and work hard to preserve the apparently fading minds of Alzheimer's patients (Gubrium, 1986). Finally, Cahill considers the ***technology of person production***. Given that information is the "raw material" of person production, control over information is an important determinant of an individual's position in the relations of person production. For example, individuals with severe disabilities and children typically have little control over the information 'hung' on them in social interaction. This final point is well illustrated by the experience of Stuart Sutherland, a former psychiatric inpatient:

> "The younger doctors and nurses [in psychiatric hospital] tended to treat patients as though they were insane, and this could be both infuriating and upsetting… [But] none of the patients were totally out of touch with reality, and their illness only affected part of their lives. Many, for example, knew better than the nurses what pills they were supposed to be taking. However doctors sometimes wrote up the drug sheets in such a hurry that nurses could easily make mistakes. It could seem very important to be given the right drugs, but when the wrong ones were handed out any attempt to argue with the nurse would be treated as part of the patient's illness and recorded as such in the day book". (Sutherland, 1977)

Interestingly, Cahill notes that Goffman and Foucault generally agree on how the technology of person production works in total institutions. As noted earlier, it is made up of the techniques of hierarchical observation (direct, visual surveillance); inmates are compared and contrasted with other inmates, and this permits a norm to be established against which inmates can be compared (i.e.

normalising judgement*)*; and the examination and confessional. Cahill's point is that those who control these means of mining, manufacturing, storing and retrieving facts about individuals exert inordinate influence over interactional processes of person production, even in their absence, and this is a key insight for the purposes of this book. In hospital or other psychiatric settings these individuals include psychiatrists, nurses, social workers, occupational therapists and clinical psychologists. Technological control of the person production process is most obvious in total institutions, but, as was noted above, it long ago emerged from these closed fortresses to permeate everyday life of the 'psychiatric society' in which we arguably now live. So, Cahill observes, even in the informal occasions of social interaction, individuals find it difficult if not impossible to escape from technological person production. However, we might expect it to be much harder to escape for individuals caught up in psychiatric encounters, both in hospital and elsewhere, especially those who have extensive case histories (ibid).

Cahill thus offers a helpful account that may be used to help understand how the person of a mental health service user is produced, both within and outside of today's 'bricks and mortar' psychiatric institutions. However, it is an empirical question as to whether today's hospitals remain as 'closed' to the outside world as they were when Goffman wrote *Asylums*. This will be addressed in depth in Chapter 7.

The three attempts at combining Goffmanian and Foucauldian approaches, reviewed above, can be summarised as follows. Hacking draws analytic attention to the dynamic relationship between systems of classification/thought (labelling from above) and the autonomous behaviour of individuals so labelled (who may challenge the categories used). While his model, or theory, offers the potential for understanding better the *process* through which new kinds of person emerge and disappear over time, it is of limited use for studying face-to-face communication in psychiatric settings. More helpful in this regard is Baron's approach, which starts from a Goffmanian analytic home base, but then draws on Foucauldian concepts as required. This makes it possible to analyse the more subtle and pervasive forms of social control that lie outside the parameters of Goffman's interactionist sociology. Baron draws on both sets of ideas in her account of the working and demise of a 'democratic' psychiatric day hospital, but does not attempt an integrated theory *per se*. For this, we need to turn to Cahill, who proposes a sociology of the person in which the processes, relations and technology of person production are incorporated. His work raises a number of empirical questions for this book, including the extent to which patients are able to influence the production of their person in the various situations in which they meet mental health professionals, including outpatient consultations, ward rounds and assessments for compulsory admission to hospital.

2.4 Discussion

Goffman was a sociologist of human interaction whose aim was to promote acceptance of the face-to-face domain as an analytically viable one. Foucault was a historian of thought, who for more than 20 years sought to create a history of the different modes by which in our culture human beings are made up as subjects. Each may be thought of as a 'founder of discursivity' (Rabinow, 1984) or a 'contributor to human consciousness' (Freidson, 1983), in that they offer a distinctive paradigmatic set of terms, images and concepts which organise thinking and experience about society. Goffman's analytic focus is unerringly on the present, while Foucault's also encompasses the past and future. My general position, is that theorists such as Foucault provide sociological researchers with, at the very least, valuable signposts directing them to parts of the interaction order that are likely to be worthy of closer scrutiny. Foucault also offers the conceptual tools needed to examine the exercise of subtle forms of power and manipulation in present-day encounters between psychiatrists and mental health service users. However, an adequate sociological account of the *interactional dimension* of psychiatric practice requires the use of conceptual tools bequeathed by Goffman. So what is the way forward for the PhD researcher wishing to develop and apply what C Wright Mills called the "sociological imagination"; that is, to further understanding of individuals' experiences in connection with larger social realities and historical trends (Mills, 1959)?

Summarising Goffman's contribution to sociology, Heath states:

> "His contribution should not rest with the complex substantive insights he provides concerning the nature of social life, however powerful they intuitively feel: rather his studies serve as a background of initiatives for the detailed, empirical analysis of situational conduct… We may find it difficult, in some cases even unhelpful, to labour under Goffman's analytic frameworks… [Yet] it is crucial, at least for the development of sociology, that we follow Goffman's example and treat the 'interaction order' seriously, as a topic in its own right, worthy of close analytic attention, and in particular explore the situational and sequential organisation of ordinary conduct, social action and activity." (Heath, 1988, p.158)

I would go along with this balanced assessment, and also with Schegloff's observations about the vulnerability of the data used by Goffman (Schegloff, 1988). The noticeable absence of the patient's voice in *Asylums* also prompts the question as to whether it is more a tale of how Goffman himself experienced the asylum rather than the inmates (Seale, 1999).[5] Williams (1988) rejects criticism about the vulnerability of the data, along with others such as those about the

---

[5] In Chapter 4 I argue that researchers can use their own experiences in such a way that the credibility of the research report is enhanced. However, this has to be done in a fallibilistic spirit (Seale, 1999), which can hardly be said to characterise Goffman's hugely self-confident writing style.

lack of cumulativeness in his writings and the "cavalier" nature of his definitions, by arguing that they do not detract from Goffman's enterprise; on the contrary "he is successful not *despite* these vulnerabilities, but rather *because* of them (ibid, p.73). And I would argue that the great ambition and scale of Goffman's endeavour – to promote acceptance of the interaction order as an analytically viable domain of inquiry – made it inevitable that his work would sometimes be painted with broad strokes. A similar response may be made to criticism that Foucault has a cavalier tendency to over-generalise (see section 2.2).

In my review of Goffman's dialogue with CA, I noted that both approaches share a concern to investigate the structure of (micro) interaction and the rules that govern its course, but Goffman's position is that talk is ritually as well as sequentially organised. The question of which of the two types of organisation is of greater importance, and has more explanatory power in the analysis of talk, remains open for this writer. I hope that this book will demonstrate the value of attending to both sets of analytic concerns and of trying to combine them in some fashion.

This chapter has attempted to show that Goffman's work provides a sound theoretical base for studying communication in psychiatric settings. It provides the theoretical base for my work, but I seek to strengthen it in three main ways. First, naturally-occurring data, where available, are examined using CA methods. This reveals a new level of skill in how people conduct themselves in psychiatric interactions. Second, Foucault's concept of disciplinary power/knowledge is used to reveal the subtle form of control through expertise that would be missed in a purely Goffmanian study. And third, Foucauldian thinking is applied to add a historical, 'macro' dimension that Goffman's work so conspicuously lacks. With this final point in mind, I begin the following chapter by reviewing some key Foucauldian texts about the rise of a 'patient-centred' approach in Western medicine.

Chapter 3

Research literature

CONTENTS

This chapter reviews research literature that has informed the data analyses presented in Chapters 5 to 9. The scope of the review is broad because it encompasses decision-making in three forums: routine outpatient consultations (Chapters 5 & 6), ward rounds in acute inpatient care (Chapters 7 & 8) and assessments for compulsory admission to hospital (Chapter 9). Relevant findings from studies of decision-making in other fields of medicine are also incorporated.

Section 3.1 considers two Foucauldian texts which account for the rise of patient-centred medicine in Western healthcare systems. I argue that while the trend towards a patient-centred approach and shared decision-making is broadly correct in terms of the direction of change, its diffusion across medicine has been uneven. Little is known about the diffusion of shared decision-making in everyday psychiatric practice nor about the obstacles preventing this. The following section (3.2) reviews some of the huge literature on decision-making in medical (non-psychiatric) settings. Key issues relevant to obstacles to shared decision-making in psychiatric practice are identified. Section 3.3 describes aspects of 'de-institutionalised' psychiatric practice. Much of my findings are concerned with how medication decisions are made, so the section discusses participants' experiences of respectively taking and prescribing medication. Two CA studies of psychiatric interactions are discussed in some detail. The next section (3.4) considers the 'elephant in the room' in psychiatric encounters – the underlying threat of compulsion – and how this distorts decision-making. It is argued that the threat is a 'problem' both for psychiatry as a profession (because it distances psychiatry from the rest of medicine) and for individual practitioners (because it inhibits their ability to build therapeutic alliances with their patients).

The next two sections review literature relating to acute inpatient care (3.5) and compulsory admissions (3.6). Both are healthcare contexts in which the whole notion of shared decision-making is problematic. This is because (a) the patient's ability to make rational decisions is often explicitly in question, and (b) the underlying threat of compulsion is typically much harder for participants to 'ignore' than it would be in a routine outpatient consultation. Findings from previous studies show that an acute ward is a difficult place in which to build concordant healthcare relationships, while compulsory admissions represent a breakdown of shared-decision making. The chapter concludes by identifying some of the research questions indicated by the review and which will be addressed by this book.

3.1 The rise of patient-centred medicine

3.1.1 A new discourse on the doctor-patient relationship

In *Medicine and the Management of the Living*, Arney & Bergen (1984) argue that a revolution in Western medicine has occurred from around the 1950s, characterised by an enlargement of the content of medical discourse to encompass the patient's subjective experience of disease. The new medical encounter became "characterised by virtual equality of the patient and physician… and elevates the patient's problems to a level of principal importance and requires that the doctor acknowledge and affirm the patient as a person." (ibid, p.112). They argue that compassion and empathy were always evident in healthcare encounters, but that the difference now is that such understanding is "within medicine". The 'new medicine' is compelled by its own logic to speak with the patient, because by locating the cause of disease outside the body (e.g. associating heart disease with an unhealthy lifestyle) patients become *accountable* to their doctor.

A similar Foucauldian line of argument is developed by Armstrong (1983), who contends that the relationship between psychiatrist and patient began to be reconstrued from the 1960s onwards, with the disciplinary gaze also beginning to turn onto the psychiatrist, who now had to be self-aware, have good communication skills, and so on. Armstrong's position is that there is a new discourse on the doctor-patient relationship, with the patient no longer a passive object containing a disease. In the new discourse, communication is problematised, with the issue of compliance becoming central. Over time, the "defaulter" became "non-compliant", which transformed the patient from someone who simply failed to follow advice to someone who *chose* whether or not to follow that advice. (The vision of concordance in healthcare interactions, discussed below, extends this idea by relegating medical knowledge to the status of beliefs, which are on a par with the beliefs of the patient.) For Armstrong (ibid), the second strand in the new discourse on the doctor-patient relationship is a shift in the location of the medical problem to the social context, and the invention of whole person medicine. The post-war discourse on the doctor-patient relationship began to constitute the patient as a subject, with an increasing concern with the psycho-social aspects of disease and with people's 'lifestyles'. Thus, for Armstrong, the "whole person" is the product of a series of smaller discourses (including on those communication and compliance) which, though intertwined, have contributed separate elements to the final perception of the patient as a subjective body.

Both Armstrong (1983) and Arney and Bergen (1984) understand modern power as operating through inclusion, not exclusion, the latter arguing: "Power that illuminates, analyses and grasps its object is more effective than power that leaves its object alone" (ibid, p.126). Thus, "every dark recess of life must be illuminated by the brilliant light of the new medical logic if you are to benefit from the new social technologies of normalisation [e.g. psychological help] available under the medical umbrella" (p.170). It is not only patient's behaviour that is regulated by this new medical field of power, the doctor's is too, because their work is accessible to anyone who reads their records (casenotes etc).

These Foucauldian histories of the (recent) present of Western healthcare systems are strongly suggestive of a general rise of 'patient-centred' medicine. Mead & Bower (2002) attempt to clarify the key dimensions of this approach:

(1) *The biopsychosocial perspective* – a perspective on illness that includes consideration of social and psychological (as well as biomedical) factors.
(2) *The 'patient-as-person'* – understanding the personal meaning of the illness for the individual patient.
(3) *Sharing power and responsibility* – sensitivity to patients' preferences for information and shared decision-making and responding appropriately to these.
(4) *The therapeutic alliance* – developing common therapeutic goals and enhancing the personal bond between doctor and patient.
(5) *The 'doctor-as-person'* – awareness of the influence of the personal qualities and subjectivity of the doctor on the practice of medicine.

3.1.2 *Meetings between experts*

The proposal for medical consultations to be conceived of as 'meetings between experts' was made forcefully by Tuckett *et al* (1985), who argued that the patient needed to be recognised as the expert in his or her own life, beliefs and priorities, and the doctor as the expert in biomedicine. The NHS 'expert patient' initiative (www.expertpatients.nhs.uk) is founded on this idea and the premise that people living with chronic illnesses are often in the best position to know what they need in managing their own condition. The expectation is that they "communicate effectively with professionals and are willing to share responsibility on treatment" (ibid). 'Concordance' is in tune with current views on how healthcare relationships should be conducted:

> "Concordance is based on the notion that the work of the prescriber and patient in the consultation is a negotiation between equals and the aim is therefore a therapeutic alliance between them. This alliance, may, in the end, include an agreement to differ. Its strength lies in a new assumption of the respect for the patient's agenda and the creation of openness in the relationship, so that both doctor and patient together can proceed on the basis of reality and not of misunderstanding, distrust and concealment." [Working Party, 1997, p.8]

In this model, the consultation becomes "a space where the expertise of patients and health professionals can be pooled to arrive at mutually agreed goals" (Bissell *et al*, 2004, p. 851). In the U.K. there are currently a range of initiatives to help patients and prescribers to put this ideology into practice (see http://www.concordance.org/).

Shared decision-making is integral to the approach and patient-centred medicine more broadly. Charles *et al* (1997) outline its key characteristics (Box 3.1).

Box 3.1: Characteristics of shared decision-making

1. It involves at least two participants - the doctor and patient
2. Both parties share information
3. Both parties take steps to build a consensus about the preferred treatment
4. An explicit agreement is reached on the treatment to be implemented.

Source: Charles *et al* (1997)

The characteristics listed above are used in this book as criteria to judge whether what participants are doing falls within or outside the boundaries of shared decision-making. That noted, a central claim I shall make is that some shared decisions are experienced by patients as considerably less 'shared' than others. This is because in the context of negotiated decision-making, they can be subtly directed or more overtly pressured into choosing the treatment option preferred by their psychiatrist. Such activities are examined very closely in Chapter 5.

3.1.3 Uneven diffusion

Concordant relationships and shared decision-making were noticeably absent from the consultations recorded by Tuckett *et al* (1985) for their major study of doctor-patient communication in general practice. There was evidently little dialogue and sharing of ideas. Doctors and patients rarely talked about the subjective experience of the patient, and while the doctors usually shared with patients some of the reasons for thinking as they did (e.g. why they recommended a treatment), the consultations were one-sided, with doctors spending much less time trying to find out about what the patient thought. The patients themselves tended to remain silent, so Tuckett *et al* conclude that doctors could have not known whether the information they offered was being correctly understood (ibid).

Research undertaken since then continues to show a separation between ideal models of communication and what actually happens in medical consultations. Models of shared decision-making do not seem to occur frequently in actual practice (Stevenson *et al*, 2002), and the failure to exchange views has been examined in studies such as Silverman's (1997a) analysis of HIV counselling. It seems, then, that if the trend towards patient centred medicine is broadly correct in terms of the direction of change, Silverman (1987) remains correct is his assessment that it is not a description that is valid for all instances (see also Perakyla, 1989).

Why might there be an uneven diffusion of patient-centred practice across medicine? Firstly, not all patients want to 'participate' in decisions about their treatment. Studies investigating patient preferences for involvement in decision-making have found wide variations between different groups, as distinguished by age, disease type and illness severity. A general guide seems to be the older the patient, and the more severe the illness, the less they are likely to want to be involved in decision-making (Coupland *et al*, 1991). Secondly, some doctors are unenthusiastic about the idea. Reasons for this include that they may misunderstand the concept of concordance (White, 2003), are reluctant to take seriously patients' perspectives (Day & Bentall, 1996) or are concerned about colluding in the provision of unbeneficial treatments preferred by the patient (Lyall & Tiller, 2001; Weston, 2001). There are practical difficulties in putting the principles of concordance into practice, especially time pressures (Weston, 2001; White, 2003; Godolpin, 2006), and some doctors are concerned that revealing the uncertainties inherent in medical care could be harmful (Coulter, 1997).

People with severe and enduring mental health problems value empathy and need concordance just as much as other patients do (Britten, 1998; Rogers *et al*, 1998). Pilgrim (1990) has called for a 'democratisation' of mental health services, so that treatment decisions become a matter of negotiation with patients, not about them. However, he has argued that the threat of coercion in specialist mental healthcare makes true collaboration impossible (see 3.4 below). In truth, there is very little research evidence for the diffusion of use of shared decision-making in psychiatry (most research is about primary care interactions), although it is thought to be integral to current good practice (see 3.3.2 below).

Few advocates of shared decision-making in psychiatry would argue it is appropriate in every clinical situation. In crisis situations there is often little time for the doctor to build a consensus with the patient about what should be done, and this is compounded in situations where the patient's capacity to make informed decisions about their treatment is in question (for further discussion, see Seale *et al*, 2006). This book examines interactions in emergency situations (MHA assessments), and so it includes encounters in which the patient may be judged by their psychiatrist to lack 'competence' (impaired capacity to make rational decisions). Szasz & Hollender's classic paper on different models of the doctor-patient relationship (Szasz & Hollender, 1955) is thus particularly relevant, because it notes that the model of 'mutual participation' is only one of a number of possible doctor-patient relationships. Others include 'activity-passivity', where the doctor does something to the completely helpless patient, and 'guidance-cooperation', where the patient with an acute condition seeks help and is ready to cooperate. From the psychiatrist's point of view it seems sensible to recognise that different types of doctor-patient relationship, or interactional styles, are necessary for the various circumstances in which they meet their patients.

My analysis will attempt to identify some of the obstacles to the diffusion of shared decision-making in psychiatric practice.

3.2 Decision-making in medical settings

This section reviews selected papers from the voluminous research literature on how decisions are made in medical settings, much of which is about primary care interactions. Three main points will be made that are relevant to obstacles to shared decision-making in psychiatric practice. First, patients in an asymmetrical doctor-patient relationship may adopt various strategies to get what they want or to resist unwanted treatments. Second, prescribing is an interactional process in which doctors sometimes prescribe 'non-scientifically' for the sake of the therapeutic alliance. And third, misunderstandings can occur when patients' preferences for medication are not elicited or expressed, but if they *are* expressed, and they conflict with the doctor's preference, shared decision-making can come unstuck.

3.2.1 Active role of patients

Observational research by Silverman (1987) found two different styles of medical intervention in outpatient consultations for adolescent diabetics. The first is the 'old fashioned' version of organic medicine, which treats the patient as passive, polices treatment compliance with an investigative stance, and seeks to impose medically-defined outcomes. The second is the 'progressive', holistic version of medicine that emphasizes patient's choices, negotiation, and allows the patient to define his or her own version of the 'problem and its management', and promotes self-regulation. These 'policing' and 'self-regulating' styles roughly corresponded with the two consultants who participated in the research, who placed a different emphasis in their work.

Sensitised to Foucauldian analytic concerns, Silverman (ibid) points to the requirement for a high level of active patient involvement in decision-making if treatment is to be a success – ensuring, for example, that the patient is prescribed a medicine they will actually self-administer. (In this respect it parallels the model of care adopted for psychiatric outpatients.) Theoreticity refers to the attribution of rational thought or 'competence', including the ability to perceive and choose between alternative courses of action (McHugh, 1970). In other words, a theoretic actor is someone who is deemed to know what they are doing. In the consultations examined by Silverman, the patients were generally granted theoretic status whether they wanted it or not, and were defined as an active decision maker. But the autonomy patients gained through being defined as such came at the cost of being morally responsible for their actions. As Silverman rightly notes, the treatment of illness inevitably occurs within a moral framework, with sufferers of chronic illness being perceived to need to show that they are doing the best they can for their disorder (e.g. adherence to prescribing). This Foucauldian analysis reminds us that policing does not disappear in patient-centred, 'self-regulating' approaches to the medical encounter (ibid).

While patient-centred medicine implies an active decision-making role for patients, we are only just beginning to understand how such a role is locally constructed by participants. Collins *et al* (2005) apply CA methods to identify the constitutive features of what they call 'unilateral' (directed) and 'bilateral' (shared) decision-making. Bilateral decision-making is constituted of activities such as the doctor concluding the decision sequence ("I don't know how you feel about (0.6) where we should go…") such that the patient's opinion is explicitly invited while explicitly conveying that the course of action is negotiable. In other words, the doctor gradually concludes the decision-making, inviting the patient to choose between options. In contrast, 'unilateral' decision-making was concluded abruptly by the doctor, for example by shifting to a new topic immediately after the decision has been made (ibid). Collins and colleagues observe minor differences in how decisions are made in the two clinical areas, and argue that it is important for researchers to study such features of interaction in other areas of medicine. This is because it can alert practitioners to how their actions may prompt or inhibit patient participation (ibid; see also Drew *et al*, 2001). This book will attempt to further understanding of such matters by considering the variability of decision-making across psychiatric settings.

Early interactionist research shows how patients in 'asymmetrical' doctor-patient relationships are able to influence the outcomes of healthcare encounters. Stimson and Webb (1975) describe the strategies used by patients to direct and control general practice consultations towards what they want. These strategies included patients rehearsing what they were going to say, partially presenting symptoms, excluding clinically relevant information, and ignoring the doctor's advice. Recent CA research reveals a new level of skill in how patients direct consultations towards their own ends. For example, Boyd and Heritage's (2007) single case analysis of a primary care consultation demonstrates how patients exert initiative by proposing alternative agendas, challenging presuppositions and maintaining their contrary preferences.

Viewed from a Foucauldian perspective, some of these activities may be understood as forms of resistance to the exercise of disciplinary power/knowledge. Drawing on fieldwork data from two independent studies, Bloor and MacIntosh (1990) argue that surveillance is an essential component of both health visiting and therapeutic community practice. Their analysis of client/patient behaviour begins with a description of different forms of surveillance, including covert and overt monitoring of the patient, supervisory surveillance (where patient activities are overseen and directed), proxy surveillance (monitoring by other people on behalf of staff), and self-reporting by the patient. The authors then show how such control may be resisted, including by concealing information from staff, ignoring their advice and telling them 'what they want to hear' (and then doing something entirely different once they are out of surveillance space). A crucial advantage of concealment is that that it is a *covert* form of resistance which neutralises the potential for the exercise of power without explicitly challenging it in ways that would lead to penalties. Bloor and MacIntosh argue persuasively that just as surveillance was an underemphasised aspect of power relations in the sociology of medical encounters prior to Foucault (see Chapter 2), so too has concealment of information been similarly underemphasised in the sociological analysis of client behaviour (ibid).

This book will consider patient concealment of clinically relevant information in ward rounds (Chapter 8) and assessments for compulsory admission to hospital (Chapter 9).

3.2.2 Prescribing to preserve the therapeutic alliance

Doctors report sometimes prescribing in order to avoid conflict or complaints, and, ultimately, to preserve the doctor-patient relationship. Bradley's interview study of more than 70 GPs in the north of England (Bradley, 1992a, 1992b) explored 'non-pharmacological', or 'non-scientific' (Schwartz, *et al*, 1989), influences on decisions about whether or not to prescribe. The focus of the analysis was on 'difficult' decisions that cause GPs discomfort, as it is argued that this can reveal non-clinical factors influencing doctors' decisions more generally. Nearly half of the doctors interviewed reported feeling uncomfortable when they had prescribed to preserve the doctor-patient relationship. This was described in various terms, such as 'avoiding litigation or complaints', 'avoiding conflict', and 'keeping the peace'. Nearly one-in-ten mentioned prescribing in order to avoid other forms of critical response, including one who was worried about being assaulted. A small number of doctors recognised that prescriptions could serve functions other than their pharmacological one, with some saying they used prescribing to 'get rid of the patient', and others that it could be used as a 'bargaining chip'. These findings highlight the *interactional dimension* of prescribing, as well as some of the non-clinical and contextual factors that influence the decisions that are made. Its limitation is that it only hints at what actually goes on in the consultation, because the analysis was based on doctors' accounts elicited via semi-structured interviews. New insights into the prescribing process can be gained from applying observational research methods, as this book will demonstrate.

Similar patterns of interaction have been observed in the context of Outpatient methadone treatment (methadone being a synthetic opiate used in substitute prescribing for dependent opiate users) (Tober & Strang, 2003). A qualitative study of the process of methadone treatment, undertaken by this writer (Quirk, 1997; Lilly *et al*, 1999, 2000; Quirk *et al*, 2003a), found that methadone has many meanings for clients and staff, including that it is 'boring' (compared with heroin), potentially 'dangerous', more 'addictive' than heroin, and occasionally 'pleasurable'. Further, its perceived uses include: to 'hold withdrawals', offer 'stability between hits of heroin', act as a 'medicine' and provide 'capital' (via diversion onto the black market) (Quirk, *et al*, 2003a). Staff in outpatient methadone clinics recognised that setting the start dose was not an exact science, and that this inexactness left room for flexibility to accommodate clients' expectations. Before starting treatment, many prospective clients had fixed ideas of the dose of methadone they wanted, and clinic staff noted the importance of not getting 'bogged down' by dose, otherwise subsequent keyworking sessions could dissolve into game playing (Lilly *et al*, 1999; 2000). In interviews, staff talked about how they attempted to accommodate clients' expectations and preferences to some degree, though not to the point where they were perceived as 'pushovers' (Quirk, 1997). This was thought by staff to allow effective keyworker relationships to be developed over time, which were thought to be the medium through which lifestyle changes were effected in this client group (Lilly *et al*, 1999; 2000).

3.2.3 Conflicting preferences

A synthesis of qualitative studies of lay experiences of medicine taking found that the main reason people do not take their medicines as prescribed is not because of failings in patients, doctors or systems, but because of concerns about the medicines themselves (Pound *et al*, 2005). On the whole, the findings point to considerable reluctance to take medicine and a preference to taking as little as possible (ibid). Britten *et al*'s (2005) CA research suggests that GPs tend to be unresponsive to patients' expressions of aversion to taking medicine. Patients used various strategies to express their dislike of taking medicine including by a direct-on-record rejection of medicines (e.g. "Well I'd like to try without it if I can"). In response, doctors tended to exhort patients to take their medication and did not engage them in any real discussion about why they may not want to do so (ibid).

Misunderstandings occur in general practice when patients' preferences for medication are not elicited or expressed, and the GP makes an incorrect assumption about what the patient will find acceptable. Britten and colleagues' (2000) study, described above, identified 14 categories of misunderstanding between patients and doctors that had adverse consequences for taking medicine (i.e. resulting in the prescription not being cashed, or it was cashed but the patient did not take the medicine). These included where the patient did not mention relevant facts about their medication because they had wrongly assumed the doctor was aware of them; where patients were confused by conflicting advice from their GP and their hospital doctor; and where the doctor prescribed and the patient took medication, both just for the sake of the relationship – one example being where the patient took the medicine thought by the doctor to be unnecessary because she feared that future treatment would be withheld if she failed to do so. All misunderstandings were found to be associated with a lack of patient participation in the consultation, including where the patient did not voice their expectations, preferences or worries about side effects. Misunderstandings also happen when the doctor incorrectly assumes a patient wants a particular medicine. An observational study of GPs' avoidance of antibiotic prescribing in consultations for sore throats concluded that doctors should attempt to elicit patient expectations for a prescription, because then they might then realise that fewer patients than expected want antibiotics, thus reducing the potential for misunderstanding (Rollnick *et al,* 2001).

Detailed conversation analysis of a single GP consultation shows how shared decision-making can come unstuck when doctors and patients have conflicting preferences and where options open to the patient are not true options (Gwyn & Elwyn, 1999). The value of the analysis for present purposes is that it underlines that situations of "equipoise" – an equally poised or balanced context for decision-making – must be *locally constructed* by participants if decision-making is to be experienced as truly shared. If not, then it is better understood as an "informed decision engineered according to doctor preference", as was the case in their example (ibid). Collins *et al*'s (2005) analysis of unilateral and bi-lateral decision-making, discussed above, gives a good insight into this.

The lessons drawn from the literature reviewed above is that misunderstandings can arise when patient preferences for treatment are not elicited or expressed. The downside of eliciting or expressing them is that it risks revealing a conflict of preferences which may not be reconciled easily, if at all. This book aims to add to this earlier work by showing how participants locally construct situations of equipoise in psychiatric interactions (i.e. how they *make* choices real or otherwise). Closely related to this is how they communicate their preferences to one another.

3.3 Contemporary psychiatric practice

3.3.1 'De-institutionalised' mental healthcare

It is claimed that mental health services in the U.K. are moving into the third stage of a progressive shift between 'care paradigms', as defined by the locus of patient care (Lelliott *et al*, 1997). The first stage was the decision, arising in 1962 from Enoch Powell's 'Hospital Plan for England', to reduce National Health Service (NHS) bed numbers and close large psychiatric hospitals. The second, which reached its peak in the 1970s and 1980s, was the development of small psychiatric units, often on district general hospital sites, with a limited range of community services to meet the needs of those who no longer required hospital accommodation. The third stage, heralded by the white paper *Caring for People: Community Care in the Next Decade and Beyond* (Department of Health, 1989), is intended to divert people from community-based residential services into their own homes. This transition from hospital to community care has parallels in mental health services across the developed world. However, the pace of change and extent to which it has progressed, as gauged for example by the rate at which bed numbers have been reduced, varies considerably between and within countries. For example, the timing and pace of de-institutionalisation in the U.S. followed closely those in the United Kingdom; in Germany this process happened later and was slower. In Italy the change was greatly accelerated by legislation, 'Law 180', which made it illegal to admit patients for the first time to large mental hospitals from 1978, and to admit any patients after 1980. From this time onwards, Italian mental health services were expected to rely solely on psychiatric units, with limited numbers of beds, in general hospitals for in-patient care.

The process of deinstitutionalisation has brought most of the old, large, remote mental hospitals to a close in many developed countries (Lamb & Bachrach, 2001; Fakhoury & Priebe, 2002), with psychiatric service provision across Europe now characterised by an increasing diversity of community-based services run by public, voluntary and private sector organisations (Becker *et al*, 2002). In the U.K., the number of hospital beds has been dramatically reduced (Pilgrim & Rogers, 2001; Becker *et al*, 2002), and those that remain have been relocated to psychiatric units in general hospitals. Although very few patients now live in a psychiatric hospital, the mental health care system retains the function of admitting people briefly in order to treat their mental disorder or to prevent them from causing harm to themselves or others. Indeed in many European countries, and elsewhere, 'acute' psychiatric (admission) wards are an important component of the system of services (Becker *et al*, 2002). It is not known how many of the estimated 1.85 million psychiatric beds worldwide, equating to 4.36 per 10,000 population (WHO, 2001), are in acute psychiatric wards. The ratio of acute to long-stay beds is likely to vary greatly from country to country and be highest in those countries that have undergone deinstitutionalisation.

The reasons for the closure of the asylums are complex and contested. The ideals of moral treatment were abandoned almost immediately in the C19th, and the system rapidly became overwhelmed by the number of people admitted with chronic conditions, however it was not until the late 1950s and early 1960s that the asylums came under sustained analysis and critique (for summary, see Pilgrim & Rogers, 1999; see also Chapter 7 for a discussion of Goffman's contribution). Numerous arguments have been advanced to account for the general trend towards the policy of care in the community (for reviews, see Prior, 1991; 1993; Nettleton, 1995; Ham, 1999; Carpenter, 2000). First, it has largely been attributed to pharmacological advances, especially the development of neuroleptic drugs, which have made it feasible and safe for people with severe and enduring mental health problems. Second, de-institutionalisation is seen to have been driven by fiscal crises and the need to reduce costs (community care being proposed as a cheaper option). And third, it has been argued that the asylum was 'destroyed from within' (Prior, 1991; 1993) due to the transformation of psychiatric knowledge – from mental illness to the domain of mental health, and from the diseased body as the object of its focus to the whole person - and its inextricable link to psychiatric practice. In short, this reconceptualisation of the medical model has meant that the rationale for confining psychiatry within the grounds of a hospital no longer exists (ibid).

Whatever the relative merits of these 'technological', 'economic' and 'discursive' explanations (reviewed in Carpenter, 2000), it is becoming increasingly clear that the radical transformation of mental healthcare has left in-patient care in an ambiguous position with regard to its functioning in the overall system. Indeed the question over its structural position and function – for example, whether it should be at the 'core' of the system, whether it has become a 'dumping ground' for people who cannot be managed by community services, or whether it is something that should eventually be phased out altogether - is arguably at the centre of debates about how acute psychiatric care should be provided (Muijen, 2002). Bowers *et al* (2007) note that, in the context of such a rapidly changing healthcare system, it is difficult, though not impossible, to articulate clearly what the role of acute inpatient care is (Bowers *et al*, 2007). It is perhaps not surprising that staff working in such circumstances orientate to *pragmatic* goals, notably 'emptying beds' as quickly as possible to make space for new admissions (see section 3.5).

It is has been argued that we have already entered a new era in mental health care; that of 're-institutionalisation' (Priebe & Turner, 2003) or the 'rebirth of asylumdom' (Morrall & Hazelton, 2000). Some see this as being indicated by the fact that service users still get institutionalised, in the sense that an individual, while living in supported (supervised) accommodation, may visit a day hospital two days a week, community centres a few other days a week, and a clinic a further day a week (ibid). Such developments were alluded to 25 years ago by Castel *et al* (1982), whose observations of the U.S. mental healthcare system led them to conclude that institutionalisation is far from obsolete as a solution to the problems of mental health and other forms of deviance.

3.3.2 Changes to psychiatric practice

Over the past 30 or 40 years, few medical specialities have changed as much with regard to clinical practice as psychiatry. These changes have been brought about by the change in the locus of care from hospital to the community and developments in psychopharmacology (Cruz & Pincus, 2002). It is argued that these forces have changed technical aspects of the psychiatric encounter, with the psychiatrist now principally a psychopharmacologist – one who values anti-psychotic medication in treating psychosis (Seale *et al*, 2006) - and secondarily a manager of care (Lazarus & Sharfstein, 1998). A parallel trend has been the growing recognition of the importance of communication in consultations and the increased interest in ensuring that patients can play active roles in decision-making about their treatment (Department of Health, 2001; Kaplan, 2004). The change in psychiatrists' overall role, accompanied by the rise of patient-centred medicine in the context of 'de-institutionalised' mental healthcare, had brought with it uncertainties about the nature and purpose of the psychiatrist-patient relationship (Cruz & Pincus, 2002). For example, what must a psychiatrist say and do within the psychiatric encounter to optimise treatment outcome? And how might a 'patient-centred' approach be adopted with patients who are periodically admitted to hospital against their will and forced to take treatments they do not want? These questions animate much of the analysis and discussion in the present in this book.

Psychiatry is a medical discipline that involves the diagnosis of mental and behavioural disorders, such as schizophrenia, bipolar disorder, clinical depression and anxiety disorders. The field is divided into various subspecialties, including adult, old age and child and adolescent psychiatry. Practising psychiatrists may specialise in certain areas of interest including psychopharmacology, crisis assessment and treatment, early intervention, and forms of psychotherapy (for useful overviews, see www.rcpsych.ac.uk and www.answers.com). Normative statements outlining the characteristics of a good psychiatrist show much overlap with a patient-centred approach (Bhugra & Holdsgrove, 2005). The core attributes listed in *Good Psychiatric Practice* (Royal College of Psychiatrists, 2004) include clinical competence, being a good communicator and listener, being sensitive to gender, ethnicity and culture, and bringing empathy, encouragement and hope to patients and carers.

An individual may come under the care of a psychiatrist by various routes, though most commonly it is through self- or GP-referral. New patients may be admitted to psychiatric hospital by sectioning under mental health legislation, if they are considered to be an immediate danger to themselves of other people (see Chapter 9). In a de-institutionalised healthcare system, most service users are managed as outpatients and supported and monitored in the community by a Community Mental Health Team (CMHT) comprised of community psychiatric nurses (CPNs), social workers, psychologists, occupational therapists, psychiatrists and support workers. Team members are often based in the same mental health centre. Psychiatric outpatients periodically visit their psychiatrist for consultation in his or her office at the centre. Appointments usually last 15 to 30 minutes (see Chapter 5). If hospitalisation is required, stays are typically two or three weeks, with only a small number of cases involving long-term hospitalisation. In the past, psychiatric patients were often hospitalised for six months or more (see Chapter 7).

An important observation for present purposes is that, over a period of weeks, months and years, psychiatrists are likely to encounter the same patients in a range of community and institutional settings. These include routine outpatient consultations, assessments for compulsory admission to hospital, and ward rounds (if the patient is hospitalised). It has been asserted that psychiatrists typically possess a range of communicative styles that have been formed through experience with patients under such varied conditions, although the ideal set of communication skills has yet to be identified for every scenario (Cruz & Pincus, 2002). The empirical materials presented in this book will add knowledge about such matters.

Psychiatry as a speciality has become increasingly focused on providing psychotropic medication (Busfield, 2005), to point where it is now the mainstay of treatment for people with severe and enduring mental health problems (National Schizophrenia Fellowship, 2000; Healy, 2002; Seale *et al*, 2006). Accompanying these developments in specialist practice has been an extensive psychiatrisation of everyday worries (Castel *et* al, 1982; Rose, 1986) and the introduction of drug treatments such as minor tranquillisers for less severe mental health problems. This has brought GPs more squarely into the terrain of what is constituted as a mental health problem (Rose, 1986; Busfield, 2005).

3.3.3 Taking and prescribing psychiatric medication

Substantial parts of this book are concerned with how anti-psychotic prescribing decisions are made. Here, I briefly review some associated research literature.

Perceived costs and benefits

Some service users report that their medications are unhelpful and avoid taking them unless they have to, such as when under supervision in hospital (Chamberlain, 2005). An in-depth interview study of people with a diagnosis of schizophrenia suggests that the main utility of taking neuroleptic medication is to control specific symptoms and to gain personal control over managing symptoms (Rogers *et al*, 1998). The costs of taking medication were perceived to be side-effects, which at times are thought to equalise or outweigh the positive benefits of medication (ibid). A survey of the perspectives of mental health service users in community and hospital care found that while many users suffer from the side effects of psychotropic drugs, most also appreciate the benefits and lessening of symptoms. In short they balance the costs and benefits of medication, and cope with the former because of the latter (Rose, 2001; see also Rethink, 2006). Surveys indicate that the majority of service users believe their medications are, on balance, helpful (Rethink, 2003).

Notwithstanding this, many users are evidently concerned about the side effects of anti-psychotic medication. A wide range of unwanted effects may be experienced, including sedating effects (e.g. tiredness), physical effects (e.g. weight gain), movement effects (e.g. shaking in the arms or legs), and mood effects (e.g. feeling agitated) (Rethink, 2006). People receiving their anti-psychotic by injection ('depot' medication) report experiencing positive consequences, such as that it improves main symptoms, brings stability, improves mood, and reduces anger (Smith *et al*, 1999). Negative consequences include that it increases tiredness and restlessness, and makes the user feel they have no choice over taking it, as compared with taking tablets unsupervised (ibid). Users say that unwanted effects such as tiredness, being unable to concentrate, and looking and sounding odd due to speech and movement difficulties have a particularly negative impact on their quality of life and ability to integrate socially (Rethink, 2006; see also Estroff, 1982). Patients on depot medication report having only limited knowledge of their medication, especially its long-term side effects (Goldbeck *et* al, 1999).

Our earlier study (Seale *et al*, 2006) is one of the few studies to have explored psychiatrists' experiences of prescribing anti-psychotic medication. The most commonly expressed view was that medication was an important, and probably the most important, aspect of treatment for people diagnosed with schizophrenia. One in three of the consultant psychiatrists interviewed qualified this, saying that medication had an important role in non-drug treatment, because it stabilised patients and made other interventions such as talking therapy possible (ibid). These psychiatrists faced a dilemma between the conviction that medications are a mainstay of treatment for severe mental health problems, and concerns that full knowledge of unwanted effects might make patients less motivated to participate in treatment. For some, this conflicted with the obligation to share information fully with patients (ibid), even though some evidence exists showing compliance is not affected by providing such information (Chaplin & Kent, 1998).

How medication decisions are made

Surprisingly little is known about how psychiatrists and their patients negotiate medication decisions, or about how they communicate about medication more generally. The available research evidence points to considerable variation between clinicians in prescribing behaviour in the same clinical context, and the deviation of prescribing practice from the ideal, as defined by consensus statements and clinical practice guidelines (Harrington *et al*, 2002a,b; Lelliott *et al*, 2002). Clues as to why this may be the case come from an unpublished qualitative study of how psychiatrists behave in prescribing situations. Using semi-structured interviews, this critical incident technique study found that the prescribing of anti-depressants by psychiatrists went beyond that of simply treating the symptoms of depression; rather they were frequently used as therapeutic tools, with the psychiatrist often being considered to be more important than medication (personal communication, Peter Pratt, Chief Pharmacist, Community Health Sheffield). These findings are consistent with those from studies of how and why doctors in other medical settings prescribe to preserve the therapeutic alliance (see section 3.2).

The exchange of information is a defining characteristic of shared decision-making (Charles *et al*, 1997). Surveys indicate that the majority of service users are able to talk about their medication with their prescribing doctor (their psychiatrist or GP), at least some of the time (National Schizophrenia Fellowship, 2000; Rethink, 2006). However, few report having been offered a *choice* over the medication they are given (National Schizophrenia Fellowship, 2000; Rethink, 2003; Rethink, 2006). People receiving an older generation 'typical' anti-psychotic prescription were reportedly less likely than those on 'atypical' medication to have been given a choice (National Schizophrenia Fellowship, 2000). Psychiatrists in our interview study (Seale *et al,* 2006) commented that to monitor adherence in outpatient consultations, they had to rely heavily on patient self-report, and additionally accounts from carers and other professionals. Typically, the psychiatrist aims to create a safe conversational environment to facilitate disclosure of information, for example by indicating that non-compliance is normal and that the reporting of it would not be followed by disapproval (ibid).

In surveys, service users report not being given enough information about their treatment and its side effects (National Schizophrenia Fellowship, 2000; Rethink, 2003). A minority report not wanting to hear about the side effects of medication for fear that this would cause them further anxiety and apprehension (Rethink, 2006). This suggests that the concern of some psychiatrists that full knowledge of unwanted effects might put off some patients from taking their medication (Seale *et al*, 2006), is not unwarranted. Psychiatrists in another study report giving large amounts of information to patients about the possible side effects of conventional (typical) anti-psychotics, although unwanted effects, such as dry mouth, blurred vision and Parkinsonism were discussed more frequently than others, such as weight gain and temperature regulation problems (Smith & Henderson, 2000). Psychiatrists in this study claimed that when they discuss side effects, they mostly do so without the patient having to ask (ibid).

Earlier research has thus provided some clues as to how psychiatric prescribing decisions are made, however it remains something of a 'black box'. For example, nothing has been published on the *patient's* contribution to the creation of safe conversational environments in which to discuss the potentially difficult issue of non-compliance. This is one of the topics addressed in Chapter 6.

3.3.4 CA studies of psychiatric interactions

The CA literature on psychiatric interactions was very limited when the present study was undertaken. Here, I present relevant findings from two CA studies; one showing how psychiatrists avoid engaging with patients' concerns in routine outpatient consultations (McCabe *et al*, 2002), the other revealing how they elicit information from patients in an 'emergency' (intake interviews to psychiatric hospital) (Bergmann, 1992). Combined, the findings represent good evidence for how psychiatrists either *block* communication about issues regarded as irrelevant to matters in hand, or *open up* communication about clinically relevant issues, through the use of veiled interrogation techniques aimed at getting to the 'truth' of the patient's condition.

McCabe *et al* (2002): avoidance of engagement with patient concerns

McCabe and colleagues' study (McCabe *et al*, 2002) involved an analysis of 32 routine psychiatric outpatient consultations, video-taped in clinics in London. The focus of the analysis was on how doctors engage with patients diagnosed with schizophrenia. The average consultation involved the psychiatrist reviewing the patient's mental state, medication and associated side effects, and their daytime activities, social activities, living arrangements, finances, and contact with other mental health professionals. Not every topic was covered in every consultation, and psychiatrists varied in how they addressed each topic. Consultations typically started with the psychiatrist asking how the patient had been and often asking specific questions about mood, sleep, appetite, thoughts and symptoms. Patients' participation in the consultation mainly involved responding to psychiatrists' questions to inform them about their wellbeing and the effect of treatment (drugs, rehabilitation) since the last consultation.

The analysis shows that patients actively attempted to talk about the content of their psychotic symptoms by asking direct questions, repeating questions and utterances, and producing those utterances in the concluding part of the consultation. In response the doctors hesitated, responded with a question rather than an answer, and smiled or laughed (when informal carers were present), indicating their reluctance to engage with patients' concerns. Patients' attempts to talk about the content of their psychotic symptoms were thus a source of noticeable interactional tension and difficulty. It is concluded that addressing patients' concerns about their psychotic symptoms might lead to a more satisfactory outcome with the consultation from the patient's point of view and improve their engagement with health services.

Illuminating though these findings may be, a question mark hangs over their generalisability to other outpatient consultations, because the activities analysed occurred very infrequently. It may also be argued that a depiction of how patients attempt to *conceal* the content of their psychotic symptoms better represents this aspect of psychiatrist-patient communication in other encounters, especially ward rounds or assessments for compulsory admission. How psychiatrists attempt to elicit information in such circumstances is addressed by the second CA study.

Bergmann (1992): 'veiled interrogation'

The study undertaken by Bergmann (1992) involved a conversation analysis of psychiatric intake interviews in various psychiatric hospitals in Germany, in which the psychiatrists' official work was to decide whether a person should be admitted, voluntarily or involuntarily, on the basis of that person's observable behaviour during the interview.

The analysis shows that psychiatrists did not 'interrogate' patients directly via question and answer sequences, but used other forms of inquiry. Very often the psychiatrist produced talk (e.g. "I just got the information that you're not doing so well"), in response to which, without having been literally 'asked' for it, the candidate patient proffered information. This can roughly be described as the psychiatrist seeking information not by asking, but by *telling* the candidate patient something about themselves. Sometimes the psychiatrists explored by "fishing": in the initiating turn the psychiatrist would indicate that s/he has only indirect knowledge of the referred-to facts, done by including in the utterance a description of this knowledge. Such fishing devices are commonly used in everyday interaction, such as when phoning someone and saying "your line's been busy", which can be heard by the recipient as an invitation to disclose the identity of the previous caller.

Bergmann offers a structural explanation for the use of such 'information-eliciting tellings'. He argues that the operational structure of fishing means that it can successfully be used as a *lie-detecting device,* which makes it highly suitable for exploratory interviews, examinations, and interrogations, for example as used by the police. This is because the recipient (in this case the candidate patient) is addressed as someone who has authoritative access to the information being sought by the interviewer, and with this locally-constructed identity he or she may be tempted to tell a profitable lie. However, the speaker (the psychiatrist), who presents him/herself as someone with limited access, may in fact have in their possession knowledge from other sources; knowledge that enables the interviewer to contest the recipient's supposedly authoritative version, or even to reject it as having been a lie.

Patients in Bergmann's study heard these "discretely exploring utterances" as one of two very different types of activity: either a 'considerate invitation' to talk about issues which they themselves would not have dared to topicalise in the first place (for example the types of concerns patients in McCabe *et al*'s (2002) study wanted discussed), or an insidious strategy to make the recipient disclose experiences, feelings or information which they would rather keep to themselves. Bergmann (1992) thus observes that "The seemingly innocent, helpful, and affiliative utterances with which a psychiatrist attempts to induce a candidate patient to disclose his feelings and opinions have structurally an inbuilt hidden or veiled morality" (p.156) and that such utterances are "extremely vulnerable to being heard by the recipient in moral terms and may therefore trigger uncontrollable, interactionally disastrous social situations". In the context of a psychiatric intake interview, an angry response to what is heard as 'veiled interrogation' risks being interpreted as symptomatic of a mental disorder.

I would argue that Bergmann's analysis links quite neatly with Cahill's (1998) theory of how persons are produced, reviewed in Chapter 2. Given that 'fishing' techniques sometimes elicit a response that is subsequently exposed to be a lie (if the psychiatrist produces contradictory information from other sources), then the psychiatrist's locally constructed identity – invoked through retrieving and manufacturing the 'raw material' of person production (information) – will be of an individual with inordinate influence over the interactional process. Bergmann's analysis, and a CA approach more generally, can thus improve our understanding of how such identities are constituted by participants in psychiatric interactions.

The two CA studies reviewed above indicate the potential for using a CA approach to examine in microscopic detail how psychiatric decisions are made. The discipline of CA has much to contribute to discussions about control, if control is understood to be a *reciprocal* process (Perakyla, 2004). As the analysis presented in Chapter 5 demonstrates, it is well suited to examining *negotiated* decision-making. However, the central CA texts have, in contrast, very little to say about the 'elephant in the room' in psychiatric encounters; that is, control as *unilateral* process where the controlled party has no choice but to obey. It is to this issue that we now turn.

3.4 The elephant in the room

> "The whole picture [concerning the provision of psychiatric treatment] is distorted by the use of compulsion, which deters people from seeking treatment, denies them the right to choose the treatment they want, and prioritises certain kinds of patient in the offer of services." [Baroness Hale of Richmond, Sieghart lecture, British Institute of Human Rights, 2004]

3.4.1 Underlying threat of compulsion

A qualitative study of patients' experiences of anti-psychotic medication found that while some see little difference between taking psychiatric medication and medication for other medical conditions, most view it as different (Rogers *et al*, 1998). Interviewees' descriptions of taking medication were frequently accompanied by a strong sense that sanctions would follow if they did not take it. Some expressed a wish to discontinue taking their medication, but felt unable to stop because of the perceived power mental health professionals had over their lives and their use of medication. Given that patients' views about compliance and medication decisions were influenced by their knowledge and personal experience of possible coercive professional action, Rogers *et al* (ibid) conclude that a collaborative, patient-centred approach will only be possible if the fear of coercion from mental health professionals is removed.

In an interview study undertaken with newly admitted patients in the U.S. (Bennett *et al*, 1993), not being permitted full participation in the hospitalisation decision was repeatedly cited as being the most "coercive" aspect of hospitalisation. With regard to whether they had been subject to persuasion, some patients were angry because no one had tried to persuade them to be admitted to hospital; instead, it had been made clear by the decision-maker that they had no choice. Views on inclusion in the decision-making were variable however, with other patients saying that they had actively *not* wanted to have been included in the decision-making, because it was more of a responsibility than they had wanted to accept. Though deceit on the part of others was reported only rarely by patients, it evoked strong reactions when it was perceived to have occured (ibid).

Evidence for the impact of coercion on users' subsequent engagement with mental health services is inconclusive. One study found that perceived coercion at hospital admission neither increases or decreases psychiatric patients' adherence to prescribing or use of treatment services after discharge (Rain *et al*, 2003), while another found that the impact of feeling coerced produces a more rejecting attitude towards psychiatric services (Rogers *et al*, 1998). What is clear is that a proportion of voluntarily admitted patients feel that they had been coerced (Rogers, 1993) while a significant number of the compulsorily detained report not perceiving themselves to have been coerced (Hiday *et al*, 1997). In short, the distinction between voluntary and legal status is experienced by patients as blurred. Qualitative research undertaken in the U.S. suggests that is probably because of *how* the process of admission was managed and, in particular, whether undue pressure or deceptive methods had been used. In a study of how admission decisions are made in a U.S. psychiatric emergency room, Lidz *et* al (1993) found that a significant proportion of voluntarily admitted patients were subjected to 'quasi-coercive' pressure. Pressure was applied in various ways, but by far the most prevalent was persuasion, such as where the attending doctor states a preference that invokes his or her expertise:

Patient: Do you want me to come in here [to hospital]?
Doctor: Yes, I think you are going through a psychotic episode. (ibid, p.272)

Other types of pressure included threats to use legal force if the patient did not agree to a voluntarily admission, and the actual use of legal force (i.e. involuntary hospitalisation). Other force typically involved the emergency room staff calling the security guards to keep the patient from doing physical damage to someone or something, or to prevent the patient from leaving (ibid). Such findings are strongly indicative of a 'spectrum of coercion' in psychiatric practice, ranging from more subtle pressures on patients to take their medication, to the use of coercion and compulsion (Szmukler & Applebaum, 2001; see also O'Brien & Golding, 2003).

An important lesson drawn for this book is that persuasion can be experienced by patients as coercion in psychiatric contexts where the underlying threat of coercion is hard to ignore, such as psychiatric emergency rooms (Lidz *et al*, 1993) and assertive community treatment (the latter being an approach that 'assertively' engages a subgroup of individuals with severe mental health problems who continuously disengage with treatment (Watts & Priebe, 2002)). Fear of explicit coercion reportedly keeps people away from mental health treatment (Rogers *et al*, 1998; Swartz *et al*, 2003), but so too do the more subtle pressures exerted on outpatients to adhere to treatment (Swartz *et al*, 2003). These findings suggest that mental health professionals must use their powers of persuasion and coercion carefully if they wish to retain existing clients in treatment.

Previous research indicates that degrees of pressure and coercion are applied in psychiatric decision-making, however little is known about how more subtle forms of pressure and tactful manipulation are applied in the context of *shared* decision-making. This book will examine how interactional pressure is applied in a range of settings, from the ostensibly voluntaristic (outpatient consultations) to the overtly coercive (MHA assessments).

3.4.2 A 'problem' for psychiatry

This section considers the 'problem' of compulsion, both for psychiatry as a profession and individual practitioners.

Concerns about the Mental Health Act 2007

Chapter 9 examines the encounter in which the policing function of psychiatry is most evident: assessment for compulsory admission to psychiatric hospital. Mental health legislation governing these encounters has been a site of considerable ideological struggle in recent years. To inform a major review of the 1983 Mental Health Act, the Department of Health commissioned a programme of research (Department of Health, 2000a), a component of which was the MHA Study reported in this book. The draft Mental Health Bill, published for consultation in 2002, was successfully opposed by a coalition of mental health organisations called the Mental Health Alliance (www.mentalhealthalliance.org.uk), which included the Royal College of Psychiatrists. The Bill was redrafted, but was successfully opposed again. A slimmed-down "amending Bill" was announced in late 2006, which after further consultation received Royal Assent on in July 2007 and became the Mental Health Act 2007. During the course of this eight-year process to introduce new legislation, the government managed the remarkable feat of provoking virtually all of the major mental health organisations in the U.K. into creating an alliance of opposition against their proposals, even though many were formerly antagonistic to one another.

Key areas of contention included the introduction of new forms of compulsory treatment in the community, and the extension of psychiatrists' powers of coercion to cover 'untreatable' conditions, such as severe personality disorder. The 1983 Act specified that patients could only be detained against their will if they posed a risk to themselves or others and if treatment is likely to alleviate or prevent deterioration of their condition. The Government's position was that the treatability test in the existing Act was too narrow a definition because any patient who failed to respond to treatment could be discharged, even if they were judged to be dangerous. Psychiatrists responded that it was their job to treat people with mental illness but not to act as jailors of people with a severe personality disorder that they were unable to treat (RCPsych Press Release, 8-8-04). Indeed, in response to the second draft of the bill, the President and Vice-President of the Royal College of Psychiatrists expressed grave concern about extending the use of compulsory powers to a wider population. While welcoming some of the proposals, they called for legislation that improved "patient choice and involvement in their care and treatment", among other things. In so doing they invoked the 'problem' for psychiatry as a profession; that this would "further distance" psychiatric practice from the rest of medicine:

> "This proposed legislation would further distance the practice of psychiatry from the rest of medicine and ensure that people with mental health problems have less rights than people with physical problems... We are worried... that the Bill will extend the use of compulsory powers to a wider group of patients than is medically necessary... The College calls for new legislation which should be about improving patient care and treatment, and about reducing stigma and discrimination... The current proposals, with their emphasis on coercion, will make people reluctant to seek help." [Royal College of Psychiatrists' Press Release, 8-8-04: quotes from Dr. Mike Shooter, President, and Dr. Peter Zigmond, Vice President]

The problem for practitioners

Psychiatry is a medical speciality that was born in the asylum and has its own history alongside the history of medicine (Rothman, 1971; Scull, 1993; Rogers & Pilgrim, 1999; Porter, 2002). Foucault's contention in *Madness and Civilisation* (Foucault, 1967) that 'kind' psychiatry, as represented by the moral treatment provided in the asylums, is more repressive and worse than the 'cruel' confinement that preceded it is, as Porter (1990) and Scull (1993) have pointed out, not subject to straightforward empirical confirmation or refutation. Scull notes that there is no single answer to the question as to whether, and in what respects, the moral treatment era marked a 'gigantic moral imprisonment'. His argument about its *fundamental ambiguity* is, to this writer, persuasive:

> "... to reduce moral treatment simply to a species of imprisonment, a more thoroughgoing form of repression, is to mask an important truth behind a screen of rhetorical excess... [W]e do better to view moral treatment (like the larger reform it spawned) as fundamentally ambiguous:... there are good grounds for preferring the tactful manipulation and equivocal 'kindness' of Tuke and Pinel to the more directly brutal coercion, fear, and constraint that marked the methods of their predecessors. Yet one must also recognize that in the not-so-long run, it was the other, less benevolent, face of moral

> treatment that came to the fore: its strength as a mechanism for inducing conformity." (Scull, 1993, p.8)

The present book holds that this fundamental ambiguity remains at the heart of psychiatric practice. Studies of users' experiences cast doubt on the commitment of psychiatrists to what may be seen as today's 'kind' version of psychiatry, namely a genuinely patient-centred practice (Day & Bentall, 1996; Rogers *et al*, 1998). In apparent contrast, in our earlier study (Seale *et al*, 2006) consultant psychiatrists reported a general commitment to achieving concordant relationships and described how they sought to minimise perceptions of the coercive dimension of their work in order to facilitate shared decision-making. To build therapeutic alliances with patients, psychiatrists reported listening to people's views about their situation, showing empathy, understanding, warmth and respect, and using language carefully and tactfully, and avoiding technical words. One psychiatrist reported using a little trick to convey to the patient that he knows something about their personal life:

> "I do realise that it's a deception, but it's a way of making the patient think that I have a personal recollection of their personal situation - I'll jot down the names of their children or whatever [in the notes] so that I'm able to at least have a person think that I know something about their personal life." (Consultant psychiatrist; quoted in Seale *et al*, 2006, p.2867)

Psychiatrists in the same study conveyed an acute awareness of the effects of episodes of coercion on their relationships with patients. While they showed themselves to be willing to use dishonesty and coercion if they judged this to be in the best interests of their patients, they described various methods for preventing, minimising and if necessary repairing damage to the therapeutic relationship. For example, patients were judged to have fluctuations in the severity of their illness and their capacity to participate in decisions. This made it possible for these psychiatrists sometimes to discuss with them *beforehand* when coercion might be necessary (negotiating what might be thought of as an informal 'advance directive'). Alternatively, after a coercive episode and once the patient was considered to have regained competence, the doctor might try to reverse the damage done to the relationship, by allowing the patient full participation in decision-making (ibid).

This raises a central question for this book: how is it that psychiatrists are able to maintain a self image as being committed to 'kind', empathetic psychiatric practice in which democratic decision making is the ideal, while being experienced by a proportion of patients as implementing a fundamentally coercive and sometimes 'cruel' treatment regime? This book will show that the question may be answered, at least in part, by examining activities at the micro-level, particularly how decision-making is accomplished.

3.5 Acute inpatient care

The sheer volume of research reviewed in this section indicates the intense level of scrutiny there has been on acute inpatient care since the mid-1990s. Empirical work has helped to trigger an avalanche of initiatives to improve the quality of care provided in the U.K. These include the mental health charity Mind's 'Ward Watch' campaign (Mind, 2004), various Department of Health policies (Department of Health, 2000b, 2002), the user-led 'Star Wards' network (www.brightplace.org.uk/starnew.html), the Royal College of Psychiatrists' accreditation scheme (www.rcpsych.ac.uk/crtu/centreforqualityimprovement/aims.aspx), and Safewards (http://www.safewards.net).

I shall now review the health service research literature relating to everyday life and treatment provision on acute psychiatric wards. Four key themes will be addressed: systemic pressures, the subjective experiences of patients, how conflict is managed, and the therapeutic superficiality that characterises staff-patient relationships. The picture that emerges is of a healthcare context in which it is particularly challenging to build concordant staff-patient relationships.

3.5.1 Systemic pressures

The decline in the number of NHS hospital beds for people with severe and enduring mental health problems (Lelliott, 1996; Sainsbury Centre for Mental Health, 1998; Audini *et al*, 1999; Lamb & Bachrach, 2001; Fakhoury & Priebe, 2002) has not been matched by the increase in the numbers of residential places in other settings (Lelliott, 1996). Studies indicate that rates of admission have increased, particularly of young people (and especially of young men) (Lelliott, 1996; Lelliott *et al*, 1997; Muijen, 1999; Lelliott & Audini, 2003). Admissions are now largely unplanned emergencies often made compulsorily under the Mental Health Act (Fulop *et al*, 1994; MILMIS, 1995; Ford *et al*, 1998; Ward *et al*, 1998; Audini et al, 1999; Department of Health 2000a). Bed occupancy rates on acute wards[6] have increased (MILMIS, 1995; Shepherd *et al*, 1997; Ford *et al*, 1998; Audini *et al*, 1999) to levels as high as 153% in some areas (Higgins *et al*, 1999). Pressure on beds is particularly intense in inner-London (Audini *et al*, 1999; Fulop *et al*, 1994; Lelliott, 1997).

Overall, the duration of stay has declined (Muijen, 1999; Rogers & Pilgrim, 2001; Thompson *et al*, 2004) while rates of admission have increased. However there is evidence that acute admission wards, which are intended for short stays, invariably accommodate some

[6] An 'acute' bed is a bed designated for the admission of general psychiatric patients of working age. This excludes beds designated as offering specialist services, e.g. drug detoxification or for the treatment of eating disorders.

people for prolonged periods (Lelliott & Wing, 1994; Lelliott, 1996; Audini *et al*, 1999) who remain even though the ward manager thinks they no longer require acute care on that ward (Fulop *et al*, 1994). Such 'bed blocking' seems to occur despite opposing pressures of an ideological ('community care') and practical (very high bed occupancy) kind, and is partly due to lack of suitable community-based residential accommodation (Lelliott & Wing, 1994; Lelliott, 1996). Difficulties in discharging young men with a severe mental illness and histories of violence are most pronounced, as there is evidence that hostels exclude people who pose a risk of violence (Lelliott, 1996).

The 'systemic' pressures described above are associated with a change in the profile of patients, with acute wards now tending to house the more 'difficult 'patients (especially young men with schizophrenia) (Lelliott & Wing, 1994; Lelliott, 1996; Lelliott & Audini, 2003). Acute wards are, in effect, the only part of the mental healthcare system that cannot refuse to accept a referral. As such they can come to function as a dumping ground for those patients who cannot be managed by community services (Muijen, 1999). At the same time, acute wards are also characterised by rapid staff turnover, extensive use of bank and agency staff and low morale (Ford *et al*, 1998).

In wards that can quickly becomes 'clogged up' if discharges are delayed due to a lack of housing and community support (McDonagh *et al*, 2000; Abas *et al*, 2003), staff are faced with the challenge of treating patients adequately and with due care while emptying beds fast enough to prevent the threshold of admission to the ward from being raised even higher (Hummelvoll & Severinsson, 2001a, 2001b; Rhodes, 1991). Rhodes' (1991) ethnographic study of an acute psychiatric unit in the U.S. found the primary concern of the multi-disciplinary team to be the discharge of patients and how to manage the shortest possible stays for them. This remit shaped a *pragmatic* use of language by the team. For example, staff would apply diagnoses that made patients easier to 'sell on' to potential receiving agencies. In a helpful review of Rhodes' (1991) and other studies of nurses' use of language in the acute inpatient setting, Hamilton & Manias (2006) note that the mechanistic image of a conveyor belt comes to mind, with staff urgently doing what is necessary to maintain momentum in the system, rather than helping people to settle.

The systemic pressures reported above point to a bleak experience for people admitted onto acute wards. Indeed, they have raised concerns that the wards offer a non-therapeutic environment for those patients who are most vulnerable (Muijen, 1999; Barker, 2000).

3.5.2 The subjective experience of patients

Psychiatric hospitalisation means different things to the people who have experienced it. Surveys show that many inpatients dislike their physical environment, and find life on the ward to be intensely boring

(Barker, 2000; Mind, 2004). Patients report filling in time by sitting on their own doing nothing, watching television or talking with other patients (Higgins *et al,* 1999). Forty per cent of patients in a national survey reported having undertaken no social or recreational activity while on the ward (Sainsbury Centre for Mental Health, 1998; see also Mind, 2004). Indeed, the Mental Health Act Commission's national survey of acute admission wards found that most patients had little to do all day and that no interest was taken in them unless they made a disturbance (Ford *et al*, 1998). At the same time, patients report feeling unsafe, and complain about the lack of basic amenities (e.g. secure lockers) (Sainsbury Centre for Mental Health, 1998; Barker, 2000; Mind, 2004) and the ward environment more generally (e.g. lack of privacy) (Leavey *et al*, 1997; Barker, 2000; Mind, 2004).

Those patients who report being particularly dissatisfied with in-patient care include women (Sainsbury Centre for Mental Health, 1998) and, among people with a first episode of psychotic illness, those admitted under the Mental Health Act (Leavey *et al*, 1997). Aspects of practice most often identified as being of poor quality include: nurses' failure to explain their actions; the negative impact of nurses' group behaviour on the ward atmosphere (e.g. congregating in the ward office for long periods, in full view of the patients); their inadequate knowledge base; and the negative consequences of inadequate staffing levels (Beech & Norman, 1995). Also criticised by patients are, perhaps not surprisingly, coercion and punishment on the part of nurses (Rogers & Pilgrim, 1994)

Recent work has added to knowledge about what patients find positive about the experience. A study of a diverse group of psychiatric inpatients in Norway identified their common needs as being security, sleep, rest and help with finding meaning, which includes finding 'new tracks in life' and an ability to cope better with difficult situations (Hummelvol & Severinsson, 2001a). Patients at an acute psychiatric unit in the U.S.A. perceived the main value of hospital care as being refuge from self-destructiveness (Thomas *et al*, 2002). A psychiatric ward can nevertheless be a difficult and bizarre place in which to live; a social context in which patients' actions can be misinterpreted and pathologised (see Rosenhan, 1973). Patients who are presumed to lack competence may find their legitimate complaints or queries recorded in their notes as symptomatic of the illness (see Sutherland, 1997, quoted in Chapter 2).

Patients report wanting more contact and communication with staff, particularly in the context of therapy. Before beginning treatment in a psychiatric hospital in Germany, a higher proportion of patients expected to receive verbal therapeutic interventions (76%) than pharmacological therapy (61%) (McDonagh *et al*, 2000). Research in Nigeria (Olusina *et al*, 2002) and Germany (Fleischmann, 2003) shows patient dissatisfaction with the limited amount of time spent talking with doctors. The lack of someone to talk to is a common source of complaint among users of both inpatient and community mental health services in the U.K. (Rose, 2001). In hospital this can largely be explained by the centrality of medication, the limited availability of talking therapy, and the passing relationships patients have with nurses (see below).

Talking therapies are reportedly popular among patients/service users who have access to them, but many seem to want a 'sympathetic ear' and a chance to talk about ordinary things (Rose, 2001). Other research shows that users value nurses who are 'active listeners', but it is equally important that nurses know when to 'back off' and 'leave people alone' (Rogers & Pilgrim, 1994). Similarly, some inpatients in the U.S. expressed a wish for a deeper connection with staff and for more insight-oriented therapies (Thomas *et al*, 2002). Other patients may meet this need; indeed one group of patients reported that peer-administered 'therapy' was the most beneficial aspect of their stay in hospital (Thomas *et al*, 2002). The centrality of pharmacological therapy on acute psychiatric wards, discussed below, is at odds with patient expectations.

Patients report experiencing pressure to accept that they are ill and often believe that they are likely to be discharged sooner if they comply with this formulation of their problems (Hummelvoll & Severinsson, 2001a). Resistance to being categorized as 'mentally ill' can cause particular problems for patients who have been aggressive and who show no remorse. This is because, unless they accept the position that they are ill/mad, as opposed to personality disordered/bad, they risk being blamed for the incident and are less likely to receive empathy or therapy (Benson *et al*, 2003).

3.5.3 Management of conflict

A large body of research evidence indicates that an acute psychiatric ward can be a dangerous environment for staff and patients, and one that is permeated with various forms of conflict. Quantitative and survey research indicates problems of violence and sexual harassment in this setting, with high proportions of patients detained under the Mental Health Act (reviewed in Quirk & Lelliott, 2001; Quirk *et al*, 2004, 2005). The focus of research has been on overt conflict and how it is managed by staff. Research undertaken in the Netherlands has shown that that clinical staff are able to predict which patients are likely to become aggressive (Nijman *et al*, 2002). On a locked Norwegian acute ward, 90% of aggressive incidents were preceded by staff attempts to set limits (e.g. stopping patients from leaving the ward), problems in communication (e.g. misunderstanding) and physical contact, either separately or in combination (Mellesdal, 2003). Further, most aggressive incidents occurred within a few hours or days of admission (ibid). In a U.S. state psychiatric hospital, physical restraint was more often used at times when certain ward activities were taking place, such as meals and medicine rounds (Vittengl, 2002).

Safety and security measures for preventing or managing dangerous behaviours include banning of items, door security, alarms, close-circuit television, use of security guards and searches of patients and visitors (Bowers *et al,* 2002). Containment methods include use of seclusion, physical restraint, the use of medication, special observation and transfer to psychiatric intensive care or a close observation area (Bowers *et al*, 2003a; O'Brien & Cole, 2003). Research in the U.K. has shown that staff in psychiatric intensive care units often consider that transfer from the acute ward is requested too soon and before alternative management options have been exhausted, a view not shared by their counterparts on the acute ward (Bowers *et al*, 2003b).

On a Norwegian ward, strategies used to manage violence or threats varied according to the sex, age and diagnosis of the patient (Wyn, 2002). Survey research, undertaken in 12 London acute psychiatric wards, explored the relationship between different forms of staff-patient conflict and containment measures (Bowers *et al*, 2003a). Patient conflict behaviours (defined as issues and behaviours likely to cause discord between patients and staff) include outwardly directed aggression against objects or others, self-harm, attempts to abscond, refusals of medication, illicit drug use and general rule breaking (Bowers *et al*, 2003a). Acute ward staff tend to respond to self-harm by using continuous observation only, whereas they use all forms of containment to manage 'angry absconding' (a behaviour type that includes physical aggression against objects and others, attempting to abscond and going missing without permission) (Bowers *et al*, 2003a).

Observational research on a London ward has revealed nurses' use of a variety of 'low level' physical and interactional manoeuvres in order to manage patients' disturbed behaviour and resistance (Ryan & Bowers, 2005). Manoeuvres include 'body blocking' (where the nurse blocks an advancing patient's path), deception (e.g. promises broken after the patient has shown compliance) and stern looks (described by patients as being given the "evil eye"). These manoeuvres were seldom recorded, discussed or reviewed by staff in their daily practice, even though there were frequently used to manage conflict situations. The study thus demonstrates one of the benefits of participant observation research; namely that it has the capacity to reveal activities that are taken for granted by practitioners and would therefore probably go unmentioned in research interviews. Research findings about such activities can help to stimulate in staff a more reflective approach (for further discussion, see Chapters 4 and 9).

In Australia, qualitative research revealed that staff generally prefer to control behaviour by using seclusion rather than medication because the latter is perceived to take control away from the patient and increase frustration (Wynaden *et al,* 2002). Furthermore, staff were concerned about the unknown effects of giving medication to patients with a dual diagnosis of mental illness and drug misuse. In this context, seclusion was viewed as a comparatively safe and less restrictive patient management strategy, and one that was less likely to damage the staff-patient relationship. The same study also hinted at how organizational and contextual factors might influence the nature of the response to, as well as the frequency of, dangerous behaviours. Although staff reported using seclusion only after other patient management strategies had failed, the decision to seclude was accelerated if inexperienced staff were on shift. The perception was that inexperienced staff are unable to apply less restrictive measures safely (ibid).

The current evidence base overwhelmingly reflects a staff perspective on conflict and risk management, and there is little evidence for how service users cope in the acute ward environment, or strategies they employ to manage the risks they face or pose to others. My own ethnographic research, reported in this book and elsewhere (Quirk *et al*, 2004, 2005), found that patients on acute wards routinely take an active role in making a safe environment for themselves, in part because they cannot rely on staff to do this for them. A range of strategies were employed by patients to manage risk, including actively avoiding risky situations/individuals, seeking staff protection, and getting discharged. Integral to these strategies are the risk assessments that patients make of one another (ibid).

To date, the focus in the research literature has been on overt methods of controlling of patient behaviours in the ward setting, rather than the more subtle forms of manipulation in treatment decision-making and patients' methods of resistance to it. This subject is addressed in Chapter 8.

3.5.4 Therapeutic superficiality

The various forms of treatment or therapeutic activity available to patients on general adult psychiatric wards are summarised below.

Box 3.2: Types of treatment and therapeutic activity on an acute ward

- Medication
- Weekly ward rounds with the patient's consultant psychiatrist and others involved in their care
- Individual sessions with the junior doctor in charge of their case
- Sessions with their senior registrar from time to time
- Weekly, or perhaps daily, ward meetings attended by staff and patients
- Occupational therapy sessions, such as art and music appreciation, and other forms of group therapy
- One-to-one behaviour therapy provided by a clinical psychologist.

Patients cannot expect to receive all of the above on a regular basis, if indeed at all. By all accounts pharmacological treatment is central to the typical inpatient's experience, with many patients reportedly valuing it (section 3.3 above). There are certainly times when inpatients value their medications, even if it means being "doped up":

> "I was given droperidol [when admitted], the 'don't give a fuck' drug, which calmed me down considerably. It was not that it made any of the symptoms go away – it was just that I did not care about them anymore. That, together with 650 mg chlorpromazine, ensured that I was well and truly doped up. But I felt okay. I was safe." (Holloway, 1999, p. 51)

But it is the "therapeutic relationship", and associated communication, between the patient and his or her named nurse that is thought by both parties to be crucial in aiding recovery from an acute crisis (Higgins *et al*, 1999). An in-depth interview study, involving patients on two admission wards, also highlights the importance that patients attach to the therapeutic functions of the psychiatric nurse, in particular the value of him or her being an active listener (Beech & Norman, 1995; see also McIntyre *et al*, 1989). Quantitative research indicates that patients value 'humane' qualities in nurses such as empathy, tolerance and respect (Rogers & Pilgrim, 1994; Leavey *et al*, 1997).

Research suggests that patients have few contacts with staff other than doctors and nurses. For instance, a national survey found little evidence of use in hospital of occupational therapists, social workers or psychologists (Sainsbury Centre for Mental Health, 1998). But even contacts with nursing staff tend to be characterised by a 'therapeutic superficiality' (Hummelvoll & Severinsson, 2001a). A number of factors were found to contribute to this on a Norwegian ward. First there was inconsistent staff-patient contact resulting from a 'primary nurse system' which allocates a named nurse to each patient (the patient's primary nurse only works certain shifts and may not be present when the patient has a problem or is discharged). Second, nurses were concerned about making matters worse by uncovering complex problems (psychological 'abscesses') that cannot be dealt with in the short time the patient is on the ward. And third, the priority placed on pharmacological treatments, with medication being administered soon after admission and before the patient's problems had been fully evaluated (Hummelvoll & Severinsson, 2001b).

It is likely that such therapeutic superficiality will be compounded on wards with a high turnover of staff, because as well as making it difficult for patients to get to know staff and develop trusting relationships, it can also be boring for them to have to go over their stories with every change of doctor and other staff (see Sutherland, 1977). The short duration of most hospital stays, combined with the unpredictable and stressful character of the ward environment, can make it difficult for ward staff to build mutually trusting relationships with patients – irrespective of the patient's perceived capacity to contribute to treatment decisions. The threat of violence can feed into a vicious circle, particularly when mistrust and fear increases 'avoidance' between patients and staff to the extent that shared decision making becomes virtually impossible:

> "There were… lots of angry young men [on the ward]. The nurses spent their time shut in the office and the door to the ward was locked most of the time. There was much overt racism among the staff. Later I found out that one of the nurses had been badly assaulted by one of the patients, and so the staff were very scared. I was scared; the nurses were scared – it could hardly be a therapeutic environment." (Holloway, 1999, p. 47)

Psychiatric nurses report experiencing intrinsic difficulties in adopting the role of 'therapeutic instrument' for acute patients. Ethnographic research in Norway examined the difficult role conflicts that may arise when psychiatric nurses attempt such work. In particular it revealed how difficult it can be for nurses to balance human closeness and professional distance in relationships in which they may at times feel 'rejected', 'demeaned' and 'provoked' (Hem & Heggen, 2003). Also they reportedly find it difficult to balance the safety and security of patients, staff and the public, while respecting the rights and choices of individual patients (Bowers *et al*, 2002). A key challenge in this regard is to know when to reduce a patient's autonomy, for example via use of seclusion or limit setting. This issue is particularly difficult when working with patients who do not perceive themselves to be ill, who have been admitted against their will, perceive hospitalisation as a violation (Hummelvoll & Severinsson, 2002), and who reject therapy as being unnecessary. Adopting a 'paternalistic' or coercive approach, even if it is motivated by a desire to alleviate suffering, risks undermining such patients' trust in staff even further (ibid).

With health service researchers' attention typically focused on overt conflict and risk management in this setting, the nature of patient participation in treatment decisions has been explored only rarely. An exception is an observational study undertaken on a Finnish acute ward (Vuokila-Oikkonen *et al*, 2002). An analysis of video tapes of 'cooperative' team meetings[7] showed that staff encourage active participation by asking open questions, presenting reasons for the questions asked and creating opportunities for patients and significant others to express their points of view freely (ibid).

This review of literature related to acute inpatient care shows clearly that this is not one of the easier contexts in which to achieve concordant staff-patient relationships and shared decision-making. There are pressures on nursing staff to orientate to pragmatic, non-therapeutic goals (primarily emptying beds), it can be a dangerous place in which to live or work, and the opportunities for developing therapeutic relationships are minimal, not least because patient stays are so short.

The following section considers the psychiatric encounter where one might least expect to find evidence of shared decision-making – assessments for compulsory admission to hospital. Indeed these

[7] These are roughly equivalent to ward rounds in U.K hospitals, as described in Chapter 8.

interactions may be understood to symbolise the *breakdown* of shared decision-making, as it is an encounter in which an individual's competence and ability to undertake responsible self-monitoring is explicitly in question.

3.6 Assessment for compulsory admission to hospital

Health service research in the 1990s indicated that admissions to psychiatric hospitals in the U.K. were mostly unplanned emergencies made compulsorily under the Mental Health Act (Fulop *et al*, 1994; MILMIS, 1995; Ford *et al*, 1998; Ward *et al*, 1998; Audini *et al*, 1999). The numbers of these made in England increased by 63 per cent between 1984 and 1996 (Hotopf *et al*, 2000), with the rate of increase being greatest among young men (Lelliott & Audini, 2003). Geographical variations in medical practice are the rule rather than the exception (Anderson & Mooney, 1990), and are determined in part by non-medical factors such as the availability of resources, patient expectation or demand (McPherson, 1990) and local operational norms among clinicians (Greer, 1988). Variations in psychiatric practice are under-researched (Gilbody & House, 1999). However, there is evidence of considerable local variation in compulsory admissions made under the 1983 Mental Health Act (MHA), both in requests to social services departments for section assessments (Huxley & Kerfoot, 1993) and rates of detention (Bindman, 2000).

3.6.1 Two stages of a compulsory admission

Two stages of a formal (compulsory) admission to psychiatric hospital need to be distinguished at the outset: the initial *'breakdown'* stage and the subsequent *'assessment and admission'* stage. This distinction is most important because the two stages are likely to be affected by different non-clinical and extra-legal factors (Lawson, 1966). Such 'social determinants' of admissions include: the environment of the disturbed person, divided into social groups according to neighbourhood, social class, family, living conditions and other factors; and the policies, procedures and administrative machinery of the services involved (Lawson, 1966). The factors influencing each stage of the assessment and admission process are summarised below.

Stage 1: *Breakdown*

This stage of a compulsory admission comprises the events leading up to the request for help and the assessment referral. It includes the perception and recognition of illness, the 'breakdown of tolerance' towards the individual's behaviour (from both community members, mental health professionals and the police), and the definition of an emergency situation. Emerson's participant observation study in the U.S.A. shows that people are admitted because their situation in the community has become untenable (Emerson, 1989). The psychiatric emergency team's decision-making was specifically attentive to the *implications* of craziness for the situation within which the disturbed persons functioned. In other words, the very "seriousness" of a case was negotiated by reference to circumstances that merged psychological disturbance and situational tenability (ibid). This shows that acceptable, 'tolerated' behaviour, and its perceived riskiness, varies according to its social context. The concept of a 'tolerance threshold' (Lawson, 1966) is useful because it conveys the interactionist idea that what is considered 'crazy' in one place, family or social group is tolerated elsewhere; psychotic behaviour in an elderly person in supported accommodation may be tolerated much longer than it would in a young person living at home; and so on (Goffman, 1969). The tolerance threshold, and consequently whether help is requested, thus varies according to the candidate patient's personal characteristics and living arrangements, the attitudes of people with whom they interact, and public opinion towards mental illness more generally (Lawson, 1966). This might be expected to be reflected in MHA detention rates, and indeed social factors such as ethnic origin, gender and age have been associated with assessment outcomes (reviewed in Wall *et al*, 1999).

Stage 2: *Assessment and admission*

This stage comprises the decision for suitable disposal of each case (i.e. the 'assessment'), leading up to the point of admission to hospital or some other option. Factors identified as influencing events at this stage include the level of resistance shown by the candidate patient (Miller & Schwartz, 1966), the diligence of the petitioner in pursuing commitment (Wilde, 1968), attitudes of professionals and the 'negotiation' between them (Peay *et al*, 2000), plus supply-side factors such as admission policies of local hospitals (Lawson, 1966) and the availability of psychiatric beds (Bean, 1980; Haney & Michielutte, 1968).[8] Emerson's participant observation research, referred to above, highlights the active role professionals play in *averting* hospital admissions (Emerson, 1989). For example, mental health professionals did not merely assess whether it was feasible and safe for candidate patients to continue living in the community; rather, they would pro-actively discover and often *create* 'tenable situations', for instance by identifying a 'candidate caretaker' (ibid). Similarly, a U.S. study of emergency apprehensions of mentally ill people (Bittner, 1967), found that police officers would sometimes identify a caretaker to "look out" for the candidate patient, such a family member or neighbour, or even a trusted shop keeper or

[8] I have written elsewhere about some of the other extra-legal and non-clinical influences on assessment decisions: see Quirk, A., Lelliott, P., Audini, B. & Buston, K. (2003) Non-clinical and extra-legal influences on decisions about compulsory admission to psychiatric hospital. *Journal of Mental Health*: 12 (2): 119-130.

bartender in the case of rough sleepers. By using their detailed knowledge of local social structures and information networks, police officers thus created tenable social situations for people to continue living in the community (Bittner, 1967).

In the U.S.A., Holstein (1993) examined how commitment proceedings focused primarily on how patients managed practical everyday affairs; non-psychiatric criteria become paramount, with psychiatric condition receding into the interpretive background. Patients were more likely to be released[9] if they, or their attorney, were able to construct a tenable situation with controls approximating those exercised in hospital (ibid). In contrast, those arguing for release into community circumstances that required independent living skills or normal social functioning often found their arguments treated as unreasonable and unwarranted. This was because such circumstances are considered untenable "for mentally ill persons". Holstein concludes that mental health care in the USA is often 'deinstitutionalised' in name alone, because commitment proceedings promote a system of "community control" where patients must agree to be monitored and supervised when they are released. The assumption of mental illness in patients reduced the likelihood that a person wanting to live in circumstances requiring initiative and

[9] In the USA, courts determine whether or not a candidate patient should be admitted to psychiatric hospital against their will. These persons have almost always been brought to court from a psychiatric facility, where they have been interviewed, observed and sometimes treated. Therefore by the time of most 'commitment' hearings, the person is already a patient who is technically seeking release.

responsibility would be allowed to do so, because of the court's tenability concerns (ibid).

The key lesson from this literature is that decisions to admit are not simply concerned with severity of symptoms – or, as Foucault would put it, dividing the mad from the sane (Foucault, 1967) – but are partly about whether a tenable situation can be created as an alternative to hospital admission.

3.6.2 Participants' experiences

Previous studies suggest that the patient's experience of involuntary psychiatric care is a complex picture of support and violation; interpreted by those on the receiving end as a "balancing act" between good opportunities and great losses (Johansson & Lundman, 2002). A substantial number of involuntarily admitted patients do not retrospectively feel their admission had been justified or beneficial (Katsakou & Priebe, 2006). Studies indicate that the 'breakdown' stage leading up to an assessment is typically accompanied by a breakdown in shared decision-making with mental health professionals: communication becomes blocked, with candidate inpatients feeling that they are seen but not heard by those involved in their care (Olofsson & Norberg, 2001; Johansson & Lundmann, 2002; Watts & Priebe, 2002). There is evidence of considerable variation in how this breakdown is *managed* by all parties (see section 3.4). This will have implications for the therapeutic alliance.

As noted above, the distinction between voluntary and legal status is experienced by patients as blurred, with a proportion of voluntarily admitted patients feeling coerced (Rogers, 1993), and a significant number of the compulsorily detained feeling that they not been coerced (Hiday *et al*, 1997). In a U.S. study of patient, family and staff perceptions of coercion (Hoge *et al*, 1993), patients' accounts focused on the nature of the relationship with the person involved rather than how coercive powers were exercised. However, the 'coercion' literature, reviewed in section 3.4, shows that at least some of the confusion and ambiguity of over legal status can be explained by *how* the process of assessment and admission was managed. This point is underlined by my own analysis presented in Chapter 9.

A qualitative interview study explored the views of the various professionals involved in the assessment process in the U.K., including Approved Social Workers (ASWs), general practitioners, ambulance crews, the police, CPNs and psychiatrists (Bowers *et al*, 2003). Interviewees spoke of the difficulties of getting all necessary personnel to the place of the assessment at the right time, other practical difficulties, and the risk of verbal aggression and violence (ibid). Professionals' views on the impact of compulsory admission on the therapeutic alliance were mixed. For example, some CPNs were subsequently accused of having 'set up' the client, while others believed that 'being there' at a difficult time had been appreciated by their client. While some nurses reported that client anger at having been sectioned generally subsided over time, one reported being sure that it undermined trust and provoked concealment in their subsequent interactions: "Clients allow less access, are less familiar and keep things back after they have been [compulsorily detained]" (Bowers *et al*, 2003, p.965).

The Mental Health Act (2007) removed the ASW role and replaced it with that of the 'Approved Mental Health Practitioner'. This allows other mental health practitioners, such as CPNs, to coordinate MHA assessments. Considering the central coordinating role of ASWs in applying the 1983 Act (Department of Health and Welsh Office, 1999), their experiences were underrepresented in the research literature. The available material suggests that their role was multi-faceted, with practitioners acting as 'gatekeepers' to inpatient care (Sheppard, 1990) who sometimes offer therapy (Thompson, 1995), and who, as social workers, ensure that the psychiatric emergency is assessed in its social context (Hatfield *et al*, 1997).

It is therefore important to consider the *multiple roles* of ASWs in undertaking what has been called the 'dirty work' of the mental health professions; that is, work involving the practitioner being compelled to do something *to* clients, in a coercive sense, rather than *for* them, in a therapeutic sense (Emerson & Pollner, 1975; Bean,

1980).[10] Findings from my research, presented in Chapter 9, flag up some of the role tensions Approved Mental Health Practitioners are likely to experience in applying the 2007 Act.

3.7 Research questions

The broad aim of this book is to identify some of the obstacles to shared decision-making in psychiatric practice. The literature reviewed in this chapter has raised a number of specific questions that will be addressed in doing this. Some are listed below:

1. How are situations of 'equipose' locally constructed by participants?
2. How is pressure applied in the context of shared decision-making?
3. How are patients' and psychiatrists' treatment preferences communicated in decision-making and how are expressions of conflict between them resolved?
4. How is adherence or non-compliance talk done such that the 'therapeutic relationship' between doctor and patient, founded on trust, is not damaged?
5. To what extent is Goffman's 'total institution' model helpful for understanding the nature of everyday life on present-day psychiatric wards?

[10] The 'dirty work' literature will be discussed more fully in Chapter 9.

6. What are the methods of non-cooperation and resistance used by patients in encounters such as the hospital ward round?
7. Are compulsory admissions to psychiatric hospital still thought of as the 'dirty work' of the mental health professions?
8. How can mental health professionals rationalise such activities while maintaining a general commitment towards a 'patient-centred' practice.

Broader themes will be identified and developed as the analysis proceeds through the findings chapters.

Chapter 4

Methodology

CONTENTS

4.1 Overview of the three studies

This book brings together findings from three qualitative, observational studies of psychiatric practice, with the overall aim of exploring obstacles to the use of shared decision-making in this field of medicine. The design and focus of each study is summarised in Table 4.1 overleaf. For each study, appropriate ethical approval was obtained from local NHS research ethics committees. Data extracts in the findings chapters have been anonymised. The data, in the form of consultation transcripts and ethnographically-derived materials, totalled approximately 1.5 million words. These were analysed with assistance from software packages for qualitative data analysis. There was a different analytic focus to the write-up of each set of findings. Broadly speaking, while 'meaning' was central to both ethnographic and conversation analysis (CA) approaches, in the former the focus was on 'insider' knowledge and meanings, while in the latter it was on the activities that make those meanings possible in the first place (Cuff *et* al, 1990). So, rather than being concerned with 'understanding as tested' (e.g. identifying the categories used by Members in sociological interviews), the CA study was concerned with 'understanding as displayed' between speakers in naturally occurring situations. Despite the potential for analytic inconsistency, I believe that this work has far greater force and persuasiveness as a result of the attempt to combine, compare and contrast findings from the three studies.

Table 4.1: Summary of the three studies

	Prescribing Decisions Project	**Acute Ward Ethnography**	**MHA Study**
General aim	To investigate how decisions about long-term anti-psychotic prescribing are negotiated	To understand what everyday life on an acute psychiatric ward is like, from the patient's point of view	To understand (a) how MHA assessments are conducted, and (b) the roles and experiences of participants
Duration	April 2003	January 2000	October 1998

	↓ March 2006	↓ March 2003	↓ December 1999
Methods	CA of transcripts of audio-taped psychiatric outpatient consultations	Participant observation and interviews, with fieldworker in 'participant-as-observer' role	Participant observation and interviews, with fieldworker in 'observer-as-participant' role
Settings	Offices of 9 consultant psychiatrists in community mental health centres, located in 2 NHS Trusts in S.E. England	3 acute psychiatric wards in different hospitals in London (inner; outer; outskirts)	Community MHA assessments organised by 5 social work teams in 2 London boroughs (inner; outer)
Sample	92 psychiatric outpatient consultations, involving 9 general adult consultant psychiatrists and 88 patients (4 were 'follow up' consultations	Events observed during the course of 3-4 months of fieldwork on each ward. Includes 6 ward rounds involving 5 consultant psychiatrists and 22 patients	20 MHA assessments (10 from each borough), undertaken in settings such as the candidate patient's home, a hotel room and a police cell

	involving patients a second time)		
Topics covered	*Chapter 5:* How pressure is applied in 'negotiated' decisions about medication *Chapter 6:* Communication about adherence to long-term anti-psychotic medication	*Chapter 7:* The permeable institution *Chapter 8:* Patients' methods of non-cooperation and resistance in ward rounds	*Chapter 9:* Doing the 'dirty work'?: the multiple roles of the Approved Social Worker

The boundaries of the two London boroughs researched in the MHA Study were nearly coterminous with the boundaries of the inner- and outer-London NHS Trusts researched in the Acute Ward Ethnography. This meant that some of the people I observed being sectioned were admitted onto one of the wards I would come to observe for the latter study. Indeed, there was some overlap between individuals observed in the two studies. For example, a consultant who undertook a medical examination for one of the MHA assessments also ran two ward rounds I subsequently observed. Similarly, one of the social workers shadowed in the MHA study visited a ward I was observing for the Acute Ward Ethnography, to check up on one of her clients.

Combining the findings from the three studies means I am able to comment not only on how people are admitted onto an acute psychiatric ward – both under mental health legislation and voluntarily (two of the audio-taped outpatient consultations resulted in an informal admission) – but also what happens to them when they get there. Further, in the Prescribing Decisions Project I observed some people's first outpatient appointment after their discharge from hospital. This offers some insight into people's experiences after a stay in hospital, as do the follow-up interviews undertaken with discharged patients for the MHA Study. In short, the observations presented in this book span events leading up to, during, and after hospital admission.

To my knowledge this is the first combined observational study to encompass all of these aspects of psychiatric practice.

In the remainder of this chapter I will first describe in more detail the three studies' methods and settings. This will be followed by a description of how the data were analysed, and a discussion of the various methods used to enhance the credibility of the findings, including member validation. The chapter concludes with a lengthy 'confessional tale' about the anxiety I experienced while undertaking fieldwork on acute psychiatric wards. This has been included to show

how some of the central claims in my book emerged as well as to offer readers further material with which to evaluate the trustworthiness of my account.

4.2 Methods & settings: Prescribing Decisions Project (Chapters 5 & 6)

4.2.1 Conversation analysis

Conversation analysis (CA) starts with the simple observation that people's utterances are not 'just talk' about things that might be more or less truthful. Rather, talk – accounts, explanations and descriptions – may be analysed as *action*. Like other forms of qualitative research, CA focuses on meaning and context in interaction. However, in contrast to a 'subjectivist' focus on 'insider' knowledge, CA studies investigate activities and *how* meanings are locally accomplished. The analytical focus is thus on how activities come to have meaning in and through the talk itself, the idea of *sequence* being central (for overviews, see Levinson, 1983, pp. 294-370; Heritage, 1984, pp. 232-292; Silverman, 1993, pp. 125-143; Heritage & Maynard, 2007, pp. 9-19).

At its most basic, CA involves describing the commonsensical rules that people use and rely on in participating in intelligible social interaction, such as those relating to management of conversational turn-taking. For CA researchers, the question of whether reality is 'out there' or 'in people's heads' is not the issue, rather it is how people *make* reality 'out there' in and through their talk (action). The rules relating to turn-taking, for example, provide a *basis for discrimination*, between inadvertent overlap and rude interruption (Sacks, Schegloff & Jefferson, 1974). As Levinson neatly summarises:

> "Participants are constrained to utilize the expected procedures... if they don't, they find themselves accountable for specific inferences that their behaviour will have generated... Conversationalists are thus not so much constrained by rules or sanctions, as caught in a web of inferences." (Levinson, 1983)

Actual examples of interaction between people, as captured by audio- or video-tape recording, are analysed. The analysis provides insights into the nature and meaning of the interaction that cannot be attained by other means. CA was originally developed as a 'pure' science, motivated by the wish to discover basic and general aspects of sociality (Sacks 1992; Silverman 1998). It has since been 'applied' to examine how interactions are organised within a wide range of institutional settings (Drew & Heritage, 1992; Heritage, 1997; Hutchby & Woofitt, 1998; Ten Have, 1999; Drew *et al*, 2001). This has included the use of CA to study aspects of professional-lay interaction and therapeutic talk (Silverman, 1997; Hutchby, 2002, 2005; Heritage & Maynard, 2007). However, there have been relatively few CA studies in mental health care settings (see Chapter

3). To my knowledge, none have examined the topics addressed in Chapters 5 and 6.

A fundamental assumption informing the orientation of CA research is that contributions to interaction are both context-shaped and context-renewing (Heritage, 1997). This step by step, sequential organisation of talk is double edged (Heath, 1997) in that it is both an integral feature of the social organization of talk and a *methodological resource* for its analysis. As Sacks and colleagues (1974) note:

> "[It] is a systematic consequence of the turn taking organization of conversation that it obliges its participants to display to each other, in a turn's talk, their understanding of the other turn's talk. More generally, a turn's talk will be heard as directed to a prior turn's talk, unless special techniques are used to locate some other talk to which it is directed... But while understandings of other turns' talk are displayed to co-participants, they are available as well to professional analysts, who are thereby provided a proof criterion (and a search criteria) for what a turn's talk is occupied with." (Sacks *et al,* 1974: 728-9)

Conversation analysis thus proceeds from the viewpoint of the participants' understandings of one another's actions; rather than from the analyst's interpretations of what is happening (Drew *et al,*

2001). In other words, in a clinical context, the contributions of the patient to the interaction are influenced by those of the health practitioner and vice versa. A sequential analysis of talk-in-interaction is a powerful method for identifying forms of patient participation, and the interactional conditions that provide opportunities for this participation (Drew *et al*, 2001).

4.2.2 Sampling and data generation

Nine consultant general psychiatrists audio-taped consultations with patients attending outpatient clinic appointments at which antipsychotic medication was discussed. The psychiatrists, working in two mental health Trusts in south east England, had been interviewed about their perceptions of such consultations for an earlier study (Seale *et al,* 2006). As principal investigator on the study, I met participating psychiatrists individually or spoke with them over the telephone, in order to identify approximately 16-18 likely candidates among their current patients; that is, those who were currently being prescribed anti-psychotic medication and whom the consultant believed would not mind being approached about participating in the research. At least one week before their next appointment, these patients were sent a Patient Information Sheet accompanied by a covering letter from their consultant. The letter explained that the Royal College of Psychiatrists' Research Unit was "doing a research study to investigate what happens during appointments that people have with their psychiatrists" and that "Alan Quirk, who is doing the research" would be at the health centre when they attended their next appointment. It added that I would tell patients more about the research, answer any questions they may have and ask if they would like to be involved. The information sheet, printed on College Research Unit (RCPsych) headed paper, made it clear that I was independent of the clinic, that subjects did not have to take part, and that their refusal to do so would not affect their health care in any way.

The recruitment sites were the Community Mental Health Teams or health centres in which the outpatient clinics were run. I arranged my visits weeks in advance and actively sought advice from consultants about how to minimise any intrusion (see Chapter 5 for a description of how a psychiatric outpatient clinic is run). On the day, I would turn up shortly before the clinic was due to start in order to elicit consent from the consultant, and give him/her the tape recorder. I stayed outside in the waiting room for the duration of the entire clinic session (e.g. 09.00 to 12.30), leaving the psychiatrist to audio-tape consultations with consenting patients (typically one or two per clinic). As they turned up, I approached patients and third parties - relatives, carers and other mental health professionals - to explain the research and seek their written consent, as described above. Of the patients who were sent a letter about the research, approximately one third agreed to take part, a third refused, and a third did not attend their appointment.

Patients' expectations of the consultation were elicited at this point via a simple, one-sided 'pre-consultation' interview schedule, which would be administered in a quiet corner of the waiting room or an adjoining office. The interviews typically lasted only two or three minutes: I was concerned not to disrupt the clinic schedule by making patients late for their appointment, so interviews were deliberately kept short and to the point. Patients were asked standardised questions about how long they had known their psychiatrist, what they wanted to achieve from the appointment (if anything), their current medication, and age, sex, ethnic group and diagnosis. As patients exited the consultant's office I approached them a second time in order to administer a 'post-consultation' interview schedule, which included questions about how satisfied they were with the appointment, and whether there was anything they would have liked to have talked about but were unable to.

At the end of the clinic I met with the consultant to collect completed tapes and fill out a 'fact sheet' for each consultation. These simple, self-completion questionnaires gathered satisfaction ratings from the consultant as well as basic contextual information about the patient, the consultation and the therapeutic relationship. I aimed to be as unobtrusive as possible throughout the recruitment and data collection process.

Ninety-two consultations were taped between November 2003 and July 2005. The tapes were subsequently transcribed at different levels of detail (see section 4.5.1 below). Some extracts were transcribed using conversation analytic conventions. The CA transcription notations are presented in Appendix A.

4.2.3 Sample

Consultations (n=92)

Characteristics of the 92 tape-recorded consultations are summarised in Table 4.2 overleaf. Consultations lasted an average of 17.7 minutes (SD: 8.2). In 32/92 (35%) consultations a decision was made to change the medication; in the remainder the decision was made to leave it unchanged. (See Chapter 6 for a profile of the different types of medication decisions.) Third parties, such as the patient's carer or CPN, were present in 41 (45%) consultations. Four of the consultations were 'follow-ups', involving patients whose previous appointment had been recorded for the study. Most patients were well known to their consultant, as indicated by the mean duration of the doctor-patient relationship of nearly four years.

Table 4.2: Consultation characteristics (N=92)

		N
Duration (mean, in minutes)	17.7	na
Decision to change medication		32
Third party present (e.g. carer, CPN)		41
Dr-Pt relationship (mean duration, in months)	47	na
Follow-up consultation		4

Participants

Characteristics of the patients who participated are summarized in Table 4.3. This shows that the patient sample is predominantly White British (76/92; 83%) and mostly male (50/92; 54%) with a mean age of 42 years (range 22-65; SD: 11.5). Antipsychotic medication can be classified into two types: typical (tending to be older drugs) and atypical (tending to be newer drugs). Atypical antipsychotics are distinguished from typical antipsychotics in that they are better tolerated due to their lower risk of the extrapyramidal side effects of parkinsonism (stiffness or shakiness), akathisia (restlessness) or dystonia (acute stiffness) and raised levels of the hormone prolactin (leading for example to osteoporosis and sexual dysfunction). In this study 60 patients were currently being prescribed a single atypical antipsychotic; 20 a single typical; 11 were on two antipsychotics and in one case the antipsychotic medication the patient was (supposed to be) taking was not known.

Table 4.3: Characteristics of patients (N=92)*

		N
Male		50
White British		76
Age (mean years)	42	Na
Age (range)	22-65	Na
Age (standard deviation)	11.5	4
Single typical anti-psychotic		20
Single atypical anti-psychotic		60
Two antipsychotics		11

**Four of the consultations were 'follow-ups'. Patients involved in these have been counted a second time because their medication may have been changed in the first consultation, e.g. from typical to atypical anti-psychotic.*

The mean age of the nine participating psychiatrists was 48 (range: 43-52). All were white and three were women.

4.3 Methods & settings: Acute Ward Ethnography (Chapters 7 & 8)

4.3.1 Ethnography

Ethnography may be defined as the study of people in naturally occurring settings or 'fields' by methods of data generation that capture their ordinary activities. It involves the researcher participating directly in the setting, if not also the activities, in order to collect data in a systematic manner but without meaning being imposed on them externally (Brewer, 2000). The rationale for adopting this methodological approach, or style of research, is that the best way to understand the social activities and cultural life of an organisation or social group is to observe them up close, from the 'inside'. The researcher is then able to engage in what Goffman (1989) regards as the "serious ethnographic task" of assembling the various ways in which individuals are treated and treat others, and to deduce what is implied about them from this treatment.

According to Hammersley, ethnography is research that includes the following features. First, people's behaviour is studied in everyday contexts rather than under unnatural or experimental circumstances created by the researcher. Second, data collection is flexible and unstructured to avoid pre-fixed arrangements that impose categories on what people say or do. And third, the analysis of data involves attribution of the meanings of the human actions described and explained (Hammersley, 1998). While data are generated by various techniques, it is primarily done by means of participant observation:

> "The ethnographer participates, overtly or covertly, in people's daily lives for an extended period of time, watching what happens, listening to what is said, asking questions; in fact collecting whatever data are available to throw light on the

> issues with which he or she is concerned." (Hammersley & Atkinson, 1982)

Ethnography and CA thus demand the use of naturalistic, observational research methods, and share an attention to the detail of everyday social activities and the meanings associated with them. Indeed, Silverman (1998) notes that Sacks found much could be learned from such ethnographic work in sociology:[11]

> "Instead of pushing aside the older ethnographic work in sociology, I would treat it as the only work worth criticizing in sociology; where criticizing is giving some dignity to something. So, for example, the relevance of works of the Chicago sociologists is that they do contain a lot of information about this and that. And this-and-that is what the world is made up of." (Sacks, 1992, *Lectures in Conversation, Volume 1*: 27)

An observational study becomes ethnographic when the fieldworker is careful to connect the facts that s/he observes with the specific features of the cultural and historical *backdrop* against which these facts occur; that is, when observed phenomena in the field are grounded in the field or setting in which they were produced (Baszanger & Dodier, 1997). Further, the analytic focus is on actors

---

[11] See Silverman (1998, pp.52-56) for a helpful summary of Sacks' points of departure from the ethnographic tradition.

and meanings rather than the CA focus on the activities which make those meanings possible in the first place (Cuff *et al*, 1990). The book thus has two distinctive analytic foci: actors and meanings (ethnography) and the sequencing of activities that constitutes such meanings in interaction (CA). I return to this point in section 4.5 when describing how the data were analysed.

4.3.2 The fieldwork process

The study was designed to provide an insider's account of life on an acute psychiatric ward. The main method for generating data was participant observation on three NHS acute psychiatric wards in England. Two of the wards were located on general hospital sites in inner- and outer-London; the third was in the grounds of an old, large psychiatric hospital on the outskirts of the city. The table below briefly describes each ward.

Table 4.4: Wards on which fieldwork was undertaken

	Location	**Beds/layout**	**Staffing***
Ward A	Outer-London; one of 6 inpatient wards in the psychiatric unit of a general hospital	25-bed mixed sex ward. Most beds were in single bedrooms	2 qualified nurses and 3 nursing assistants during daytime shifts

Ward B	Inner-London; one of 6 inpatient wards in the psychiatric unit of a general hospital	15-bed mixed sex ward. Beds were in male or female dormitories (n=6 in each) or single rooms (n=3)	2 qualified nurses and 1 nursing assistant during daytime shifts
Ward C	Outskirts of London; stand-alone ward in the grounds of an old psychiatric hospital	25-bed mixed sex ward. All beds were in the male or female dormitories	2 qualified nurses and 3 nursing assistants during daytime shifts

**Based on mean number of staff on shift during the fieldwork period. Excludes student nurses.*

The fieldwork was conducted between July 2000 and April 2002. I worked for three to four months at each site and attended the ward on an average of two days a week. I visited on different days and at different times, including at night and at weekends, and attended the range of events that characterise the ward routine, such as ward rounds, group meetings and medication rounds. Although many interactions involving staff were observed and recorded, much of my time was spent in informal contact with patients; observing social interactions and talking with patients in lounges, dining rooms, corridors and other parts of the ward. My fieldwork role may be adequately summarised as an overt "participant-as-observer" (Gold,

1958);[12] I introduced myself to patients and staff on the wards as a researcher and handed out information sheets. Informed, written consent was obtained from those who were interviewed and a written summary of the purpose of the research was provided to all participants (see Information Sheet in Appendix B).

The methodological approach adopted is probably best described as 'combinative ethnography' (Baszanger & Dodier, 1997), of a type that incorporates a grounded theory approach (Glaser & Strauss, 1967). Unlike forms of integrative ethnography, which considers the context of events as a whole (a culture or society) to be discovered, or forms of reflexive, narrative ethnography (Marcus, 1998), this approach involved focusing on a geographic space (i.e. the hospital or a ward) and the situations, encounters and types of activity that occur within it. As Baszanger and Dodier (1997) rightly note, such an approach makes it closer to Chicago School interactionist sociology than anthropological forms of ethnography. In this study my participation in daily activities in hospital was as much about collecting facts as it was about gaining access to the meaning of situations for the subjects being studied. The implications of adopting such an approach for analysing the data are discussed below (see section 4.5.2).

[12] Following Brewer (2000), I fully recognize that this role is best seen as an ideal type. Later in this chapter I describe some of the challenges faced in managing my identity in a highly 'permeable' institution characterized by a rapid turnover of patients and staff.

4.3.3 Data generation and management

Sampling, data collection and data analysis were guided by grounded theory, meaning that fieldwork was interspersed with periods of coding and analysis so that emerging concerns could inform further fieldwork (Glaser & Strauss, 1967). Thus the study followed a progressive focusing design. Hundreds of events were observed and recorded during the fieldwork periods. Some of these were unexpected events that occurred while I was present; others were more predictable or could be timetabled, such as ward rounds. This allowed for visits to be timed or planned so that certain types of events could be observed repeatedly. The phases of fieldwork were separated by intervals of about two months. These intervals were used for preliminary data analysis, reflection and the generation of hypotheses to be tested during the next fieldwork phase, as agreed by members of the research team (including my PhD supervisor). This sequencing of fieldwork and data analysis is discussed further below in section 4.5.2.

Brief notes of observations and informal interviews were made at the time: these were typed up in the word-processed fieldnote book in the days following each visit. The notes were organised under the same standardised section headings I had used before in the MHA Study. These included: *Issues & themes* (emergent hypotheses), *Methodological issues* (e.g. relating to gaining access), *Field relationships* (i.e. about my relationships with people on the wards), plus headings relating to specific events, such as ward rounds. Organising fieldnotes like this made it easy to keep track of developments of thinking, for example the ongoing testing and modification of specific hypotheses (under *Issues & Themes*). This was especially the case once the Word files had been transferred into the QSR N6 software programme, because all data recorded under such headings were more easily retrieved and viewed together. Observational data were supplemented by 26 tape-recorded in-depth interviews with patients, patient advocates and staff who had been identified as key informants and with whom I had developed sufficient rapport. Analysis of the resulting database, which amounted to more than 600,000 words, was assisted by QSR N6 software (Richards, 2002).

A more reflexive account of the fieldwork process is offered in section 4.7 below.

4.4 Methods & settings: MHA Study (Chapter 9)

4.4.1 The fieldwork process

The observations made in Chapter 9 draw on qualitative data gathered in the course of a 14-month project funded by the

Department of Health (DH). The research aimed to complement quantitative studies for the DH- commissioned review of the 1983 Mental Health Act (Department of Health, 2000), by exploring the processes involved in conducting MHA assessments, and the roles and experiences of participants. The premise on which this observational study rests is that the process of MHA assessments will be better represented if the researcher has observed them as they naturally occur, rather than relied solely on participants' *accounts* of such activities (for example, Katsakou & Priebe, 2006).

Fieldwork was conducted in two London boroughs between December 1998 and July 1999. As the principal researcher, I spent approximately eight weeks in each borough, shadowing professionals to observe how MHA assessments are planned and undertaken. Fieldwork was conducted in five teams: two hospital-based social work teams in outer London, and two community mental health teams (CMHTs) and an out-of-hours emergency duty team in inner London. This made it possible to compare the modus operandi of a range of teams in local authorities with markedly different sectioning rates: approximately 350 Part II formal admissions (civil detentions) per 100,000 at risk in inner London, compared with 50 per 100,000 in outer London.

I spent two distinct periods in the field. Initially 10 MHA assessments were observed in the outer London local authority (LA 1). After a gap of approximately three months I then moved on to observe a further 10 assessments in the inner London local authority (LA 2). Each fieldwork period lasted eight weeks, which gave me sufficient time to type up my observations and reflect upon them. This period also allowed hypotheses to be identified and modified in light of new observations, within each fieldwork period. The three-month gap between each fieldwork period was reserved mainly for the more detailed and systematic analysis of the data. This allowed emergent hypotheses from one area (outer-London) to be tested and possibly modified in the other (inner-London).

4.4.2 Data generation

A grounded theory approach was adopted (see section 4.5.2 below for further description). The unit of analysis or 'event' was the Mental Health Act assessment, as made under Part II of the Act. As expected, these assessments were sometimes discrete (e.g. a co-ordinated assessment completed in the space of a few hours) but often fragmented and protracted (e.g. spanning many days as attempts were made to co-ordinate the availability of professionals and tie in with the movement of an unpredictable person in the community). In practice, this meant that it was not always possible for each assessment to be observed in its entirety, from start to finish, such as when a new assessment came in while a prolonged assessment was being tracked.

During assessments I consciously attempted to adopt a less participatory field role than the one used in the Acute Ward Ethnography: the gloss 'observer-as-participant' (Gold, 1958) probably best summarises it. In practice, this meant generally 'keeping out of the way' during assessments and keeping inter-personal contact with candidate patients and professionals to a minimum. One way I did this was to observe activities from a short distance away - perhaps from an adjacent room or the hallway. Events were discretely noted by me at the time or immediately afterwards. I also spent considerable amounts of time in the social work teams to which I was attached, and participated in what went on (e.g. I attended multi-disciplinary team meetings where upcoming assessments were one of the items on the agenda). This was useful in that it offered me the opportunity to contextualise MHA assessments in relation to mental health professionals' other work.

Handwritten notes were subsequently typed up in the word-processed fieldnote book. Additionally, tape-recorded interviews with seven key informants, and numerous informal interviews, were undertaken with professionals. In-depth follow-up interviews with four of the 20 candidate patients and one carer were used to elicit the views of these participants (the other candidate patients either refused to be interviewed, were still acutely unwell, or could not be traced). A purpose-designed topics guide was used for the patient/carer interviews. This covered the broad areas to be addressed, which had been identified as important, but allowed flexibility within these areas for interviewees to talk about specific issues that were important to them (see topics guide in Appendix C). The field observations and transcribed interviews yielded more than 33,400 lines of typed text (roughly 400,000 words): these constituted the qualitative database.

The plan had been to complement the field research by audio-taping assessments and applying CA methods to transcripts of them. This was strongly recommended by one the reviewers of the original grant application, and is something that I would have valued doing. However, ASWs in the participating teams were understandably concerned that requesting to tape record the assessment might inflame an already tense and potentially volatile situation. The ASWs would not persuaded otherwise (for example, see section 4.4.4) so the plan was quickly dropped and I made a handwritten record of the talk in assessments instead, to the best of my ability. These notes were subsequently typed up as part of the fieldnote book.

4.4.3 Sampling and sample profile

The way in which MHA assessments are organised varies greatly between geographical areas. In some areas, there are small teams of ASWs dedicated to this task, while in others ASW duties are shared across a large number of social workers who have other duties. It is common for teams that work outside of office hours (sometimes known as Emergency Duty Teams) to be quite separate from those working 09.00 to 17.00, Monday to Friday. Likewise the organisation and availability of both psychiatrists and GPs varies. There is thus no 'typical' configuration. The two local authorities were selected because they were known in advance to differ substantially in the organisation of staff who conducted assessments. (Appendix D compares how the five participating teams operated.)

Twenty assessments were observed (10 from each borough), selected via theoretical sampling. This is integral to the constant comparative method of grounded theory development and involved choosing assessments to study and settings to observe, as well as people to interview, which were likely to challenge and develop the emergent theory (summarised in Seale, 1999). For example, the first two assessments involved candidate patients held in police custody under Section 136 of the MHA. Various hypotheses – or, more crudely, 'ideas to check out' in subsequent fieldwork - emerged from an initial comparison of these two cases. It was decided that these initial hypotheses would best be tested against events in a markedly different setting in the community. I therefore decided to wait for such a referral, and chose not to attend the team's next assessment which again involved someone held in police custody.

This sampling technique yielded observations of a range of assessment types and outcomes. Eleven of the assessments were for possible admission for assessment (Section 2) and nine were for admission for treatment (Section 3). One Section 4 assessment (emergency admission for assessment) was observed as part of the 'build up' to a subsequent Section 3 admission. Fourteen lead to a formal (compulsory) admission, two to an informal (voluntary) admission and four to no admission. Assessments occurred in a variety of community and institutional settings, with nine of them in the candidate patient's home. They were initiated by general practitioners (GPs), psychiatrists or other members of the CMHT, social workers, the police and members of the candidate patient's family. The mean number of professionals directly involved in assessments - excluding staff working behind the scenes - was five. The profile of assessments is described more fully in Chapter 9.

The time I spent attached to each team, and the number of assessments observed, are summarised in the table below.

Table 4.5: MHA Study fieldwork

	Time (weeks)	**No. of assess'ts observed**
LOCAL AUTHORITY 1 (OUTER-LONDON)		
Hosp SW team A	2	4
Hosp SW team B	6	6

LOCAL AUTHORITY 2 (INNER-LONDON)

CMHT A	3	5
CMHT B	4	5
Emergency Duty Team	1*	0
TOTAL	16	20

*Comprised of three out-of-hours shifts: 2 x 16 hrs & 1 x 24 hrs

4.4.4 Gaining access

There are some long stories to be told about how I gained and maintained access to each of the many research settings observed for this project. There is, however, not the space in this chapter for me to recount them all. I reflect on how this process was managed in the MHA Study because it tended to be more precarious and time-consuming in this project than it was in the other two.[13]

My research role was negotiated before I entered the field, first with senior management and then with local staff. I also telephoned and/or met many other local gatekeepers and interested parties in order to inform them about the research and, if possible, elicit their support.

[13] Only just, though, in the case of the Acute Ward Ethnography: maintaining access to the wards was a major source of anxiety (see section 4.7).

These individuals included the chair of a local mental health service user group, a divisional manager for mental health, a police chief inspector responsible for liaising with mental health services, the head of a patient advocacy service, and lead clinicians in both areas. The trust and co-operation of staff (especially ASWs) was crucial to the success of the project, so I attended whatever staff meetings were necessary in order to explain the study and give them a chance to voice any concerns.

Predictably, there was variable staff co-operation both between and within teams. One of the hospital-based social work teams was particularly resistant, if not downright hostile, to my approach. In our first meeting, I was forced to defend the research passionately, in response to an onslaught of criticism, scepticism and suspicion from the 14 social workers in the room. Fortunately, this reaction had not been unexpected, and I had come prepared. The team's senior manager had warned me beforehand that while he supported the research, my association with the Royal College of Psychiatrists would be a major hindrance. Indeed he invoked long-standing antagonisms between social workers and psychiatrists by advising me that there would be little I could do to prevent ASWs from seeing me with an "RCP [Royal College of Psychiatrists] label across your forehead". If ever there was a time to invoke my identity as a *sociologist,* then this meeting, I knew, would be it. Also, I subsequently found out that the team had been "stitched up" in a TV documentary; most unfortunately by a reporter who had used similar observational methods to those I was proposing. The field had thus been "spoiled" (Bulmer, 1982), making it even harder for me to gain access to this particular team. Under these circumstances it is perhaps understandable that I quickly dropped the plan to tape-record the assessments (see section 4.4.2).

Generally, though, the trust and cooperation of ASWs tended to increase as I became more accepted into the work environment. Indeed, the 'resistant' social work team mentioned above turned out to be one of the most helpful I encountered. I attempted to make it clear that the wishes of staff who wanted to be 'left alone' would be respected. In practice, this entailed 'backing off' from attempting to observe certain assessments and not 'pushing my luck' with ASWs who seemed antagonistic towards the research.

Accessible and brief summary sheets (one-side of A4) were prepared; one designed for staff involved in assessments and one for candidate patients and relatives. These were handed out during assessments at what I judged to be the appropriate moment. The sheets were similar to those used in the Acute Ward Ethnography (see Appendix B) in that they explained the purpose of the research; stated that people could at any time refuse consent to allow the researcher to observe all or any part of the MHA assessment process; and emphasised that refusal to participate would not result in any adverse repercussions for an employee, patient or carer/relative. I negotiated with the ASW beforehand how best to obtain patients' consent in the upcoming assessment. In some assessments the ASW or another practitioner explained why I was present, while in others I did this directly. As with staff, any indication - implicit or explicit - that the candidate patient wanted to be left alone was respected and acted upon. The ASW or I gained verbal and, if required, written consent from the workers involved and verbal agreement from the patient and carers/relatives. Separate information sheets were produced for the follow-up interviews with patients and carers. These formal, tape-recorded interviews were subject to written, informed consent.

Two points should be emphasised about the study design. First, the analytical focus was inevitably on the later part of compulsory admission – that is, from the referral onwards – because events leading up to the candidate patient's 'breakdown' or crisis were not observed directly. And second, my close association with the assessment teams, and in particular the ASW, meant that events were observed much more from a professional perspective than a service user's perspective. Originally, the study had aimed to generate a richer, more in-depth account of the experiences of candidate inpatients. Their views are represented in Chapter 9, but there is a limit to what can be claimed on the basis of an analysis of four follow-up interviews.

4.5 Data analysis

The data were in two main forms: transcripts of talk-in-interaction, and ethnographically-derived materials (mainly fieldnotes of observations and informal interviews, and tape-recorded research interviews). I shall now describe how each type of data was analysed.

4.5.1 Transcripts of talk-in-interaction

Using different levels of transcription

I started the analysis of data from the Prescribing Decisions Project by first 'actively listening' to each of the 92 tapes at least twice to familiarise myself with the material. On the first run-through I typed up a summary of the talk, highlighting any mention of medication (*) and sequences of talk that seemed particularly relevant (**), such as prescribing decision sequences. Listening a second time, I checked and edited the summary and added detail as required. Tape marker numbers were added to make it easy to retrieve key sequences. An example of this first level of transcription is shown in the box below.

Box 4.1: Transcription level 1 (summary of consultation talk)

Opening to Consultation 49:

000: **Opening. P [patient] says she's less paranoid, not taking the Olanzapine anymore, put on weight, erratic eating.
014: **C [consultant] says they always had different views on Olanzapine, his view being that she shouldn't take it, wasn't convinced it was helpful. P's mother says that she had been in favour of it once, but not now, because P is much less paranoid. C suggests finding something else that doesn't make her put on weight.
((Consultation continues))

This gave me a general 'feel' for the data, including a sense of the frequency of particular activities (e.g. how many prescribing decisions were made) and their structural location within consultations. For example, I noted at this early stage in the analysis that patients sometimes volunteered a report of non-compliance at the opening to the consultation, an example of which is shown above (see where P reports "not taking the Olanzapine anymore").

Next, all the tapes were fully transcribed by a typist. Each tape was listened to and transcription errors were corrected. An example of this 'second' level of transcription is shown in Box 4.2 below. It offers a new, more detailed version of the opening to the same consultation as is shown above.

Box 4.2: Transcription level 2 (typist-level transcription)

Opening to Consultation 49:

C: Right. Well, how are things?
P: Yea not too bad. I think sort of, getting better slowly. Um not feeling nearly as paranoid as I was. I'm not taking the Olanzapine any more. I have put on weight but that's partly my own problem.
C: About how much weight have you put on, if I might ask?

Some analyses of these typist-level transcripts are presented in the findings chapters, including the 'who gets what they want' table in Chapter 5. CA-transcribing all the tapes in their entirety would have taken far too long, so having these typist-level transcriptions made it possible to examine, analyse and summarise the content of all 92 recordings, rather than selected extracts only. Further, these 'level 2' transcripts allowed me to identify analytically relevant extracts for CA-level transcription. The final stage was to CA-transcribe such extracts, an example of which is shown below. The opening to Consultation 49 is shown for a third time, making it possible to compare different levels of transcription of the same sequence of talk.

Box 4.3: Transcription level 3 (transcription using CA notations)

Opening to Consultation 49:

1	C:	°Right° well how are things Sarah?

2	P:	.hh Yeah not to bad um::: I (think um) (0.4) .hh sort of (0.4)
3		getting better slowly, (0.4) erm:: (1.0) .hh not feeling nearly
4		as paranoid °as I was°, .hh I'm not taking the Olanzapine any
5		more, .hhhh
6		(0.2)
7	C:	[°Right°
8	P:	[°Erm°
9		(1.0)
10	P:	I have (over-) put on weight (.) but (.) that's (.) partly (.) my
11		£own problem .hhh erm:::£
12	C:	H-how much weight have you put on °if I might ask°

Analytic strategy

As in any qualitative inquiry, there is no 'one best strategy' for selecting which data extracts to focus on in the analysis (Ten Have, 1999). In CA there is a preference for the investigator being 'open' to discovering phenomena and examining materials via "unmotivated looking" (Psathas, 1995; Schegloff, 1996). At its purest this analytic strategy is arguably less well suited to the 'applied' form of CA used for the Prescribing Decisions Project: one that required me to orientate the analysis towards addressing both sociological *and* social problems (Bloor, 1997). The objectives of the study, as outlined in the grant application, included to (a) describe and create a typology of the persuasion techniques employed by psychiatrists, and (b) explore the circumstances in which decisions about antipsychotic medication are truly negotiated, involving active participation by the patient. The parameters of the analysis were thus pre-given, however the decision as to which *specific* research questions to pursue was left open. My choice of topics - how pressure is applied in 'negotiated' decision-making (Chapter 5), and communication about adherence to long-term anti-psychotic prescribing (Chapter 6) - was based, pragmatically, on what I considered would be relevant to practitioner, service user and academic audiences, rather than one such audience alone.

The level 2 (typist-produced) transcripts were indexed with a coding scheme, and NVIVO qualitative data analysis software was used to code and retrieve segments of text. To analyse communication about adherence to long-term anti-psychotic prescribing, for example, transcripts were inspected to retrieve segments where this occurred. Exchanges about non- or partial adherence (i.e. where the patient reports having not taken medication as prescribed) occurred in 22 out of the 92 (24%) consultations recorded. Sensitised to CA concerns, I summarized these sequences in a table showing the three key parts of each exchange: that is, how each report of non- or partial-adherence was elicited, reported and responded to. This marked the beginning of a *sequential* analysis of the data: the table allowed me to identify patterns in the data, both within sequences (e.g. how does the psychiatrist respond to a report of non-adherence produced 'voluntarily' by the patient?) and across sequences (e.g. do psychiatrists respond differently to such reports compared with those elicited via a direct question?). The table also made it possible to generate frequency counts of activities, and identify extracts that needed to be CA-transcribed (e.g. negative instances/deviant cases). The table was large, covering nine sides of A4 paper. Part of it is reproduced below.

Table 4.6: Extract of table used in analysis of adherence exchanges, reported in Chapter 6 (Prescribing Decisions Project)

Note: C = Consultant, P = Patient, CPN = Community Psychiatric Nurse

No.	Elicitation	Adherence report	Psychiatrist response	Decision
32	C asks a direct compliance question: "Have you stopped your medication then?". C evidently hears this to have been invited by P's preceding turn: "My mood's been	P reports having carefully and slowly cut down her medication, adding that she feels "100 times better" for it *[Anti-psychotic = Sulpiride]*	C cautiously accepts P's decision, after having carefully checked on her moods, sources of support, risk awareness etc. C announces that he is sure P will take appropriate steps is she feels herself getting unwell	Post-hoc acceptance/ agreement, albeit done very much more cautiously than in consultation PDP08

	fine but you're not going to be very happy with me (unclear)"			
49	Voluntary disclosure in response an innocuous opener ("Well how are things?")	P reports "not taking the Olanzapine any more". P reports having "put on weight but that's partly my problem". 3rd party (Mother) reports that she had been in favour of P taking it in the past, and that it had helped *[Anti-psychotic = Olanzapine]*	A clear 'no problem' response: C indexes previous convers-ations in which he had disagreed with P about taking Olanzapine in the first place. A deviant case in this regard (normally the assumption is that C wants P to comply)	Post hoc ratification, plus an attempt to find non-drug solutions for P's anxiety
88	C asks if P has any worries in terms of treatment. CPN	P reports having stopped taking her morning dose of	'No problem' response. C replies that this sounds "eminently	Post-hoc acceptance/ agreement for P to

	evidently knew about the non-compliance	Quetiapine, unless she feels racy *[Anti-psychotic –= Quetiapine]*	sensible", and checks whether P wants to continue with this. C thus hears/ constructs it as a decision-in-need-of-ratification. C normalises the report ("we've found plenty of people taking it at night have done fine")	continue taking 175mg at night and none in the morning

Finally, the Level 3 transcriptions were analysed using CA methods, which essentially involved a detailed turn-by-turn consideration of the turn-taking process. The results of this analytic strategy can be seen in Chapter 6. A similar procedure was employed to examine how pressure is applied in negotiated decisions about anti-psychotic medication (Chapter 5).

4.5.2 Ethnographically-derived materials

The general aim of the two ethnographic studies was to provide audiences for the research with 'insider' knowledge, although rather than claim to reproduce the meanings of staff and clients (see Schwartz & Jacobs, 1979), I endeavoured to 'represent' them as best I could , in part by taking on board the methodological assumptions of subtle realism (Hammersley, 1992). Informed by Layder's (1993) resource map for research, the analytic focus was on inter-related levels of social organization, encompassing 'micro' (e.g. situated activity) and 'macro' (e.g. organizational context, historical process) elements.

I will now describe in some detail how I actually did this; that is, how I used the aggregation of specific events recorded in the fieldnote books for the Acute Ward Ethnography and MHA Study.

It is probably helpful to clarify what I did *not* attempt to do with these materials. First, I did not try to discover from my data a cultural 'whole' in relation to which these sequences of ethnographic observations could be integrated. Such 'integrative ethnography' (Baszanger & Dodier, 1997) is associated with classical social and cultural anthropology, and involves producing an account in which all data are integrated into a whole (monographic totalization). In other words, the ethnographic text is presented as a picture of a culture or society as it was revealed to the ethnographer at the end of an intense learning period, by which point s/he had become able to see it as a whole. Also, I have chosen *not* to produce a hyper-reflexive ethnographic text which preserves the temporal dimension of the sequence of events recorded, and in which my encounter with the study populations is viewed as a *dialogue* between individuals who themselves belong to different collective wholes. Such 'narrative ethnography' (Baszanger & Dodier, 1997) starts from the valid and important observation that the switch from experience in the field to the ethnographic text is an extremely complicated and very personal activity, in which the researcher's biography and the actual work of writing are essential elements.

Instead, my approach is best described as 'combinative ethnography' (Baszanger & Dodier, 1997), because it incorporated a process of grounded theorising and sought to construct a 'saturated' or 'thick' theoretical account that is comparatively well defended against threats to its truth status. The aim was not to integrate the data collected around a collective whole in terms of a common culture, but in terms of a *territory of geographic space* in which social and occupational groups interacted. The main point was to make a detailed list of the activities occurring in a given space (psychiatric hospitals; acute wards; ward rounds; offices of community mental health teams; MHA assessments) and record the interaction between the different communities that encounter and confront each other in that space. The ethnographic material thus aims to identify certain types of activities and experiences as examples of more general phenomena, this allows for some level of *generalisation rather than totalisation*. The methodological implications of grounded theory (Glaser & Strauss, 1967) include that the analytic focus should be not so much on collective entities/cultures as on *situations or types of activity,* classified by a sociologist and studied in their relationships to each other, with a view to revealing their compatibility or the contrasts between them. My aim, therefore, was not to gain access to some collective whole that governed behaviour; rather, it was to reveal a *combinative inventory of possible situations* in a given institution or space.

This approach has made it possible to generalise at different levels. For example, certain types of activities, roles and experiences that are possible in certain spaces have been identified, including patients' methods of non-cooperation and resistance in ward rounds (Chapter 8) and the multiple roles of the Approved Social Worker during MHA assessments (Chapter 9). The central claim to have emerged from the Acute Ward Ethnography is that Goffman's metaphor of the total/closed institution (Goffman, 1961) fails to capture the highly permeable nature of the psychiatric institutions studied, so the "permeable institution" is today a better ideal type against which to examine and compare empirical cases (Chapter 7). This ideal type is constructed on the basis of an analysis of related events recorded in the study's fieldnote book.[14]

[14] This takes the analytic strategy closer to 'integrative ethnography' than is the case elsewhere in the thesis. In other words the analysis involved (a) constructing typologies of activities and the meanings associated with them, and (b) presenting these as evidence for factors associated with an increased permeability of today's 'bricks and mortar' psychiatric institutions.

Sequencing of fieldwork and data analysis

Qualitative data analysis packages QSR N6 and NUD*IST (4.0) were used to facilitate data analysis in the acute ward and MHA studies respectively. The sequencing of fieldwork and data analysis reflected my aspiration to adopt a grounded theory approach. In both studies, fieldnotes were written during each fieldwork period, as described above. These, plus taped-interview transcripts, were transferred into the software analysis packages during the time-period between each phase of fieldwork, allowing for an intensive period of 'interim analysis' and theory building (see Figure 4.1). This was valuable because it gave me time away from the field (periods of approximately two to three months) when I could reflect on the material already gathered, develop the analysis, and think about how best to gather data in the next phase of fieldwork. In short, this sequential ordering of fieldwork and data analysis assisted in generating theory from the data.

Figure 4.1: Sequencing of fieldwork and data analysis for the MHA Study[a]

PROJECT START

↓

Fieldwork in outer-London borough:

Observation of 10 MHA assessments, plus formal and informal key informant interviews with staff, accompanied by ongoing data analysis and theory-building (using fieldnotes typed up as Word files)

↓

Computer-assisted interim analysis (NUD*IST)

↓

Fieldwork in inner-London borough:
Observation of 10 MHA assessments, plus formal and informal key informant interviews with staff, accompanied by ongoing data analysis and theory-building (using fieldnotes typed up as Word files)

↓

Computer-assisted interim analysis (NUD*IST)

↓

Follow-up interviews with patients/carers:
Ongoing data analysis and theory-building (using Word fieldnotes and transcribed interview data)

↓

Computer-assisted final analysis (NUD*IST)

<u>PROJECT FINISH</u>

[a] The sequencing of fieldwork and data analysis followed a similar pattern in the Acute Ward Ethnography, albeit with a third phase of fieldwork in place of follow-up interviews

Coding for interim and final analyses was undertaken on-line and segments were retrieved for theory-building and writing-up (Buston, 1997). The 'index tree' or coding frame was modified as appropriate during each of the three distinct phases of computer-assisted analysis (see Appendix E for the final version). Throughout the text I have attempted to offer plenty of illustrative examples of key concepts so that readers will know what I am referring to. And, I have attempted to adhere to the subtle realist principle that the more central the claim, the more the evidence needed in support of it (Hammersley, 1992).

Analysis of talk in ward rounds (Chapter 8)

Transcripts of talk in ward rounds were recorded by me during the course of six ward rounds observed for the Acute Ward Ethnography. These were run by a total of five consultant psychiatrists and involved 22 patients. Tape recording was possible in only one of the ward rounds, so I attempted to take detailed notes on exactly what was said in the others, to the best of my ability. This is not a perfect substitute for tape recording but they are good 'field notes' in the sense that they captured well the sequence and sense of what was said. Analysis of these data was broadly informed by knowledge of CA techniques, allowing comparisons to be made between ward round interactions and outpatient consultations. The ethnographically-derived transcriptions look contrived when compared to those made using reliable CA conventions. Inevitably the transcripts have been tidied up, but I believe that they are adequate for the analytical purposes to which they have been put. (Holstein, 1993, used similar data for his CA study of psychiatric hospital commitment proceedings).

It can be argued (for example, Hammersley, 1992) that the theoretical descriptions produced by ethnographers are often little different from the descriptions and explanations employed by us all in everyday life. What distinctiveness they ought to have concerns not their theoretical character but the explicitness and coherence of the models employed, and the rigour of the data collection and analysis. I believe my account of life on an acute psychiatric ward is more credible and generally *better* than a scandal-mongering TV documentary,[15] but how can I prove it?

4.6 Credibility

Here, I outline how the credibility or trustworthiness of a qualitative research report may be judged. With a subtle realist approach, the validity of truth claims is judged on the basis of *adequacy* (Hammersley, 1992). This "pragmatic" approach means that (a) we must consider whether the claims made are sufficiently plausible, given our existing knowledge, (b) that where a claim is central, more

[15] For example, Channel 4's Dispatches documentary *'Britain's Mental Health Scandal'*, broadcast on 9 October 2006, which covertly filmed events on three acute psychiatric wards.

convincing evidence will be required than where it is marginal, and (c) we need to distinguish between definitions, descriptions, explanations and theories (ibid, pp. 69-72). In sociology, truth claims cannot be validated through replication by a subsequent investigator, as it can in the natural sciences. This is because, as Bloor (1997b) notes, while social life contains elements that are generalisable across settings (thus providing for the possibility of the social sciences), other elements are particular to given settings (thus forever limiting the predictive power of the social sciences). Instead of attempting to replicate findings across settings, sociologists have developed techniques which may be considered alternative methods of validation (for example, Bloor, 1997b; Seale, 1999).

Trust in the findings presented in this book will hopefully have been enhanced in a number of ways. First, all three studies having been undertaken in a ***spirit of grounded theorising***, with attempts made to search and account for negative instances. Second, various methods of ***triangulation*** have been used (Denzin, 1978). In the two ethnographic studies various types of evidence were collected before concluding that a thing is true (Becker & Geer, 1957; Glaser & Strauss, 1967; Becker, 1970a), and in the Prescribing Decisions Project, the CA research complemented our interview study (Seale *et al*, 2006). It did so because while the analysis of consultation transcripts revealed activities that psychiatrists failed to mentioned in research interviews (e.g. what patients do to construct safe conversational environments in which to discuss non-compliance -

see Chapter 6), the interviews helped one-off psychiatric consultations to be understood in the context of the unfolding doctor-patient relationship in which they take place. Third, ***simple counts*** of well-defined phenomena have been included in the findings chapters where appropriate. This is aimed at increasing the credibility of claims and guarding against accusations of anecdotalism that can be levelled at certain qualitative studies (for example, McCabe *et al*, 2002). And fourth, ***member validation*** techniques were used. The remainder of this section will focus on how such techniques fed into the development of two central truth claims presented in later chapters – one derived via the CA research and one that was derived ethnographically.

4.6.1 Member validation

The philosophical justification for this approach comes from Schutz (1967) in that member validation essentially assesses continuities between 'common-sense thinking' of community members (first order concepts) and 'scientific thinking' of the social scientist (second order concepts). As Bloor (1997b) rightly notes, a problem with member validation is that the exercise is never context free, so member endorsement is provisional and subject to change. For example, practitioners may be wary of perceived criticism and concerned about the implications it may have for their funding, and so will respond accordingly (ibid). Rather than regard it unproblematically as a simple 'validation' exercise, it seems more helpful to view member validation as a method for testing researchers' claims by gathering *new* evidence (Bloor, 1997b; Seale, 1999). That noted, it can only enhance the credibility of a research report if it is perceived to have been undertaken in a fallibilistic spirit; that is, if the researcher is genuinely ready to revise claims rather than merely confirm them as true (Seale, 1999).

Testing a CA-derived claim

Given that member validation is an ongoing feature of conversation (see section 4.2.1 above), it can be argued that CA research is self-validating, in the sense that the mode of analysis offers demonstrably true interpretations of members' reasoning (Perakyla, 1997). As Seale (1999) rightly notes, CA allows for a highly 'positivist' reading of social reality, emphasising singular, fixed interpretations that can be judged as either true or false. For this writer, this is one of the great appeals of adopting a CA approach, as it requires a less overtly 'fallibilistic' reporting style than is the case for 'subjectivist' qualitative research. (This, I hope, is reflected in the different writing styles used in this book to report findings from CA and ethnographic components of the work.) Even so, I agree with Seale's (1999) argument that there is potential value in adopting a fallibilistic approach, implied by more conventional member validation exercises, in CA research.

It was in such a spirit that I sought feedback on interim findings from a consultant who had participated in the Prescribing Decisions Project. One of the consultations in which he was involved included a decision sequence which is claimed, in Chapter 5, to exemplify a 'directed' decision. The consultant and I talked about the following extract from that sequence at length.

Extract 4.1 (Consultation 50)

Outcome = Swapping of anti-psychotics (from Olanzapine to Sulpiride)

1	C:	Wha- what d'you think you'd like [to do (about)
2	P:	[Well I think I-I would
3		like to try the new medica[tion
4	C:	[Yeah
5	P:	(French) new medication ( )
6	C:	Yeah .hhh the:::: (0.2) I'm just trying to think the-
7		<u>pos</u>sibly the most (0.6) likely side effect (.) are (0.6) yer
8		sexual performance °might be affected by it° (0.5) in
9		terms of (0.2) delayed ejaculation. (.) (But) that's the
10		most likely thing that °can happen° (0.4) (that) doesn't
11		happen with everybody or [(.) a lot of people
12	P:	[.hhh (.) (fine) actually I am
		single so=

Two key observations may be made for present purposes. The first is about when information about side effects is delivered by the consultant. Notice how this is done, on lines 6-11, only after the patient has already chosen to swap anti-psychotics, on lines 2-3 (this was the first time that side effects of Sulpiride were discussed in this consultation.) The second observation is that the consultant delivers information on one potential side effect only - delayed ejaculation (line 9) – rather than, say, the three or four most likely side effects. Without presenting the full analysis at this point, it can be observed that these actions function to reinforce the decision, and do not 'encourage' the patient to change his mind about trying the new medication. The analysis, presented in full in Chapter 5, reveals some of the methods used to 'direct' decision-making such that the consultant's 'preferred' treatment option is chosen.

In the first, very rough draft of these findings, the consultant's activities were presented as evidence of a subtle form of *coercion*. Discussing this with the consultant, he took my point, but believed it to be a harsh interpretation, because he did not remember *feeling* having been at all 'coercive' in this instance. Indeed, I had to admit it did not *sound* like a particularly coercive encounter either – far from it - so I conceded that he might have a point. This prompted me to examine the data again. After further inspection I spotted a vital piece of evidence that had previously been missed; namely, the complete absence of patient resistance throughout the entire decision sequence. More specifically, further examination of the transcript found the patient to be following the psychiatrist's recommendations, cooperating with the decision-making, and at no point orientating towards the doctor's actions as 'pressure' or 'manipulation'. This made me revise my claim (or theory) and present this as an example of 'directed' rather than 'coercive' decision-making (see Chapter 5).

When we met to discuss the next draft, it was evident that the consultant had read the text carefully. He was now persuaded by the revised claims, and reported finding the analysis "fascinating". It had evidently stimulated a reflective mood in him because he reported having "changed his practice" as a result of reading and thinking about it. Specifically, he told me that it had sensitised him to the decisive influence of the *timing* of side-effects information delivery in prescribing decisions – something that neither he nor his colleagues had considered before. The reported findings thus enabled taken-for-granted skills to be perceived and made into objects of thought for the first time (see Silverman, 1997). Further, this feedback reassured me of the potential relevance of these findings to a practitioner audience.

The member validation exercise generated evidence that was reassuring and valuable in itself, because it also adds credibility to the claims made in Chapter 5 about how pressure is applied in negotiated decision-making. The consultant's feedback certainly made *me* feel more confident in the claims I was making. However, the consultant's account went beyond feedback and validation because he voluntarily disclosed new evidence for an even more subtle form of manipulation in the consultation – one that could not be inferred from the transcript. The consultant explained that of all the many potential side effects of Sulpiride, he chose to deliver information about delayed ejaculation because *he knew this patient was sexually inactive* and did not believe it would be perceived to be a major problem. The consultant certainly did not believe it would make him change his mind about trying the new medication, which he confirmed had been his preferred option in this case. I was only able to elicit feedback from the psychiatrist in this encounter, and not the patient, but I believe it supports the general argument, presented in Chapter 5, that this was an example of 'directed' decision-making. It certainly does nothing to *falsify* it.

This then is a comparatively strong version of member validation (Seale, 1999), in that a member commented on the analysis of a transcript in which he was a speaker. The exercise generated new evidence that (a) supported the emergent theory of how prescribing decisions are 'directed' and (b) suggested how this theory might be developed or extended. Not only did it confirm the potentially decisive influence of the timing of side-effects information delivery in prescribing decisions (a CA-derived claim), it suggested that doctors may also consciously choose to deliver on some side effects and not others, in such a way that their 'preferred' treatment option is chosen.

Clearly, members/interviewees might lie about their motives in order to portray themselves in a morally good light, but this seems unlikely in the present example. This begs the question: why would this consultant psychiatrist 'own up' to the dubious practice of manipulating one of his patients? From an interactionist perspective, there are three plausible reasons for this.[16] First, the consultant and I had developed a trusting relationship over a period of many months; this would have made him more inclined to be open with me about such matters. Second, the decision sequence is a deviant case in the sense that the consultant had pressing reasons for wanting the patient to stop taking his present anti-psychotic immediately.[17] I knew it was not typical of this consultant's practice, he knew that I knew this, and I tried very hard to convey that the research was being undertaken in a spirit of understanding rather than evaluation. Finally, and perhaps most importantly, my perception was that this consultant had approached the member validation exercise in an admirably fallibilistic spirit himself, with the aim of improving his practice.

The consultant's account of his motives does not appear in the findings chapter, due to pressures on space and because the truth claims presented are sufficiently well-supported by CA-derived evidence. However, I hope the present discussion has served its

---

[16] From a CA perspective, part of the answer for this consultant's candour is rather straightforward; namely, that he was not doing 'manipulation' (or 'coercion') in the first place – as I take great pains to demonstrate in and through the detailed analysis presented in Chapter 5.

[17] The consultant was responding to the patient's report of having experienced seizures as a side effect of taking his present anti-psychotic (see Chapter 5).

purpose in showing the potential value of applying conventional methods of member validation in CA research. In this example, the new evidence sheds light onto a level of manipulation that could not have been revealed through CA methods alone.

Testing an ethnographically-derived claim

Findings from the MHA Study were also subject to a strong version of member validation. Copies of the final report on which Chapter 9 is based were distributed to 15 selected individuals, including at least one representative of each of the five participating CMHT/social work teams, for their views on its content (e.g. factual accuracy, interpretation of data) and to help identify the key conclusions and implications for practice. Overall, the response of ASWs to the final report has been very positive, indicating that it offers a fair representation of their experiences. This is evidenced by the fact that ASWIG (the Approved Social Workers Interest Group) recommended it as an "excellent piece of research" in their written evidence to the UK Parliament's Joint Committee on the Draft Mental Health Bill (www.publications.parliament.uk). The immediate reaction of participating ASWs was more mixed, though, partly because some evidently felt that they had been 'exposed' through their work being portrayed in a critical light.

For example, the central question addressed in Chapter 9 is whether assessments for compulsory admission are still considered part of the 'dirty work' of the mental health professions. It is argued that in portraying such interventions as 'dirty work', to outsiders (e.g. researchers) and each other, practitioners invoke their organisational goals. In other words, displaying the morally dubious and *anomalous* nature of the coercive dimension of this work, practitioners are able to communicate what they are *really* in the business of doing; that is, some kind of caring or social support role in which shared decision-making is the norm. Evidence is presented in support of the claim that while this remains the case in certain institutional contexts, the meaning of such work has been transformed by the new social and institutional context in which it is being undertaken; that is, 'deinstitutionalised' mental health care.

This claim was included in draft interim reports circulated for comments, including to participating teams. While there was unanimous agreement with the general thrust of the argument, some social workers were concerned about how this discussion of 'dirty work' made them appear in print. This led me to clarify some points in the analysis and emphasise that it bore no reflection on the humane qualities of the ASWs concerned. It also alerted me to the need to proceed cautiously in reporting findings on this particular issue. This, in turn, gave me greater confidence in the 'dirty work' claim, because in and through 'taking issue' with it (and accusations of 'blasé' or 'cold-hearted' coerciveness some thought it implied), they once again invoked the morally dubious nature of this work, albeit in a research

context. Such ongoing analytical input from practitioners thus proved to be an important and effective validation method.
Is reflexive methodological or 'confessional' accounting of aspects of the research process another way to enhance the credibility of qualitative research report? I will now argue that it depends on the spirit in which such accounting is done.

4.7 Anxiety in ethnography: a confessional tale

Seale (1999) is correct to note that researchers' confessional tales are not always produced in a fallibilistic spirit; they are sometimes used as a rhetorical claim to authenticity. The confessional tale offered here – about the anxieties I experienced too often while undertaking the Acute Ward Ethnography – is intended to help readers understand how some of the central truth claims emerged; namely those about how patients on the wards assess and manage risk (see Quirk *et al*, 2004; 2005), and about the greater 'permeability' of today's wards as compared with those in total institutions (reported in Chapter 7). I hope readers will be assisted in evaluating the quality of the report presented, by seeing how I used my emotional responses and experiences in the field to help generate such findings.

What crystallised about half way through the second phase of fieldwork, in a comparatively rough inner-city ward, was that I simply was not enjoying the research. Indeed my overwhelming feeling was one of anxiety – especially during the fieldwork – and this contrasted with my experience of undertaking other research, such as depth interview studies with marginalised social groups (Quirk *et al*, 1998; Rhodes & Quirk, 1998) and participant observation in methadone clinics (Lilly *et al*, 2000; Quirk *et al*, 2003). At the same time I was aware from the outset that understanding the experience of psychiatric patients was never going to be an easy ride, so I began to think about how I might use my own emotional responses in this process; hence my decision to monitor and reflect on the topic of anxiety in ethnography.

4.7.1 Some sources of anxiety

Throughout, I regularly had good reason to doubt ***whether I would be able to pull the study off.*** I am referring here to project management issues, logistical problems, and various other threats to the successful completion of the study. For example I experienced a whole host of problems in gaining and maintaining access to acute wards in three NHS Trusts (see section 4.4.4). I suspect it is not uncommon for researchers to share my worries about whether the study would ever get off the ground – for example, through failing to gain approval of local research ethics committees or to win over highly sceptical staff and management. Numerous difficulties were associated with ***recording data during fieldwork***. For example, there were a number of instances when I thought my surreptitious recording of aide memoir notes in the ward toilet had been rumbled (e.g. nurse: "Where've you been Alan? I've been looking for you for ages – I need the keys you borrowed to the interview room."). Yet at other times I was concerned about holding back from such note-taking: first, because things were likely to be forgotten when it came to writing up field-notes later; and second because the quality of the notes would probably suffer too. Another source of anxiety related to the ***amount of data being generated***. While I was initially concerned that I was not recording enough data, my worry later was that I had collected far too much (600,000 words for the Acute Ward Ethnography alone) and would be unable to manage it all in the final analysis.

Identity management was particularly difficult on the wards, and I suspect that this is partly why the research was so difficult to do. I am referring here to issues such as the presentation of self – what to wear, how to behave and so forth (Goffman, 1989) – but also more broadly the different roles ethnographers are likely to adopt or have cast upon them – especially in settings frequented by numerous and varied social and occupational groups. For example, the three wards I spent time on held an ever-changing population of patients, visitors, and a wide range of different professionals, and amongst these groups notions of acceptability varied greatly (see below). There were also many times when I was made to feel like an ***unwanted guest*** on the wards. Certainly, I did not always feel welcome, especially at the start of each fieldwork period on a new ward when people were at their most guarded. Aside from general worries about being snubbed, or at worst being stopped from coming on to the ward, I had to manage some excruciatingly embarrassing moments, for example as a result of trying to strike up conversations with unwilling participants. If patients on the ward do not want to know you, and the nurses and other staff are suspicious of your motives, then what on earth do you do, and where do you actually *go*? These could be very difficult situations to manage, especially on wards where there were no quiet corners into which you could retreat. Such moments literally brought me out in a cold sweat on more than one occasion.

From time to time I worried (and occasionally still worry) about ***how people will respond to the findings***. My formal aim, as a health service researcher and paid employee of the Royal College of Psychiatrists, was to portray service users' experiences of acute psychiatric care as best I could, so I knew that some of the nurses would be unhappy with what they might perceive to be a partisan account. However, if I watered down implicit or explicit criticism, service user organisations would probably view the report as a 'cop out', especially in the light of my association with the Royal College. The last thing I wanted was an indifferent response, but then again I did not want people involved in the research to feel they have been exposed or, worse, betrayed. The final source of anxiety came from ***threats to my physical and mental health***. This acknowledges the fact that some studies require the researcher to put him or herself into comparatively risky situations. I will return to this issue shortly.

Other researchers have reported experiencing similar anxieties during fieldwork (for example, Lareau, 1996). Indeed, while undertaking the other two studies reported in this book I carried with me similar concerns about how participants would respond to the findings and whether they would feel I had betrayed them. So, in the remainder of this chapter I will reflect on what it was that made the Acute Ward Ethnography especially anxiety-inducing. I will argue that this was largely due to the peculiar nature of the setting and the risks that people face within it (participant observers included), combined with the unusually unstable field role that I had on the wards.

4.7.2 Difficult to get to know strangers

The fieldnote extract below (Box 4.4) was recorded early on in the fieldwork on the first ward I studied. It offers an example of social ineptitude on my part; in response to what, at that time, seemed to be strange behaviour by one of the patients. My "crap" reaction to being stared at told me that I had a long way to go before I would be seen as 'fitting in'. It also indicates that this can be a particularly difficult setting in which to get to know strangers. The patient concerned became one of my closest, most helpful and trusting key informants, but this took the two of us many weeks to achieve, after an unpromising start.

Box 4.4: Fieldnote extract ***[recorded on Ward A for the Acute Ward Ethnography]***

I had been chatting to student nurse-Michael in a quiet corner of the TV room/day room for some minutes, when I became aware of a patient [Helen] watching us. She was staring at me intensely, from about 3 metres away, to my left. After a while she walked slowly over to the doorway to my right, and stood there for 30 seconds or so, still staring at me and occasionally Michael. To my eyes it looked like she wanted to say something but was holding back. This is the first time I could recall seeing her.

N.B. AS A NEWCOMER TO THIS ENVIRONMENT, I FOUND HER BEHAVIOUR EXTREMELY DISCONCERTING *[emphasis in original]*. I really didn't know what to do – should I maintain eye contact or look away? I really didn't know what it meant – I couldn't 'read' her, as it were – but I sensed that she was very suspicious of me and I didn't know how to deal with the situation. I ended up feeling, and possibly looking, very shifty – I made eye contact with her a couple of times, did a nervous half-smile, and looked away again. Her facial expression remained the same throughout and she never averted her gaze for an instant. Mine was a crap reaction and I knew it. Student nurse-Michael carried on talking to me, and was not in the least bit disturbed by this, but I went into 'weird behaviour' mode in that when he asked me a question, I would respond hesitantly, look blankly downwards at the coffee table between us (i.e. at neither Michael nor Helen, who I knew was still staring at me), then stop talking altogether mid-sentence, hoping for Michael to say something. I had a real feeling of being scrutinised intensely by Helen, who was still staring at me from the doorway, and felt anxious that she may have thought we were talking about her (which we weren't). She finally left the room, at which point I explained to Michael why I might have seemed so odd (he had been unaware that Helen had been staring at us).

Crucially, I then asked him what he thought had been going on in her head – while acknowledging that it might be hard for him to say. But as an experienced student who knew the patient, and who had been on three acute wards as part of his training and had completed 2.5 years of his 3-year nursing diploma, he evidently knew much more about this than I did. He told me that Helen would normally eventually have said something to him, but didn't because she didn't know who I was and was suspicious of me. I asked what was best to do (thereby invoking a teacher-pupil relationship between us). He replied that I should say hello, introduce myself – which is what I did at the earliest opportunity, approximately 5 minutes later.

In between times, Michael and I talked further, but on seeing Helen continuing to stare at us, through the glass window-wall between the TV room and corridor in which she was standing, I asked if he felt he really should speak to her now, which he did.

Altogether she had been staring non-stop at me and Michael (mostly me) for about 10 minutes.
She came back into the room, at which point I approached her. I sat down and said something like "Hello, my name's Alan, I'm here doing some research trying to find out what it's like to be a patient on a psychiatric ward…"

When I said that I was from the RCPsych, she visibly recoiled, although I quickly tried a repair by saying that I'm not a psychiatrist or nurse, and that "I'm a social scientist." At least twice she said "well that sounds VERY interesting". The final time she did that as part of the closure of the conversation, saying "That sounds VERY interesting. But I'm not able to help you with it", and looked like she was about to rise from her of her chair. I pre-empted her 'escape' by quickly replying "Yeah, that's fine, I just wanted to say hello and to let you know why I'm here". I added, while getting out of my chair to 'leave her be' in the room, that I would be around for a couple of months, so I'd be seeing her.

4.7.3 Risk & vulnerability

I tended to play it safe on the wards and kept clear of situations that looked like they might be about to get out of hand. Even so I was surprised at how badly my time on the wards affected my 'nerves'. This, I believe, had much to do with being in closer proximity to danger and risk than I am used to in my everyday life. Indeed, the research required me to place myself into the types of situations I would usually actively try to avoid. For example, on the wards I saw fights breaking out, people being verbally abused and was abused myself, I was told all sorts of disturbing stories, and I saw vulnerable patients being preyed on and exploited by others – in fact all the things that my reading of previous research accounts had led me to expect (reviewed in Quirk & Lelliott, 2001; 2003).

Observing such things first-hand was disturbing enough, but a turning point in the study was when I started to feel vulnerable myself. This began during a phase of fieldwork on the inner-London ward, and it got to the point where I sometimes felt too scared to go in. I was usually able to compose myself before each visit, in a café around the corner from the hospital, but occasionally I had to phone the ward from there on my mobile, make my excuses and take the day off. The feeling of relief bordered on exhilaration at such times, even though I had travelled 90 minutes across London only to return home empty-handed.

All this was going on at a time when two or three patients were having a major and disturbing impact on the atmosphere of the inner London ward, which was undermining a lot of people's sense of security, including my own. I will now briefly describe an example of an event that added to my growing feeling of vulnerability at that time. It culminated in the most troubling time I experienced during the fieldwork.

4.7.4 A bad place to be vulnerable

One of the patients – who I will call Katherine – was, for a week or so, probably one of the most abusive people I had ever met. As well as directing her invective and racist comments at other patients and nursing staff, she regularly used the ward phone to make abusive phone-calls, both anonymously to people at random and to those known to her. For example, one of her hoax calls brought out the fire brigade and police to her parents' house at two o'clock one morning.

Despite this I felt she and I were getting on quite well under the circumstances, and I felt personally unthreatened by her. However, on one of my visits we entered into a conversation that disturbed me, partly because she started asking me questions about my partner, such as where she worked. In principle I have absolutely no problem in exchanging such personal information – and have often done this during fieldwork – but I realized that it was risky in these circumstances. In fact, I was truly horrified at the thought of how this information might be used – would my partner start receiving abusive phone calls at work from Katherine? – so I answered vaguely and evasively.

This definitely added to my feelings of anxiety and vulnerability around that time, yet equally I was aware that I needed to 'go there', as it were, if I was to come to terms with just how difficult life on the ward can sometimes be. Below I present extracts from my 'anxiety diary' recorded around that time as part of my fieldnote book. This indicates the personal cost of attempting to gain 'insider' knowledge in this particular setting.

Box 4.5: Extracts from 'Anxiety Diary' ***[recorded during fieldwork on Ward B for Acute Ward Ethnography]***

Context: *These notes were recorded at the end of an intensive phase of fieldwork on a 'rough' acute psychiatric ward in inner-London. It was my lowest moment – I had been feeling scared to go onto the ward, partly due the 'threatening' behaviour of a couple of patients (including Katherine, mentioned above). Also, I was more than two months into the fieldwork on that ward but had yet to speak about the research with two of the ward's four consultants. I was getting increasingly worried about how they would respond to being told that a researcher had been on their ward without their knowledge or consent. My line manager at work was on sabbatical, and I had felt unable to approach his temporary replacement (a very eminent psychiatrist) or my PhD supervisor for support. Rightly or wrongly, I had been keeping such worries to myself.*

Diary extracts

Sunday, 2.10am

I woke up 40 mins ago, feeling v anxious again; thinking thru some of the bad things I've seen and heard. For example, I was imagining what on earth [a patient] had been thinking when she literally attempted to scratch ward manager-Julie's eyes out. A scene from the film 'Red Dragon' came to mind (reflecting eyes).

At a particularly difficult moment I lay there in bed thinking that I was "looking into the jaws of the beast", i.e. I was confronting the reality of mental illness. But I've calmed down a bit now! Couldn't get back to sleep so thought it better to leave [my partner] there and make these notes.

This is all very worrying, but has probably got a lot to do with the fact that I'm very tired, due to lack of sleep, yet my brain is still racing, having been intensely focused over the last three days. I've been working non-stop, either typing up notes before the visit, doing the fieldwork visit itself, or handwriting notes immediately afterwards.

I have reduced my anxiety by deciding: (a) to go onto the ward again only when I feel ready to. That means maybe not at all next week; (b) to speak to the consultants only when I feel able to. I have been getting increasingly worried about the possibility of them reacting negatively, yet I know that I have got to speak to them before it's too late [i.e. before the fieldwork ends in three weeks' time]. I'm sure they could get most upset if they find out that a researcher has been speaking with and observing their patients without the consultants' knowledge or consent. That said, my response must be that I thought Professor Taylor [their lead consultant] had spoken to them about the research (as he said he would) and that I have spent a lot of time observing activities in the day hospital [rather than the ward] up until now; (c) finally, I could, if really necessary, phone in sick for Dad's 70th birthday party. A calming thought (re my generalised, free-floating anxiety, in this example about making a speech), but a last resort.

Two days later... Tuesday, 11am
I've come into the office having taken a lieu day in Clacton on Sea. Sat in the sun, pigged out on sausages, chips and beans at a beach café, followed by donuts and ice cream on the pier. I had a great motorbike ride up there and back, and felt good. Feeling back to normal, if a little concerned by my experiences over the last few days. Then again I feel pleased to have 'gone there' as it will no doubt help the research. Etc etc.

Later that week...
P.S. I had a phone conversation with my sister, a former nurse, about boundaries. This clarified my thinking about my unique role on the ward. Basically members of staff typically maintain boundaries, fielding 'personal' questions with the likes of "That's an interesting question, why do you want to know?" But ethnographers typically don't or can't, and choose to exchange personal information. A good example of where this approach worked well was with patient-Helen on ward A [referred to in Box 4.4 above], e.g. I showed her photos of my partner and talked freely about myself. This felt dead right and I certainly did not think she would use such information against me. Indeed Sue Estroff in *Making it Crazy* [a community ethnography

conducted in the USA: Estroff, 1981] effectively sells her research by saying she had 10 or so of the people she interviewed round to her house, i.e. 'I really got in there close'. But in this study I do have to be very careful with people as 'ill' as Katherine about.

This may be a good way of explaining my unique role on the ward and how it differs from those of both staff and patients.

4.7.5 An unstable & permeable space

An acute psychiatric ward can therefore be a difficult place in which to be a participant – and this applies to patients, staff and researchers alike. But it quickly became apparent to me that it is an especially difficult one in which to do *participant observation*. A major factor in this was the difficulties one has in developing *long-term* relationships with people there, given that participants in the territory under observation change throughout the day and week. This is brought about by having three nursing shifts per day, the widespread use of agency staff, and short patient stays. This made it very challenging to get to know people, tell them my story, earn their trust, and find out about their experiences – as in many cases people who had been there one visit, were absent the next. Further, it threatened to undermine one of the major benefits of participant observation; namely that it offers you the potential for a deeper familiarity and understanding than you can get through one-off research interviews.

Not only is this a space characterised by lots of comings and goings of participants throughout the day and week, it is one made up of an unusually varied set of social and professional groups (see Box 4.6). These different participants are likely to have hugely different understandings as to what is going on, so in this one setting there will be many different perspectives on the same events. The fieldworker will therefore come into contact with numerous groups in relation to which he or she will feel, and be perceived as, an 'outsider'.

Box 4.6: Participants in everyday life of an acute psychiatric ward

- Current patients
- Former patients (e.g. on a social visit)
- Patients visiting from other wards in the psychiatric unit
- Care assistants
- Nurses
- Police (e.g. for an MHA admission)
- Junior doctors
- Domestics/cleaners
- Porters
- Pharmacists
- Social workers
- Lay visitors (family/friends)
- Patient advocates

- Hospital-based researchers (e.g. research psychologists)
- Consultant psychiatrists
- Occupational therapists
- Clinical psychologists
- NHS Trust managers

4.7.6 Ambiguous institutional role

Linked with the previous point, I believe much of my anxiety resulted from having a relatively ambiguous and unstable role – one which I routinely had to explain to people – namely that I was a sociologist without direct experience of using mental health services, working as a Research Fellow at the Royal College of Psychiatrists' Research Unit, aiming to understand the experience of patients, while trying to keep the range of staff groups 'on side' otherwise I would be ejected from the setting. I certainly felt tensions over the classic fieldwork question as to whose 'side' I was on (c.f. Becker, 1967), as perceived by the many hundreds of people I met on the wards. For example, on one visit I was sitting in the smoking room with some patients whom I knew quite well, listening to their complaints about the ward and the criticisms of some of the staff. When the ward manager came in for a cigarette, people immediately stopped talking and carried on only after she had left – the relevance here being that I had been allowed in on their conversation because I was seen as somewhat removed from staff, otherwise they would have refrained from talking in front of me too. Therefore a key point is that what I was *allowed* to observe, and the quality of the observational data recorded, was largely determined by other people's perceptions of my role and affiliations with other groups. My job was to get as close to sets of individuals on the ward as possible, but this was difficult in a setting with multiple groups, in which getting on well with one group (e.g. nurses) could jeopardize 'getting in' with others (e.g. patients). As Goffman (1989) sagely advises, you have to "control your associations" in the field and be strategic about how you handle these social relationships.

By contrast, in the MHA Study, my close affiliation with the ASW was easily invoked, for example through my overt 'shadowing' of this particular participant, or through the ASW introducing me to other people (e.g. ASW to police officer: "This is Alan Quirk… He's come along with me to observe how we do these assessments…"). Thus, I was much less likely to get caught up in managing the shifting allegiances that characterised my time on the wards. While this limited my ability to earn the trust of some participants (especially candidate patients), it helped to make the fieldwork a far less stressful experience for me overall.

4.7.7 Active positioning in fieldwork

That noted, participant observers, and I believe researchers more generally, can actively position themselves such that they observe events and report findings from a particular perspective. A good illustration of this was where I started off observing ward rounds by sitting in the interview room with staff throughout each session, watching one patient after another come in, and taking notes throughout. An advantage of this, as demonstrated in Chapter 8, is that it enabled me to observe what the clinical team said to one another in the patient's absence; that is, before and after the patient was in the room with them. However, after a few ward rounds I began to feel uncomfortable in this role: first, because it constructed me as yet another 'professional' clogging up an already crowded room, and second, because it gave me little insight into the patient's experience of the event. I therefore consciously changed tack, and in future ward rounds waited outside with individual patients – sometimes nervously – and entered the room with them. The whole experience felt entirely different and helped me understand much better how daunting it can be to enter a room packed with professionals who are in the business of scrutinising your every move and utterance.

4.7.8 Fallibilistic spirit to confession

As recommended by Seale (1999), I have attempted to offer my 'confessional tale' in a fallibilistic spirit. It has been argued that an acute ward is both a difficult place to be a participant and a comparatively difficult place in which to do participant observation. Anxieties arose because I was routinely managing a series of tradeoffs during fieldwork – for example, striking the right balance between visiting the ward often enough to become a familiar face, yet leaving myself enough time to write up my notes between visits. Getting on with staff was essential – even if it sometimes jeopardized my 'getting in' with patients – as it helped me understand ward procedures that would otherwise have remained hidden. These anxieties were amplified in two main ways. First, the research required me to spend a lot of time in a volatile environment in which I was uncomfortably close to the sort of dangerous and risky situations I actively avoid in my everyday life. And second, I experienced difficulties in forming good field relationships in a highly unstable and permeable space; one in which I was, too often, just one more unfamiliar face to patients and staff alike.

The MHA Study, reported in Chapter 9, was certainly challenging to pull off and it had its fair share of anxiety-inducing moments. However, having done the hard work to get the social workers on my side (discussed in section 4.4.4), I found my field role was generally far less stressful to manage. Compared with the process in the two ethnographic studies, generating data for the Prescribing Decisions Project was an absolute breeze. Hanging around in outpatient clinic waiting rooms was sometimes boring, but I enjoyed spending time in a comparatively 'voluntaristic' psychiatric context – not dissimilar in feel to the waiting room of a primary health care centre - in which it was generally quite easy to strike up friendly conversations with service users and staff. It was rarely a stressful experience. Having experienced the havoc played on my social life by doing ethnographic fieldwork, I can only agree wholeheartedly with the view that you have to be young to do fieldwork (Goffman, 1989), and that conversation analysis, by contrast, has a great deal to recommend it to the middle-aged (Dingwall, 1997)!

In conclusion, I hope that my confessional tale demonstrates the value of reflecting on one's own experiences and awkward and embarrassing moments during ethnographic fieldwork. In the Acute Ward Ethnography, such reflection fed directly into the development of central claims about institutional permeability, presented in Chapter 7, and how patients assess and manage the risks they face on the wards (see Quirk *et al,* 2004; 2005).[18] Thus, it offers the reader further material with which to evaluate the trustworthiness of the report. As Seale (1999) rightly notes, in the last analysis the writer must then trust in their readers' capacity to make their own judgements about the account.

4.8 Summary

This chapter has attempted to describe how the three qualitative, observational studies on which this book is based were undertaken: (1) the Prescribing Decisions Project, which investigated how decisions

[18] To put it at its simplest, with regard to the second claim it was not only patients who were using certain methods to assess and manage risk on the wards - during fieldwork, I was using them too.

about long-term anti-psychotic prescribing are negotiated; (2) the Acute Ward Ethnography, which explored the patient's experience of everyday life on an acute psychiatric ward; and (3) the MHA Study, which examined how MHA assessments are conducted, focussing on the experience of the coordinating ASWs. The research was undertaken between 1998 and 2005, while I worked as a Research Fellow at the Royal College of Psychiatrists' Research Unit.

The decision to include three sets of findings opened up the possibility of comparing and contrasting how psychiatric decisions are made in different forums. These range from the comparatively voluntaristic outpatient consultation to encounters in which the threat of coercion is difficult for participants to ignore, namely the ward round and the MHA assessment. This, I believe, offers a solid foundation for making evidence-based claims about the conditions in which shared decision-making is possible in contemporary psychiatric practice.

Chapter 5

How pressure is applied in 'negotiated' decisions about medication

---

CONTENTS

5.6 Spectrum of pressure in shared decision-making

5.7 Discussion

Communication research in psychiatry has tended to focus on the overt forms of pressure or coercion; that is, the blunt instruments of control used by mental health professionals to achieve their preferred treatment outcomes and to manage or overcome patient resistance (reviewed in Chapter 3). Much less is known about encounters in which the threat of coercion is generally perceived to be less immediate, such as routine outpatient consultations. Our interview study (Seale et al, 2006) found that psychiatrists reported preferring co-operative relationships with patients involving shared decision-making, negotiated agreements and a sense of partnership. Pilgrim & Rogers (2005) have argued that psychiatrists' legal powers of coercion ultimately undermine initiatives designed to promote trust in psychiatric solutions. So it seems that while some psychiatrists maintain a self-image of 'patient-centredness' and are committed to democratic decision-making as an ideal, they are perceived by a proportion of patients as implementing a non-democratic treatment regime (Seale et al, 2006). That noted, a national survey of a broad spectrum of mental health service users in the UK found that 90 per cent of respondents (n=3,033) felt able, at least some of the time, to talk to their doctor or nurse about the medicines prescribed to treat their mental health problem (Rethink, 2003). Previous research, reviewed more fully in Chapter 3, indicates that different degrees of pressure are applied in healthcare decisions. Unilateral (non-negotiated) and bilateral (shared/negotiated) practitioner approaches in decision-making about treatment have been identified (Collins *et al*, 2005), as has a 'spectrum' of coercion exerted by psychiatrists (Szmukler & Applebaum, 2001). Overall, though, there is an absence of observational research evidence for how shared medication decisions are made in psychiatry.

Perakyla (2004) notes an intriguing paradox in the discipline of CA in relation to issues of control. On the one hand, there are very few, if any, explicit discussions about control in the central CA texts; that is, if control is understood as a unilateral process where the controlled party has no choice but to obey (i.e. coercion). But, as Perakyla rightly notes, if *reciprocity* is allowed in the notion of control, then many CA findings are very relevant:

> "CA studies show how parties to any interaction constrain the actions of one another, and how the constrained parties construct their subsequent responses in terms of alignment, misalignment or resistance… Therefore, CA has developed, off record as it were, pivotal means for the study of the 'microphysics' of control in social interaction, understood as a reciprocal process… [B]y starting from the case-by-case analysis of actual instances of interaction, CA has gained access to the details of the operation of sequences where control is exercised and resisted." [Perakyla, 2004, pp.6-7]

For conversation analysts, then, the primary site of control is neither in persons nor in their relations, but in actions and sequences of actions.

With this lesson in mind, I will in this chapter examine how pressure is applied by psychiatrists in the context of negotiations about anti-psychotic medication. By applying methods of conversation analysis (CA) to data generated for the Prescribing Decisions Project, I hope to capture a new level of complexity in how people conduct themselves in these encounters (see Chapter 4 for discussion of method). Part of this involves looking very closely at how the participants communicate their preferences to one another, and examining how such actions constrain freedom of choice. I will demonstrate that the application of such pressure occurs even in the context of negotiated decisions that are understood as belonging to the patient. The focus is on a small number of exemplary decision sequences, ranging from 'open' decisions to decisions in which pressure is applied heavily. The analysis will reveal some of the subtle and not-so-subtle ways that patients are pressurised into agreeing to 'choose' the treatment option preferred by their psychiatrist.

The emphasis in the chapter is on how psychiatrists apply pressure. Future analyses of Prescribing Decisions Project data will focus on the methods used by patients obtain their preferred treatment option.

5.1 How an outpatient clinic is run

'Dr Mann' is an experienced consultant psychiatrist who works half-time, and runs his outpatient clinic on one morning per week from a community mental health centre. On average 13 patients are booked into the clinic. Appointments are organised with assistance from the computerised Patient Information Management System (PIMS). This records appointments up to six months in advance. Existing patients tend to book their next appointment immediately after seeing their consultant: they see the receptionist on their way out, who logs the agreed appointment date onto PIMS. Whereas most of the other consultants in the study tended to phone the appointment date through, Dr Mann usually leaves this to the patient. He reported that nobody "slips through the net" (i.e. leaves without booking their next appointment) because he always checks such things with the receptionist at the end of the session. Patients who have not attended ("DNAs") are identified at that stage too. Default systems are in place so that standard letters are sent out automatically to DNAs.

Dr Mann usually schedules the first appointment of the session for 08.45 (PIMS does not allow anything to be recorded before 09.00, so it is put down as a '09.00' appointment). The list of appointments is prepared in advance by administrative staff, who also assemble the relevant patient casenotes. On arrival at the centre, Dr Mann picks these up, goes upstairs to his office and waits for patients to arrive. Existing patients are allocated a 15-minute slot. New patients are allocated a one-hour slot for a full assessment (none of which were recorded for this study). Sometimes double-bookings are deliberately made, in the expectation that some patients will not turn up. If they all do, this means that patients will have to be seen by the consultant in double-quick time to keep the clinic on track. The last appointment is scheduled for 12.15, allowing the session to finish at 12.30. Dr Mann reported that he tries to stick to this, so he can get himself some lunch from a café across the road, before attending a regular team meeting a 13.00. Other consultants are more flexible and will allow their clinic to over-run, sometimes by as much as an hour.

On arrival at the centre, patients report to the receptionist who logs their arrival time in PIMS, next to the time of their appointment. Dr Mann keeps an eye on this throughout the session: on the computer screen in his room he can see who is waiting to see him and when they arrived, allowing him to bring forward their appointment if needs be, for example to see them in the place of a DNA or late-arrival. The receptionist sends patients up to the first floor waiting area, which is outside the consultant's office. They often make themselves known to the Consultant by showing their face in the glass panel of his door. Dr Mann keeps an eye on who is in the waiting area, and calls people in when he is ready to see them.

After every appointment Dr Mann dictates a letter to the referrer, who is usually the patient's GP. This is typically a couple of pages long for new patients; and gives information on the person's history, mental state, and so on. For existing patients the letter might be anything from a line to one side in length. Dr Mann dictates these letters into a tape recorder as he goes along, between one appointment and the next. Most of the other consultants in the study dictated letters as and when they could; sometimes leaving them all or most of them until the whole session had ended. The letters are copied to relevant professionals (e.g. the patient's Community Psychiatric Nurse) and sometimes to the patient him or herself. Dr Mann tends to do this as a matter of course for new patients, and most follow-up patients get copies.

Sometimes Dr Mann dictates the letter while the patient is with him in the room, so that the patient knows "exactly what you think". He said there is very little information he would hold back from patients, and thinks it is important that patients know this because it helps to build trust between them. The only major exception he could think of would be when he has received sensitive information from a third party. One example of this was where a patient's mother has reported being on the receiving end of a direct threat of violence and asked for this report not to repeated back to the patient.

Dr Mann generally issues prescriptions to his patients whereas other consultants will ask/advise the patient's GP to do this. Such letters are not always acted upon.

5.2 Negotiation is the norm

The data generated for this study suggest that the psychiatric outpatient consultation is a comparatively 'democratic' forum for decision-making. Evidence for this is summarised in Table 5.1, which shows that consultants and patients achieve their 'preferred' decision outcomes (e.g. dose increases or stoppages of the medication) in roughly equal proportions. It also indicates that consultants are just as likely to suggest a reduction or stoppage, as they are to suggest an increase.

Table 5.1: Who gets what they want in negotiations about anti-psychotic medication?

	Did this happen?		
	Yes	No	TOTAL
Consultant			
Wants patient to reduce or stop med	**5**	**5**	10
Wants patient to increase or switch to a new med or change frequency of med	**9**	**2**	11
TOTAL	14	7	21
Patient			
Wants to reduce or stop their med	**13**	**4**	17

Wants to increase or switch to a new med	**3**	**2**	5
TOTAL	16	6	22

This table covers only 43/92 consultations. In the other 49 the following applied:

- 2 consultations – the medication was either reduced or stopped, but the initiation of this was a joint action
- 1 consultation – the consultant wanted more medications, the patient wanted less medications, and the outcome was that things stayed the same
- 1 consultation – the consultant initiated some exploration of changing medications without indicating a preference and the medications stayed the same
- 1 consultation – both parties jointly initiated some exploration of changing medications without indicating a preference and the medications stayed the same
- 44 consultations - there was no change and no expression of any desire for a change by either party.

It can therefore be reported that roughly one third of consultations (32/92) involved a change to an antipsychotic medication, of which 16 were initiated by the patient, 14 by the doctor and two by the initiation of both. None of these outcomes was enacted without explicit agreement having been signalled by the patient. To put it another way, all resulted in some form of 'verbal contract' between the doctor and patient. This means that *no 'coerced' decision outcomes, forced through against the patient's will, were recorded.* On the surface, then, this evidence for symmetry indicates that negotiated decision-making is the norm in this psychiatric setting – among this group of psychiatrists at least. This finding is consistent with their self-perception of 'patient-centredness' (Seale *et al*, 2006).

I shall now examine how some of these decision outcomes were produced, focussing on how pressure was applied in a small number of exemplary decision sequences. Examples of an 'open' decision, a 'directed' decision, and a 'pressure' decision are examined in turn. On the basis of this analysis, the concept of a 'spectrum of pressure' in negotiated decision-making is proposed, onto which prescribing decisions may be approximately located. This analysis will help to explain how and why certain shared decisions *feel* a lot more 'democratic' or 'open' to the patient than do others.

5.3 An 'open' decision

The first decision sequence to be examined is shown in Extract 5.1 below.

It involved a consultant psychiatrist (C) and patient (P). The consultant
was very softly spoken and it proved impossible to transcribe all of her talk. This is indicated by empty single parentheses. Other CA transcription symbols are provided in Appendix A.

Extract 5.1 (Consultation 45)

Outcome = Prescribing change (from taking 17.5 mg of Olanzapine every day, to taking 17.5mg and 15mg on alternate days)

1	C:	.hh Well (1.0) why don't we leave things as (.) they are
2	P:	Mm
3	C:	(with this now) especially as you've had worries about your
4		mum and ( )=
5	P:	=Mm=
6	C:	=( ) and so on .hhhh and maybe if things stay on a
7		level (0.4) we might:: ( ) alternate to seventeen point
8		five and fifteen? ( )
9	P:	What alternate days sort of thing?
10	C:	↑Yeah::: ↓ (.) that might be one way of doing it, (yes)
11		(0.5)
12	P:	D'yer wanna do that now-°or° (0.4) next time
13	C:	Well- thhhhh (.) I think it would be reasonable to give to give
14		it a ↑try↓=
15	P:	=Alright then (.) yeah
16	C:	Yeah? Is that gonna be ↑fiddly↓ (.) doing [that?
17	P:	[That'll be alright

18 C: Yeah (0.4) .hhhh I think ‹that would be:::› (for the next-) (0.2)
19 well that's a fair bit of Olanzapine that you're taking
20 P: I know
21 C: And I think you need to have (0.2) (   ) so .hhh it
22 might be that we could get down to fifteen (you know)
23 (0.4)
24 P: Mm
25 (1.2)
26 P: So I take seventeen and a half one day (0.2) [fifteen the next
27 C: [(Fifteen another)
28 (.) and just just see how you find that.
29 (0.2)
30 P: Yeah=
31 C: =And-if (0.4) it seems fine (then) ›what I'm hoping is you
32 won't really notice much difference‹
33 P: °No°
34 C: And then that's a good sign that it's okay to (.) to move on to
35 fifteen
36 P: °(Right) °
37 (1.2)
38 C: Your lithium level's fine ((continues))

5.3.1 Organisation of preference

Certain actions, typically those which follow other actions, such as proposals and invitations, can be marked as dispreferred or problematic in some way (for overviews, see Heritage, 1984; Atkinson & Heritage, 1984; Levinson, 1983; Silverman, 1997). For example, a silence or pause, or the item 'Well', occurring after a proposal, can be taken as displaying either potential or upcoming rejection ("Well, I'd love to come but…"). The CA concept of preference organization can be compared with Goffman's concept of 'face' - the idea that we persistently consider, and characteristically seek to protect, one another's moral standing during the course of social interaction (Goffman, 1959). The different slant of the CA concept is that, by focusing on 'system' rather than 'ritual' constraints on social interaction (Goffman, 1981; Schegloff, 1988), it highlights the *devices* which interactants use to maintain social solidarity (Silverman, 1997). It is useful concept for understanding how we are able to make inferences about each other's preferences in negotiated decision-making and it is highly relevant to understanding Extract 5.1.

5.3.2 Detailed analysis (Extract 5.1)

Returning to the transcript, we can observe various things that the participants do to make this a 'open' decision.

On line 1, the consultant (C) proposes keeping things as they are for now (17.5mg of Olanzapine every day), but puts the decision to alternate daily between dosages of 17.5 and 15mg on the agenda for their next meeting (lines 6-8). It is the patient (P) who reformulates the decision, on line 12, to being about when, and not whether, the decision to alternate dosages should be made. C's response, on lines 13-14 - "Well- thhhhh (.) I think it would be reasonable to give to give it a ↑try↓=" - is a very weak or gentle form of proposal (compared with, for example, "Actually, I would strongly recommend doing that if I were you", which would have strongly projected acceptance as the preferred response). P accepts without hesitation ("=Alright then (.) yeah"). Notice that C does not specify when to "to give it a ↑try↓" (i.e. 'now' or 'next time') and thus does not literally answer P's question. However P chooses not to attend to the potential ambiguity of this response (e.g. by asking C to specify when she means) and instead produces an acceptance without delay. P thus evidently hears it as a proposal to change the prescription immediately; one that her earlier utterance, "D'yer wanna do that now-°or° (0.4) next time", had 'invited' in the first place.

During the course of this decision sequence, P asks three questions of clarification. These are on lines 9 ("What alternate days sort of thing?"), 12 ("D'yer wanna do that now- °or° (0.4) next time"), and 26 ("So I take seventeen and a half one day (0.2) [fifteen the next"). Each is followed by clarification statements that are hearable as proposals from C. P's responses to the second and third of them indicate that they are heard that way, because P offers an acceptance each time: respectively "=Alright then (.) yeah" (line 15) and "Yeah=" (line 30). The important observation here is that this offers P numerous opportunities to reject the proposal for an immediate change to prescribing. Notice how C might have chosen to initiate a change of topic after P's first acceptance. Instead, C's utterance "Yeah? Is that gonna be ↑fiddly↓ (.) doing [that?" (line 16) extends the decision sequence by offering P a chance to 'reconsider' the decision she has just made. In other words, C could have quite easily have exited from the decision sequence on line 16, after P had uttered ""=Alright then (.) yeah" in response to C's proposal give the prescribing change a try. However, C chooses to extend the sequence so that P is offered further conversational slots in which to reject the proposal and reconsider her acceptance of it.

Notice also how C, by asking P to "give it a ↑try↓" (line 13-14) and "just see how you find that" (lines 28), downplays P's commitment to this as a permanent change to prescribing. Thus C's actions construct the decision as one that will be easy to reverse should the patient subsequently experience difficulties with the prescribing change.

5.3.3 'Letting the patient decide'

Continuing with the analysis of Extract 5.1, it can be observed that C's preferences are communicated weakly and the decision is constructed as one that is open to the patient. C invokes her long-term goal of getting P to cut down her anti-psychotic by observing that P is on a "<u>fair</u> bit" of it at present (line 19) and that it could be reduced to 15 every day if the prescribing change does not make a difference (see lines 32-35). Therefore, while the decision to change prescribing immediately 'belongs' to P, the outcome chosen is one that takes P along the 'preferred' treatment pathway signalled by C. In other words, C's actions communicate that P is heading in the preferred direction (i.e. towards a reduction), but apply no pressure for this to be done immediately. P is offered multiple opportunities to reject the treatment proposal for an immediate change (which she had 'invited') or to reconsider the decision once it had been made. On top of this, the decision is constructed as one that will be easy to reverse or abandon should P find it difficult.

This sequence may therefore be categorised as a consultant-initiated decision in which C achieves her preferred decision outcome; that is, a reduction, albeit sooner than expected. However, no pressure was applied in order to achieve it. Both parties carefully negotiated the decision, to the extent that we (and they) may understand it as 'belonging' to the patient. In short, it is a decision sequence in which the participants are 'letting the patient decide'.

5.4 A 'directed' decision

Viewed out of its conversational context, the following extract appears to offer another example of a consultant and patient together doing 'letting the patient decide'. Notice how C asks what P would like to do and accepts P's proposal to "try the new medication" (Sulpiride).

Extract 5.2 (Consultation 50)

Outcome = Swap anti-psychotics (from Olanzapine to Sulpiride)

1	C:	Wha- what d'you think you'd like [to do (about)
2	P:	[Well I think I-I would like
3		to try the new medica[tion
4	C:	[Yeah

However, a key insight from CA is that the meaning of such an exchange depends upon, and may indeed be completely transformed by, the conversational context in which it is produced. To illustrate this point, I shall examine the structural location of the 'patient's' decision to try a new medication; that is, the point at which it was produced in the consultation. I will then look closely at its more immediate context; this being the talk produced beforehand and immediately afterwards. The analysis will show that we are in fact looking at an example of *directed* decision-making, constituted, in part, through the consultant's actions to 'steer' the patient into choosing a new medication and reinforce the decision once it has been made.

The full consultation is summarised in the box below. The exchange shown above (Extract 5.2) is marked in bold in order to draw attention to the context of its production. The summary conveys the fact that the exchange constitutes only a tiny fragment of a convoluted decision sequence, one that spanned the course of an unusually lengthy, 24-minute consultation. It commences at the very beginning of the consultation with the patient's announcement that he has been experiencing seizures.

Box 5.1: Summary of Consultation 50 Outcome = Swap anti-psychotics (from Olanzapine to Sulpiride) In response to C's opening question, P reports having been "not so well" lately because he has had an "epilepsy thing" (experiencing seizures). He reports not knowing if it had had anything to do with the medication he has been taking (Olanzapine). After exploring exactly what had happened, C informs P that all medication for psychosis lowers the threshold for seizures, and suggests that one option would be to stop the medication altogether. C then successfully 'persuades' P into doing this. After further discussion, C has second thoughts and checks for an alternative anti-psychotic in the British National Formulary. After a lengthy pause while he refers to the book, C reports back that he recommends Sulpiride as a less risky drug, re. seizures, and offers P three choices: (a) to stop the medication, (b) to cut down the dose of Olanzapine, or (c) to start on different medication at low dose. **C asks what P would like to do; P chooses to try the new medication ((summary of exchange shown in Extract 5.2 above))**. C informs P about side effects of the new

medication, then reaffirms that the best thing is to stop the Olanzapine straight away. C writes a prescription, and apologises to P for what has happened. P asks if he can finish his medication. C says no, "I wouldn't take any more of that", and says that P should "go for your choice and take a different medication". C explains that ordinarily he'd get P to take both anti-psychotics at the same for a while to help the transition from one to the other, but "we can't do that because that would make you more likely to have a fit". After advising P when and how to take the new medication, and discussing with P how he is doing at University, C repeats that P should stop his present anti-psychotic immediately, and then initiates closure.

We now turn to examine *how* the decision-making was 'directed', such that consultant's 'preferred' treatment option is chosen. Two data extracts will be examined. The first (5.3) shows the talk produced shortly before P chooses to try a different anti-psychotic. The second (5.4) shows what C and P do immediately after P makes his choice.

5.4.1 'Steering' the patient

Extract 5.3 (Consultation 50)

Outcome = Swap anti-psychotics (from Olanzapine to Sulpiride)

1 C: So:::: I think we've got (0.2) three choices (0.8)

2 P: Mm hm=

3 C: =one is to stop your medication. (0.2) But (.) we've talked

4 about what would happen if you ↑stopped↓ your medication is

5 that the (0.2) psychosis (0.2) is likely to come back (   )

6 P: (Yeah fair enough)

7 C: Not straight away but (0.4) sometime.

8 P: ° (Okay) °

9 C: (0.6) The second choice is to (.) cut the dose down of

10 Olanzapine further still (0.6) °yeah to five or two and a half°

11 (0.2)

12 P: Mm

13 C: but (0.2) ‹we don't know how much you need›

14 P: (Right)

15 C: to keep you well (.) and it may be (.) going down too low.

16 (0.6)

17 P: Mm

18 C: .hh the third choice is to (.) give you a different medication in

19 a low dose (0.2) that (.) we (.) think (0.4) is (0.2) not (.) as

20 dangerous °with (.) fits °

21 (1.4)

22 P: Who will decr- (right) okay (.) will decrease th- the risk

23 of [(them)

24 C: [Yeh (.) yeah

25 P: (Oh fine (.) I think)

26 (0.8)

27 C: And if we were to give you a different medication if wouldn't

28 have the same problems with (.) weight gain or (diabetes) °or

29 anything like that°

30 P: Okay=

In the exchange above, C presents P with three treatment options: to stop his medication (lines 3-5, 7), to cut the dose down (9-10, 13, 15), or to try a different medication in a low dose (18-20). Notice how the first two are marked as 'dispreferred', and ruled out of contention, by C's production of a "but" with a caveat attached to each of them. In contrast, the third option is 'sold' to P with claims that it is not as dangerous with fits (the troublesome side effect reported by P at the very beginning of the consultation), and does not have the other side effects associated with his present medication (weight gain or diabetes). After all of this work to mark it as the only sensible option, it would be difficult for P *not* to choose the third option in a way that did not threaten C's face. Put simply, C's actions constrain free choice over this matter, though we can also observe that P 'co-operates' with this.

5.4.2 Reinforcing the decision once it has been made

The extract below shows what happens immediately after P chooses to try the new anti-psychotic. The analysis that follows will pay particular attention to how C delivers information about the side effects of the new drug such that the patient is not deterred from trying it.

Extract 5.4 (Consultation 50)

Outcome = Swap anti-psychotics (from Olanzapine to Sulpiride)

1	C:	Wha- what d'you think you'd like [to do (about)
2	P:	[Well I think I-I would like
3		to try the new medica[tion
4	C:	[Yeah
5	P:	(French) new medication ( )
6	C:	Yeah .hhh the:::: (0.2) I'm just trying to think the- <u>pos</u>sibly
7		the most (0.6) likely side effect (.) are (0.6) yer sexual
8		performance °might be affected by it° (0.5) in terms of (0.2)
9		delayed ejaculation. (.) (But) that's the most likely thing that
10		°can happen° (0.4) (that) doesn't happen with everybody or
11		[(.) a lot of people
12	P:	[.hhh (.) (fine) actually I am single so=
13	C:	=yeah=
14	P:	=( )
15	C:	But it's not -n'it doesn't make you gain weight-gain a lot of
16		weight it doesn't (.) cause diabetes and it doesn't .hhh er it
17		doesn't cause as much <u>sleep</u>iness as °Olanzapine°
18	P:	Mm (0.8) okay,
19	C:	Yeah?
20	P:	(Yeah that's fine)=
21	C:	Sh- shall we try that I think the best thing to do is to stop the
22		Olanzapine straight away and just start taking this new one
23		instead
24		((C gets prescription pad out of bag))

The decision to try the new medication is reinforced in various ways. First, C chooses to disclose information about side effects only *after* P has chosen to try the new medication. This approach does not conform to models of 'informed' decision making which assume such information is delivered before the patient decides. That noted, C's "Yeah?", produced at the end of his turn on line 19, is hearable as a 'request for confirmation' of the choice made, in the light of the information subsequently provided about side effects. P's accepting "(Yeah that's fine)", on line 20, shows that this is indeed how he interprets it. Second, C chooses to deliver information on only the "most likely" side effect (delayed ejaculation) rather than the full range of them (discussed further below). Third, the chance of P experiencing this side effect is downplayed by C's 'qualifier', on lines 10-11, that it "doesn't happen with everybody or [(.) a lot of people". Fourth, the advantages of this medication over P's current anti-psychotic is repeated (on lines 15-17), and C chooses not to discuss other adverse effects in relation to which the new anti-psychotic would have rated less well. And fifth, C brings the decision sequence to a close by getting his prescription pad out of his bag, and chooses not to offer P an opportunity to 'reconsider' the decision: an action that in this context - after all C's work to direct P into making a safe treatment choice – would appear inconsistent.

5.4.3 Conversational solution to a central dilemma for psychiatrists

Our interview study (Seale *et* al, 2006) identified a central dilemma for psychiatrists; namely, that while most are convinced about the value of antipsychotic medications, they worry about the consequences of fully explaining adverse effects for fear of compromising patient adherence to prescribing.[19] Additionally, psychiatrists mentioned the difficulty in providing comprehensive or precise information about side effects, either because they found it hard to know these themselves or because it was impractical to discuss every single one, including those that might be extremely rare, in the time available (Seale *et al*, 2006). So how might this central dilemma be resolved in naturally occurring situations?

In the transcript above (Extract 5.4) we can observe C applying one particular conversational solution to this dilemma which, in this specific context, simultaneously functions to reinforce the decision to swap anti-psychotics. The key to this is in how C refers only to the *"most likely"* side effect of the new medication and glosses over the rest (line 7).[20] By specifying in advance the precise number of side

[19] Communication about adherence to prescribing is the subject of the following chapter.
[20] Section 4.6.1 of the methodology chapter presents further evidence about this consultation, gathered for the purpose of member validation (the consultant was sent a draft of this chapter for comments). The consultant's account of his motives for choosing to deliver information on this *particular* side effect

effects about which information will be imparted (in this case "most likely" = 1; although C might have chosen to discuss, say, the "top three"), this allows a doctor to imply there are other adverse effects *without having to say what they are*. In turn, this puts the onus onto the patient to request further information should they feel they need it (which in this case P chooses not to do). Thus, the consultant is able to impart only a very limited amount of information about side effects, but in a manner that is not overtly misleading (compared with, for example, not mentioning side effects at all, or denying that the drug has any adverse effects). Further, in and through *ranking* side effects by their likelihood or importance, the psychiatrist invokes his or her expertise. Compared with, say, a psychiatric trainee who refers to the British National Formulary and dutifully reads out every single side effect to the patient, then it is quite possible that patients would have more faith in the implicit knowledge of the consultant - even though they have been given less information. In other words, it is a method in and through which doctors can deliver minimal information, and quickly, such that it conveys they are 'prioritising' what the patient really needs to know. Clearly, there is a risk of this being interpreted as the doctor withholding information about the many other possible side effects, but that was evidently not so in this example.

(delayed ejaculation) supports my claim that the decision-making was 'directed' in this case.

5.4.4 'Letting the patient have it the doctor's way'[21]

To summarise, the convoluted decision sequence in Consultation 50 was initiated by C, however P put it squarely on the agenda with the troubles talk (about experiencing epilepsy) offered in the opening to the conversation (summarised in Box 5.1). C subsequently marked swapping anti-psychotics as the 'preferred' treatment option and diplomatically 'steered' the patient towards making that choice. The patient was presented with three options, two of which were immediately ruled out of contention, leaving only one sensible choice. Once the 'preferred' option had been chosen, the consultant then reinforced the decision in various ways, for example by delivering information about side effects such that it did not deter the patient from swapping anti-psychotics. P followed C's recommendations, cooperated throughout, and no point oriented to C's actions as a form of 'pressure' or 'manipulation'.

Compared with the 'open' decision examined earlier, the consultant's actions in this case constrained free choice. Despite this, C still attempted to package this 'directed' decision as having belonged to the patient. In everyday decision-making, people very often use the item 'we' to invoke 'collective ownership' of a decision, or perhaps 'democracy'. C's instruction for P to "go for <u>your</u> choice and take a different medication" (emphasis added; see Box 5.1), invokes patient

---

[21] Adapted from the Daniele Vare quotation: 'Diplomacy is the art of letting someone have your way' (www.worldofquotes.com).

ownership; which in this case the patient does not refuse. Thus, this is a negotiated decision in which the participants are *'letting the patient have it the doctor's way'* – a meaning produced, collaboratively, by the 'diplomacy' of the consultant and absence of resistance by the patient.

It seems fair to conclude, then, that we have been examining the real-life enactment of Szasz and Hollander's (1955) 'guidance-cooperation' model of doctor-patient interaction (reviewed in Chapter 3).

Both 'open' and 'directed' decision sequences are characterised by an absence of patient resistance to the consultant's actions. But what happens if the patient resists the consultant's attempts to direct decision-making? Further, how can this response be managed while still maintaining the sense that the decision-making is negotiated rather than coerced? To answer these questions, I shall now examine how patient resistance affects profoundly the meaning of what is going on, and how it is transformed further still by the way the consultant chooses to respond to that resistance. Two types of response to patient resistance are presented. The first is an example of where the consultant 'backs off' in response to patient resistance; the second shows the consultant 'pressing on' to achieve his preferred outcome, even though it is evidently not what the patient wants.

5.5 A 'pressure' decision

5.5.1 'Backing off' in response to patient resistance

Extract 5.5 (Consultation 40)

Outcome = Prescribing change to omit anti-psychotic (Olanzapine)

1	P:	The only one that agrees wi' me (.) (the two)
2		(.) Carbamaza[pine
3	C:	[(I know)=
4	P:	=they go down alright
5	C:	Yeah=
6	P:	=and the- (.) that iron tablet
7	C:	(Ye[ah)
8	P:	[But they (.) make me sick=
9	C:	=It's just while you're- because you're I mean i-it's only
10		because of the stress I realize, (.) you're in-in you're-you're
11		very stressed at present .hhhh taking a small dose of
12		Olanzapine or something a bit similar might help to (.) relax a
13		little bit:: and be less uptight and anxious
14		(1.4)
15	C:	No? You- just want to carry on your- with the
		Carba[mazapine
16	P:	[Aye (0.2)
17	C:	You- are you tak=
18	P:	=You want ta drug me up ain't yer!
19		(0.2 – C turns page in case record)

20	C:	And you take four hundred of that don't you
21	P:	(1.4) °(Yes)°
22	C:	°Okay°
23	P:	.hh doctor .hh with the help ( ) I pulled myself oot the
24		gutter and I'm no going back in the gutter! .hhh I've got ma
25		money the day an I'm determined I'm not gonna buy drink!
26	C:	°Yeah: okay°
27	SW:	You've done well ((P's first name))
28	P:	I know I have done I'm proud of maself

In the talk leading up to the extract above, C enquires about P's use of medication, in response to which P reports having not taken her anti-psychotic (Olanzapine) because it makes her "sick" (line 8). On the face of it, C's actions in this sequence hardly seem to constitute 'pressure'. Indeed, in attempting to persuade a 'non-compliant' patient to take a "small dose of Olanzapine or something a bit similar" to help her "relax a little bit" (lines 9-13) this consultant appears to be treading cautiously. However P evidently interprets it as pressure, as evidenced by her angry 'accusation' on line 18: "=You want ta drug me up ain't yer!". In this context, the accusation is easier to interpret as having been about "a small dose of Olanzapine or something a bit similar" (lines 11-12) that C had just been persuading P to take. However, C's utterance on line 20 "And you take four hundred of that don't you", produced in response to the accusation, refers instead to the dosage of P's *Carbamazapine* (a mood stabiliser) – the only drug that "agrees with" P (lines 1-2).

On the face of it, C is ‘dodging’ P’s accusation by choosing not to respond to it directly, and in and through choosing not to revisit the topic for the remainder of the consultation (data not shown). However, the post-consultation questionnaire shows that the outcome of this exchange – though not expressed verbally by the consultant in the consultation – was that the consultant decided to omit the anti-psychotic from P’s prescription. This is something that P would discover subsequently – at which point she would know the consultant *did* in fact hear what she had been saying. Further, in and through his ‘backing off’, C *demonstrates* that the substance of the accusation is incorrect. In other words, C’s decision to ‘back off’ in the consultation, and his subsequent decision to omit the anti-psychotic, has every chance of communicating to P that he was not trying to drug her up. Had he chosen to deny the accusation, but then continued pressurising P to commit to improving adherence to prescribing, then P, and we, would probably have drawn a very different conclusion.

This analysis shows that C evidently heard this accusation as a form of resistance, and responded by hastily exiting from the sequence of adherence talk before it became even more turbulent. (This sequence is examined again in Chapter 6, as part of an analysis of adherence talk).

5.5.2 Cycle of pressure and resistance

The final decision sequence, examined below, is unusual for the *concerted* nature of the pressure applied by the consultant, who refuses to 'back off' in the face of patient resistance. Though the decision-making is, at times, on the very margins of 'coercion', the analysis will reveal what the participants do to maintain an understanding that it was a 'negotiated' decision.

In the conversation leading up to Extract 5.6, P voluntary discloses that she has not been taking her anti-psychotic – presumably in the knowledge that her social worker, sitting next to her, would probably have disclosed this in any case.[22] P reports having not been taking any tablets because they were doing more harm than good. After an extended cycle of C pressurising P to commit to taking her medication and P resisting this, C eventually 'changes tack' and

[22] Interventions by a 'proxy supervisor' such as this – that is, someone who is in a position to monitor the patient's behaviour outside of the consultation and feed information about it back to the psychiatrist - are discussed in Chapter 8.

proposes that P tries a new medication which she is more likely to take, rather than pressurise her into committing to take one to which she is evidently so resistant. This action creates the context for the conversation that follows, shown in the extract below.

Extract 5.6 (Consultation 74)

Outcome = Swap anti-psychotics (from Olanzapine to Sulpiride)

1	C:	You know Olanzapine isn't the only drug?
2	P:	(0.4) .hh no I know it isn't no=
3	C:	=No
4	P:	Mm
5	C:	›There are others as well-lots of others‹
6		(0.4)
7	P:	Mm
8	C:	(0.6) and (.) Olanzapine (.) you may have found isn't the drug
9		for ↑you↓
10		(2.2)
11	P:	Well=
12	C:	=You used to have Sulpiride
13	P:	(0.4) Yes
14	C:	°What d'you think of that?°
15	P:	(That) was alright tha- .hh that solved the problem
		immediately
16		[when I was in ((prison))
17	C:	[°Would you take it now? °
18	P:	she gave me Sulpiride and that was it

19 C: °Would you take [it°

20 P: [no [problem at all

21 C: [would you take it now instead of

22 Olanzapine?

23 (0.2)

24 P: Sorry?

25 C: Would you take it now instead of Olanzapine?

26 P: Yeah (.) if I had to

This particular consultation is examined further in the following chapter, in relation to the issue of adherence talk. Here I make a few observations of some key features in the transcript. First, C's proposal for P to take a different anti-psychotic (Sulpiride), among other actions, invokes the 'negotiated' character of the decision-making, because it shows his attendance to P's earlier resistance to committing to taking her present one (Olanzapine). However, rather than package this as 'backing off' (see section 5.5.1) C instead 'changes tack'. P's 'grudging' acceptance of the new proposal "(Yeah (.) if I had to)", on line 26, shows P's orientation to C's actions as 'coercion'. P might have chosen to try to bring the decision sequence to a close at this point (e.g. via a 'firm' commitment), but instead this weak acceptance provokes further 'bartering' and pressure work aimed at eliciting a firm commitment from P that she will take this new medication (data not shown).

The second extract from this consultation, shown below (5.7), picks up from where C asks whether he can write P a prescription for the new anti-psychotic. The most striking observation is that the cycle of pressure and resistance continues unabated. First, P makes it plain that she does not want to take *any* anti-psychotic; attributing her improvement to having *stopped* taking tablets - "I-I-I have improved greatly that way yeah .hh er- since I've stopped takin all those tablets" (lines 30-31). And second, C continues to refuse to back off in the face of this resistance (e.g. line 17: "It's [not really quite what I had in mind").[23]

Extract 5.7 (Consultation 74)

Outcome = Swap anti-psychotics (from Olanzapine to Sulpiride)

1	C:	=So it'll be one tablet per day
2	P:	°Mm°
3	C:	Can I give you a pre[scription (for that)?
4	P:	[One tablet?
5	C:	Mm
6	P:	One tablet. (1.2) Okay you can give me a prescription but I
7		won't take them unless I'm (.) goin a bit (.) off [(the wall)
8	C:	[Aaah now
9		that's [not quite what I had in mind£
10	P:	[£(Aaaah)£ that's not a good deal is it-I've (.)

[23] A similar extended cycle of pressure and resistance was produced in one of the hospital ward rounds observed for the Acute Ward Ethnography. It is examined in detail in Chapter 8, section 8.3.3.

11 C: No=

12 P: =£Aah[:::::::£

13 SW: [(It's a better deal) (0.2) (if er)

14 P: £(See) he's a hard man£

15 SW: ([ )

16 P: [He is a hard man

17 C: It's [not really <u>quite</u> what I had in mind

18 SW: [( ) £he's fair he's fair he's a fair man

19 [as well£

20 P: [Heh heh

21 C: I'm thinking about your neighbours as well and I'm=

22 P: =heh=

23 C: =thinking about

24 P: .hh £yeah I-I've improved greatly I ha-ha-have improved

25 greatly£

26 C: Oh you ↑have↓

27 P: Yeah [I have

28 C: [but y-you're risking throwing that all ↑away↓

29 that's [the problem.

30 P: [I know (.) no no I-I-I have improved greatly that way

31 yeah .hh er- since I've stopped takin all those tablets and I

32 just take .hh (every) one or two (0.2) [(and)

33 C: [I (.) I'm not <u>dou</u>bting

34 that for one minute.

35 P: ↑Mm↓

36 C: (.) <u>But</u> (.) the schizophrenia does <u>not</u> come straight away.

37 (0.2) If you're gonna get schizophrenia it creeps up on you

38 P: Does it?

39 C: Yeah? And before you know it (.) you're under the spell of it
40 and you'll [be a changed person
41 P: [yeah I know (0.4) yeah
42 C: A::nd (0.4) there could be something dangerous happens.
43 (1.2)
44 C: And I'm just thinking
45 P: Mm=
46 C: =particularly if you've (0.2)
47 P: Mm
48 C: <u>Dru</u>nk as well (0.4)
49 P: Mm (0.4)
50 C: You could put y- yer safety severely at risk
51 P: °Mm hm°
52 C: °Yeah? °
53 P: °Okay°
54 C: That's my worry
55 P: Alright
56 C: And that of your neighbours you know (0.4) but yeah – if
57 there was a <u>fire</u> and=
58 P: =Mm=
59 C: =you'd had something to drink (0.4)
60 P: Mm=
61 C: =who knows what would happen to you
62 (3.4)
63 P: Okay (then) I- I- I- oh (.) I- I don't know I mean I don't know
64 all these things you know but erm (1.0) as I say I feel alright
65 now and I'm not y'know and I- I'm not going off the rails or
66 anything .hhhh

67	C:	(Fine) [I'm gonna I'm gonna
68	P:	[But but if you- if you I might do, (.) you think I might
69		do in time.
70	C:	I think you might ((sound of C opening briefcase to get out
71		prescription pad))
72	P:	Yeah okay (.) alright then (0.2) well I [I'll take your advice
73	C:	[Yeah it's not (.) yeah
74		it's not a risk I'm (.) very happy with
75	P:	Mm (0.2) °mm°
76		((sound of C writing prescription))

Even in the context of the 'pressure' work evident in Extract 5.7, which wavers on the margins of 'coercion' at times, the participants still orient to what they are doing as bartering or doing a "deal" (see lines 10 and 13). Such actions demonstrably keep the decision-making on a 'negotiated' footing (Goffman, 1981). Further, P's eventual *agreement* to the prescribing change on line 72 – "Yeah okay (.) alright then (0.2) well I [I'll take your advice" - is an action that marks the decision as having been non-coerced. However, note how in that turn P orients to C's preceding talk *as "advice"* rather than, say, a command over which she has no choice. This action stabilises decision-making on a 'negotiated' footing, a move that C, crucially, chooses not to challenge, for example by demanding a firmer commitment. P's orientation to C's talk as advice is risky in this context because the withholding of 'fulsome' agreement is very easy to interpret as continued resistance. Yet, from P's perspective it is probably a risk worth taking because it functions to downplay her accountability should she subsequently fail to keep to her side of the bargain.

5.5.3 Conversational solution to the downside of patient autonomy

Chapter 3 reviewed previous research which shows how attributions of theoreticity (patient competence) are double-edged in the sense that the autonomy a patient gains through being defined as an active decision maker comes at the cost of being morally responsible for his or her actions (Silverman, 1987). In the present example, the advantage to the consultant of producing a decision sequence with a negotiated rather than coerced outcome is that it *co-implicates the patient*, making her accountable should she choose not to take the new medication. By orienting to C's talk as advice, however, P minimises her accountability and thus manages the downside of being actively involved in decision-making. In other words, at her next appointment she would be able to present partial or non-adherence to prescribing as having been the outcome of decision not to follow the consultant's advice rather than a refusal to follow orders. This reduces the risk of provoking a 'disciplinary' response from the psychiatrist.[24]

5.6 Spectrum of pressure in negotiated decision-making

The concept of a 'spectrum of coercion' (Szmuckler & Applebaum, 2001) is a useful device for conveying the idea that there are degrees of coercion in psychiatric interactions (see Chapter 3). However, the concept is less helpful for interpreting the more subtle forms of manipulation and pressure applied in negotiated or shared decision-making. I therefore propose an alternative *'spectrum of pressure'* on to which decision sequences resulting in an explicit agreement, or verbal contract, may be located.

Figure 5.1 overleaf summarises key features of the three types of negotiated decision presented earlier, as well as their position on a spectrum of pressure.

---

[24] In reporting partial or total non-compliance, patients use various methods to reduce the risk of receiving a disciplinary response. These are discussed in Chapter 6.

Figure 5.1: Types of 'negotiated' prescribing decisions, positioned on a 'spectrum of pressure'

Level of pressure applied

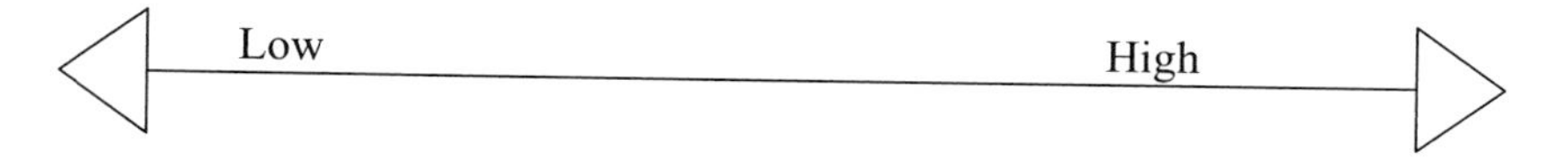

Open decisions

Doctor's actions

The doctor's preferences are communicated weakly, if at all: both parties construct this as a decision that is truly open to the patient. For example, the patient is offered multiple opportunities to reject any treatment proposals and to reconsider the

Directed Decisions

Doctor's actions

The doctor marks a given treatment option as preferred and diplomatically 'steers' the patient towards choosing it. For example, the doctor may rule out alternative options, leaving only one sensible choice. Once the 'preferred' option has been chosen, the doctor reinforces the

Pressure Decisions

Doctor's actions

The contrary preferences of doctor and patient are communicated very clearly. The doctor does not 'back off' in the face of patient resistance (see below), though may 'change tack' in order to achieve a 'preferred' outcome by another means. The doctor

decision once made. The decision is constructed as one that will be easy to reverse if the patient experiences difficulties	decision and actively works to prevent the patient from having second thoughts (e.g. via reassurance)	pressurises the patient to agree to some outcome the patient evidently does not want
Patient's actions	***Patient's actions***	***Patient's actions***
The patient takes the initiative to some degree, e.g. by asking questions of clarification before making his or her choice, or reformulating the decision to being about when, not whether, the prescribing change should be made	The patient follows doctor's recommendations and cooperates with the decision-making. At no point does s/he orient towards the doctor's actions as 'pressure' or 'manipulation'	The patient overtly resists the doctor's proposals, attempts at persuasion, etc, and orients to the doctor's talk as 'pressure'. The patient does not 'back down' in the face of continued pressure from the doctor. Acceptance is offered 'grudgingly'
Ownership of decision	***Ownership of decision***	***Ownership of decision***
The patient is 'allowed to decide' and accepts	The patient 'has the doctor's way'. The patient literally	It is difficult for the decision-making to be concluded without

ownership of the decision. This excludes sequences where the patient refuses ownership, e.g. "You're supposed to be the expert, you decide"	'chooses'. However, both parties will have to work hard to construct it as having belonged to the patient, given the preference work done by the doctor to 'steer' the patient	one side losing face. The decision is owned by the patient only if his or her preference is eventually accepted. Otherwise it is clear to all involved that it is the doctor's decision
Outcome agreed? Yes	***Outcome agreed?*** Yes	***Outcome agreed?*** Yes

At one end of the spectrum there are 'open' decisions, where the patient is 'allowed to decide'. In the middle are 'directed' decisions, where the patient co-operates with being diplomatically 'steered' by the doctor; and at the other end are 'pressure' decisions where the contrary preferences of the doctor and patient are clear for all to see, in a decision sequence characterised by an escalating cycle of pressure and resistance and from which it is difficult to exit without one side losing face. 'Coercion' is not represented, only decisions resulting in a verbal agreement. Coercive powers are exercised in other psychiatric settings, such as psychiatric wards (Chapters 7 & 8) and assessments for compulsory admission to hospital (Chapter 9), the implication being that the spectrum of pressure would need to be extended to encompass decision-making in other, less voluntaristic, psychiatric settings.[25]

The figure demonstrates clearly that one must examine the activities of both doctor *and* patient in order to understand how pressure is applied by doctors in 'negotiated' prescribing decisions. For example, patient resistance to being 'directed' will transform the sequence into a 'pressure' decision, in response to which the doctor may choose to either 'back off' or continue to apply pressure to achieve his or her 'preferred' outcome. These two responses will produce what can be conceptualised (and will experienced by participants) as a different 'level' of interactional pressure. In short, to understand how doctors apply pressure in negotiated decision-making one cannot examine their actions in isolation.

5.7 Discussion

This chapter has examined how pressure is applied in 'negotiated' decisions about anti-psychotic medication, focusing on how the activities of psychiatrists and patients produce a certain level of interactional pressure in decision-making. The findings suggest that the psychiatric outpatient consultation is a comparatively democratic forum for decision-making. The consultations recorded for the study were highly negotiated, with some level of agreement signalled to all

[25] I attempt this in Chapter 10.

medication decisions. Indeed there was surprisingly little evidence of overt coercion or compulsion. Even so, the analysis reveals that negotiated or shared decision-making can be done in such a way that the patient is likely to feel they have had little real influence over the outcome. Some forms of patient-centred psychiatry are evidently a lot more 'patient-centred' than others, although examples of heavy pressure being applied were rare.

Why the absence of overt conflict and resistance? Commitments from patients to take their medication as prescribed do not necessarily equate with what is going to happen outside of the consultation. *Both parties know this.* Thus, in these psychiatric encounters, as in many other health care encounters, the doctor and patient choose to play along, and *act as if* this will be the case. This allows both parties a dignified exit from decision making when the conversation looks like it might be about to become turbulent (e.g. where the consultant chooses to 'back off'). Given that patient agreement to treatment decisions made in this setting is essentially unenforceable, due to minimal or non-existent surveillance over the client once he or she has left the consulting room, it seems unnecessarily risky to the therapeutic relationship for the consultant to press for an agreement that means little. Overall, psychiatrists in this setting seemed better able to achieve their preferred decision outcomes via 'diplomatic' forms of decision-making where they direct patient toward the preferred treatment option.

Two of the main goals psychiatrists orientate to in these consultations are adherence to prescribing and client retention.[26] Often not shared with the patient, adherence to prescribing and client retention both are *long term* goals, unlike those for the more focussed psychiatric encounters I shall be examining in subsequent chapters. That noted, the immediate aim of the encounter was not always obvious, to participants and analyst alike. For example, one particular patient who had been discharged from hospital four weeks before the consultation, and who was attending an outpatient appointment for the very first time, reported to me in the post-consultation interview that he had entered the doctor's office without the faintest idea of what to expect. This added to his anxiety about the encounter. The psychiatrist may be equally in the dark as to why the patient has turned up, because appointments are often booked by another healthcare professional, such as the patient's care co-ordinator (e.g. their Community Psychiatric Nurse), with the consultant not having been told why. While the psychiatrist will probably assume that it will be related to one their main areas of expertise (medication, symptoms and risk), the participants still have to work this out for themselves and negotiate appropriate immediate goals.

---

[26] A further goal is the assessment of risk the patient presents to him/herself or other people (for example, see Extract 5.7). My impression from listening to all of the tapes and reading the typist-level transcriptions – though not through any detailed conversation analysis - is that psychiatrists tended to do risk assessment in these encounters with a comparatively light touch. This contrasts with how it is done in crisis situations, such as MHA assessments, where risk assessment is typically the main goal oriented to by practitioners (see Chapter 9).

Our interview study (Seale *et* al, 2006) suggests that these psychiatrists probably view adherence to prescribing and client retention as *pre-requisites* for the construction and maintenance of good therapeutic relationships with this client group. Their orientation to the goal of client retention – encouraging patients to return for their next appointment - is perhaps not surprising given that this is a 'chronic' group of patients with severe and enduring mental health problems.[27] The deferral of decisions to change medication ("Okay, let's leave things as they are for now, but think about changing things next time") seemed quite common, and this not only helps the consultant save face in certain situations (e.g. offering him or her a dignified exit from an escalating cycle of pressure and resistance), it also minimises threats to the therapeutic alliance resulting from the patient feeling pressurised into agreeing to something they do not want.

Our earlier research (Seale *et al*, 2006) raised the question as to why psychiatrists are able to maintain a self image as being committed to democratic decision making as an ideal, while being experienced by a proportion of patients as implementing a non-democratic treatment regime (Seale *et al*, 2006). It seems plausible that for psychiatrists, their defining moments in their relationships with patients are when trust is achieved in the context of patient-centred practice, with

---

[27] The following chapter examines communication about adherence. There, it is argued that the avoidance of confrontation in these consultations is most likely to be related to the desire of the psychiatrist, if not also the patient, to preserve a cooperative relationship in which shared decision-making is the norm.

episodes of coercion considered as exceptions to the rule. For example, one consultant described to me the sense of achievement he felt when patients started addressing him by his first name rather than his honorific, because this generally indicated that an important level of trust had been achieved in the doctor-patient relationship. In contrast, for service users, the defining moments are those very 'exceptions', especially compulsory admissions to hospital, because that they can have profound, life-changing consequences (discussed in Chapter 9).

As we shall soon see, an analysis of those exceptions paints a very different picture of psychiatric practice to the one presented here. The central challenge for practitioners, then, is how they may adapt their consulting styles to the different contexts in which they meet their patients.

Chapter 6

Communication about adherence to long-term anti-psychotic prescribing

CONTENTS

Partial or non-adherence to medication prescribed for chronic conditions is a common phenomenon that occurs across medical specialties and in different countries (WHO, 2003). Previous research, reviewed in Chapter 3, found a range of factors that influence adherence behaviours, such as the complexity of the dosing regimen and whether the patient's beliefs about their condition conflict with those of professionals'.

Psychiatric outpatient consultations are routine encounters in which practitioners have the opportunity to monitor adherence behaviours, identify partial or non-adherence and explore the reasons behind it, and negotiate or impose some change to the medication aimed at securing improved adherence in the future. As noted in Chapter 3, psychiatrists in our earlier interview study (Seale *et al,* 2006) reported having to rely heavily on patient self-report, as well as accounts from carers and other professionals, to monitor adherence in outpatient consultations. Typically, the psychiatrist tries to create a safe conversational environment to facilitate disclosure of information, for example, by indicating that non-compliance is normal and that the reporting of it would not be followed by disapproval (ibid). However, because a third party is rarely present when the patient actually takes their prescribed medication (unlike in hospital, where the taking of medication is mostly supervised – see Chapter 8), a practitioner in this situation can only ever estimate adherence. Previous research evidence suggests that psychiatrists generally over-estimate it (Marder, 2003; Babiker, 1986). From a psychiatric point of view, then, communication about adherence to anti-psychotic prescribing is important for two main reasons. First and foremost, it is necessary for informing safe and effective prescribing decisions. And second, it is a key component of clinical risk assessment, given that the risks facing a non-adherent patient are generally thought to be higher than for those taking their medication as prescribed.[28]

---

[28] This is not to deny the side effects and other risks associated with the taking of

This chapter examines how psychiatrists and patients communicate about adherence to long-term anti-psychotic prescribing. Informed by conversation analysis (CA), my focus is on how reports of partial or non-adherence are elicited, delivered and responded to in outpatient consultations. The dynamics of the relationship between the process and outcome of adherence talk is examined. To my knowledge this is the first observational study of compliance talk in psychiatric practice.

6.1 Proximal outcomes

Exchanges about partial or non-adherence were produced in 22 out of the 92 (24%) consultations recorded. The analysis starts by identifying the immediate or 'proximal' outcomes of these exchanges; that is, the decisions made, agreements reached and commitments given. These, then, are outcomes directly attached to the communication and achieved *within* the consultation, rather than 'distal' outcomes achieved subsequently, such as changes in the patient's adherence behaviour, related attitudes, and so on. Table 6.1 summarises the within-consultation outcomes.

---

psychotropic drugs (see for example, Healy, 2002; Busfield 2005).

Table 6.1: Proximal outcomes of communication about 'poor' adherence (n=22)

Outcome	N
Prescribing change	
Omit anti-psychotic	3
Swap anti-psychotic	2
Reduce dose	2
Increase dose	1
Tablets prescribed in lower dose (PRN)#	1
Consultant informally endorses adherence behaviour	
Acceptance of partial adherence	4
Patient doesn't commit to improving adherence	
Unchallenged assumption	2
Overt patient resistance/refusal to change	1
Consultant doesn't accept adherence behaviour	
Patient's reasoning is challenged	1
Rejection of 'request' for prescribing change	1
Consultant organizes vol. hospital admission	1

Other	
Prescription issued (patient had run out)	1
None	2

The anti-psychotic was a secondary medication for a patient with diagnosis of bipolar disorder, who reported not wanting to take his tablets because they came in too high a dose to take at any one time.

The most common outcome (9/22) was a decision to change prescribing, including omitting the anti-psychotic. Four exchanges culminated in the consultant informally endorsing the patient's reported adherence behaviour, with prescribing remaining the same. Three concluded with the patient not committing to improving adherence; the consultant exiting from the exchange before this had been elicited from the patient. The psychiatrist refused to accept the reported adherence behaviour in only three consultations.

Two adherence exchanges are categorised as having no associated outcome (Consultations 18 and 50). The first was where the consultant chose not to topicalise the issue of adherence, mentioned in passing in the context of 'jokey' anecdote about how the patient had forgotten to take his Olanzapine on the day of a flying lesson. The second was the 'directed' decision, examined in Chapter 5, where the swapping of anti-psychotics was driven by participants' concerns about an alarming adverse effect (seizures) reportedly suffered by the patient (see section 5.4). In that context, the participants understandably marked the patient's report of occasionally missing doses as irrelevant to the task in hand, so the prescribing change cannot be attributed to it.

Some of these outcomes may well be associated with improved adherence after the patient has left the consulting room. The clearest example of this is where the prescription is changed in order to re-align it with what the patient is reportedly ready to take (for example, see Box 6.2). Either way, behind any one of these outcomes there is a complex sequence of interaction. This is illustrated by the transcript-summary shown in the box below.

Box 6.1: Prescribing change (Consultation 65)

Some minutes into the consultation, the patient (P) reports having "halved everything", by biting her 15mg Aripiprazole tablets into two. She reports having not noticed a difference on the lower dose, states that this shows she does not need them anymore, and so proposes further reduction, "slowly and surely". The initial response of the consultant (C) is laughter at P's report of biting her tablets in half. C cautiously accepts P's decision, but says she wants P to stay on this dose, and this proposal ("Let's carry on with what you're taking in terms of the tablets") is accepted. The negotiated proximal outcome, therefore, is a decision to reduce P's prescription by half, to re-align with what she has reportedly been taking. However C signals that she does not agree with P reducing it any further.

I shall now turn to the various ways in which outcomes such as the one above were collaboratively produced. The analysis proceeds, sequentially, through the structure of a typical adherence exchange: from how reports of partial or non-adherence were elicited, delivered and responded to by the psychiatrist.

6.2 How adherence reports are elicited

Seale *et al* (2006) explored methods used by psychiatrists to encourage patients to be honest about adherence. Typically, they indicated that non-compliance was normal and that reporting it would not be followed by disapproval. I shall now examine this process much more closely, using naturally-occurring data rather than psychiatrists' accounts. This will reveal something that the psychiatrists did not mention when interviewed (ibid); namely, the active role patients take have in creating comparatively 'safe' conversational environments.

Table 6.2: How reports of partial or non-adherence were elicited (n=22)

Elicitation	**N**
Patient volunteers report	7
Consultant asks about patient's use of medication	5
Consultant asks about adherence directly	4

Consultant/other professional delivers report to patient	2
General enquiry by consultant (e.g. “Any worries?”)	2
Carer/partner volunteers report	1
Adherence not disclosed explicitly	1

Table 6.2 above shows that 4/22 reports of partial or non-adherence were elicited by a direct question about adherence and a further 5/22 by a more general enquiry about the patient’s use of medication. However, in 7/22 cases the patient volunteered the report of partial or non-adherence without a prompt. This is illustrated in the transcription extract below (6.1) where the patient does this at the start of the consultation, in response to an ‘innocuous’ opening question by the psychiatrist.

Extract 6.1 (Consultation 49)

Outcome = C acceptance of partial adherence

1 C: °Right° well how are things Sarah?
2 P: .hh Yeah not to bad um::: I (think um) (0.4) .hh sort of (0.4)
3 getting better slowly, (0.4) erm:: (1.0) .hh not feeling nearly
4 as paranoid °as I was°, .hh I’m not taking the Olanzapine any
5 more, .hhhh
6 (0.2)
7 C: [°Right°
8 P: [°Erm°
9 (1.0)

10	P:	I have (over-) put on weight (.) but (.) that's (.) partly (.) my
11		£own problem .hhh erm:::£
12	C:	H-how much weight have you put on °if I might ask°

The act of volunteering morally dubious information about oneself is something that generally puts the speaker in a good light ('owning up' before being asked). This is perhaps consistent with a finding from our earlier interview study, in which psychiatrists spoke of how they attempted to foster trusting therapeutic relationships in which patients feel safe enough to speak openly about such matters (Seale *et al*, 2006).

Patients sometimes enlist the doctor to help them deliver the upcoming 'bad news' about partial or non-adherence. This is another method through which conversational safety may be created. Box 6.2 summarises an adherence exchange in which this is done. Notice how the patient invites the doctor to guess the worst (that she has stopped taking medication altogether), allowing her to 'downplay' it, by announcing that the news was actually not as bad as all that: she had in fact only "cut it down (0.2) very slowly".

Box 6.2: Adherence exchange in Consultation 32

SUMMARY OF CONSULTATION

Duration = 10 minutes. Adherence exchange starts 40 seconds into the consultation. Participants = Consultant (C), Patient (P), Social Worker (SW). Duration of doctor/patient relationship = approximately 24 months

ELICITATION

P 'invites' C to ask a direct question about adherence (see lines 6-7 in the extract below):

1	C:	How are things at home
2		(0.2)
3	P:	Yeah great
4		(0.6)
5	C:	But your mood has been okay is it?
6→	P:	My mood's been fine (0.4) ↓but↑ (.) you're not gonna be very
7		happy with me °(probably not)° .hhh [(.) I
8	C:	[Have you stopped [your
9		medication then?
10	P:	I haven't <u>stopped</u> it (.) I've cut it down (0.2) very slowly (0.4)
11		but erm (0.6) I feel a hundred times better °(not) taking as
12		much°

DELIVERY

As shown above, P reports having "very slowly" cut down her medication, adding that she feels "a hundred times better" for not taking as much *[Sulpiride]*

CONSULTANT RESPONSE

C cautiously accepts P's decision, after having carefully checked on her moods, sources of support, risk awareness etc. C announces that he is sure P will take appropriate steps if she feels herself getting unwell

OUTCOME

Prescribing is changed to re-align it with what the patient is reportedly taking

PARTICIPANTS' SUBJECTIVE RATINGS

Satisfaction with consultation: P *"Very satisfied"*, C = *"Satisfied"*. Happiness with outcome/medication decision: P *"Very happy"*, C *"Neither happy nor unhappy"*.

The patient in this example was thus able to deliver bad news about adherence in a hospitable conversational environment; created in a way that mirrors doctors' use of the 'perspective-display series' (PDS) (Maynard, 1991). This is a "device by which one party can produce a report or opinion after first soliciting a recipient's perspective" (ibid, p.464). Put simply, it involves soliciting an opinion from someone else before making one's own statement, and typically has three parts: a question from speaker A, an answer by speaker B, and a statement by speaker A. As Maynard notes, the PDS has a special function in circumstances requiring caution because it helps to create a hospitable conversational environment in which to break bad news – for example, by allowing the doctor to *confirm* the recipient's understanding as to what the problem may be. This inherently cautious manoeuvre contrasts with the outright offering of a report or assessment (ibid).

This analysis indicates that patients as well as doctors work to create a safe conversational environment in which to talk about this potentially contentious issue.

6.3 How patients report partial or non-adherence

In only 5/22 instances patients reported poor adherence as having been result of "forgetting" to take their medication and/or being "confused" about doing so (e.g. "I take so many tablets I dunno what I'm supoosed taking to be honest"). In the remainder, patients presented not taking medication as something they had done on purpose; that is, as what Goffman calls a 'guided doing' (Goffman, 1986). Reasons provided by patients included that they had been suffering from side effects (6/22), they felt they did not need their anti-psychotic or were better for having not been taking it (6), or believed that anti-psychotic medication "hides the truth" of what you are really like (1) and that it drops you "down" badly (1). One patient explained that she had been "unwell" on the reduced dose agreed at their last outpatient appointment, so went to see her GP to arrange an increase (a decision that was endorsed enthusiastically by the psychiatrist).

'Owning up' to poor adherence before being asked generally puts the patient in a good light morally, but presenting it as *wilful* makes the patient accountable for their action. So why would these patients do this, given that it opens them up to blame and a disciplinary response?

This can be explained by the fact that presenting non-adherence as wilful functions to construct it as *an informed decision that has already been made*. In this context, it also functions to disguise a request for a change in their medication as 'honest reporting' of partial adherence, which helps to invoke trust and thus create a sound footing on which to proceed into negotiations about medication. Indeed in most instances, patients appear to be doing so in the hope of receiving official ratification (marked by a prescribing change) or, at least, informal endorsement (for example, the doctor 'accepts' the patient's reported adherence behaviour but does not change prescribing). Examples of this have already been presented in Boxes 6.1 and 6.2 above. Indeed all three decisions to omit the patient's anti-psychotic (Table 6.1) were arrived at via this route.

Overall, patients tended to deliver their reports in ways that minimised the risk of receiving a 'disciplinary' response from their psychiatrist. This is exemplified by the actions of the patient in Extract 6.2 below, who uses a number of devices to achieve her 'preferred' outcome; that is, of the consultant's continued acceptance of partial adherence. The sequence below is started by the consultant referring back to the patient's complaint, made shortly beforehand (data not shown), that she had been feeling "medicated up to the eyeballs".

Extract 6.2 (Consultation 52)

Outcome = C acceptance of partial adherence

1	C:	.hhhhhh medicated up to the eyeballs hh[hh
2	P:	[Well [I feel-
3	C:	[Er do you feel
4		like that at the moment?
5	P:	.h erm (.)
6	C:	Cus we did increase yer medication at the last er (0.3) the
7		[last meeting
8	P:	[I feel okay (0.2) it's=
9	C:	=Yeh=
10	P:	=okay but I really don't want to take– if I <u>ha</u>ve to ta- if I get
11		really psychotic I <u>wi</u>ll take more. .hhh but you see um (.)
12	C:	How-how much Pimozide are you taking at the moment

13 P: Three milligrams but I must=

14 C: =(right)=

15 P: =confess=

16 C: =(mm)=

17 P: That about once a week because I feel so tired=

18 C: =mm [hm

19 P: [I only take two. (0.4) .hhh but you see I don't=

20 C: =mm=

21 P: think I took– I am <u>rel</u>atively good with medication .hh but

22 I've got a feeling I missed out but I don't know I took the

23 large tablet .hhh it's like every two months I .hh=

24 C: =°Mm°

25 P: I seem to drop a tablet on the floor or something when I put it

26 on my bedside table.

27 C: That's re<u>mark</u>ably (0.6) good (.) taking of medication

27 ju[st to miss the odd one like that

28 P: [Yes I am not too bad

29 C: Ye[ah

30 P: [I'm not too bad I .hh=

31 C: =Yeah

32 P: I would never go more=

33 C: =yeah=

34 P: =than three days without it

35 C: Yeah

36 P: .hh there are some [days

37 C: [Wh- what happens if you do:: go [(   )

38 P: [Well I

39 probably –I've very rarely done it .hh

40 C: (Yeah)=

41 P: =perhaps if I’m really tired=

42 C: =yeah=

43 P: =I might miss=

44 C: =yeah=

45 P: =a couple of (nights)- I just=

46 C: =yeah=

47 P: =go to bed .hhhh but I think the longest I’ve been without

48 medication=

49 C: =yeah=

50 P: in twenty years

51 C: Yep

52 P: .hh is probably about (.) ten days when I was about twenty

53 one .hhh doing my Spanish degree as an experiment .hh and

54 then I did get a bit ill and I went on it=

55 C: =Yeah=

56 P: =and I was fine. .hh but you know [I

57 C: [(unclear)

58 P: .hh I’m not (.) I I’m reas- I’m fairly compliant you know

59 there’s .hhh a couple of=

60 C: =mm hm=

61 P: =days I just fall asleep but (.)

62 C: (I I think that’s) as good as a- a- anyone’s

63 er [taking of medication

64 P: [I do sometimes cut it down a bit but=

65 C: =(Well) I think .h (.) the last time we met ›you were you were

66 we‹ we did increase to four did you did you (go)=

67 P: Four for two weeks you sa[id

68 C: [Nm- yep {continues}

It was observed in the previous chapter how patients sometimes manage the downside of being defined as an autonomous decision-maker; in one case to minimise their accountability for future poor adherence (see section 5.5.3). The extract above exhibits a number of the devices used by P to elicit the consultant's acceptance of her autonomy over her use of medication. P achieves this primarily through presenting herself as someone with the capacity to make rational decisions about taking her medication; in other words by doing 'being theoretic' (c.f. McHugh, 1970). P does this by:

(1) aligning herself with medical discourse and the doctor's perspective, for example through using psychiatric terms such as "psychotic" and "compliant" (lines 11 and 58 respectively)
(2) displaying 'insight' into her condition, for example by showing that she monitors her symptoms and takes medication accordingly: "if I get really psychotic I <u>wi</u>ll take more" (lines 10-11)
(3) presenting her adherence report as a 'confession'; thereby showing that they know she knows she is accountable to her psychiatrist in this regard (line 15)
(4) presenting poor adherence as always time-limited (see lines 32-34), and

(5) presenting it as something that is done "very rarely" (line 39).

This analysis indicates that patients in this institutional setting use two main methods to create a safe conversational environment in which to talk about not taking medication. The first is to 'own up' to partial or non-adherence before being asked about it; the second is to present the report in such a way that it makes it difficult for the psychiatrist to respond in a disciplinary manner.

6.4 How psychiatrists respond

The most common proximal outcome of an adherence exchange (9/22) was a change to the patient's prescription (see Table 6.1 above). These resulted from the psychiatrist agreeing to either (a) re-align the prescription with what the patient has reportedly taking, such as formally ratifying a reduction or omitting an anti-psychotic the patient has stopped using (n=5), or (b) negotiate changing the prescribed medication to something the patient is more likely to take, for example swapping one anti-psychotic for another (n=4).

As noted in Chapter 4, CA and ethnomethodology more broadly are fundamentally concerned with understanding how it is that people generate and maintain their experience of the world as a factual object. This means that we cannot assume adherence to prescribing is an inherently important, problematic or delicate issue to these psychiatrists and patients.[29] Instead, we should examine whether and if so how the importance of the issue is invoked. It is therefore interesting to note that only once in 22 adherence exchanges did the psychiatrist choose not to pursue a report of poor adherence. This was Consultation 26, where the patient mentioned not taking his medication in the context of a jokey anecdote (referred to section 6.1 above). In every other instance the psychiatrist responded in some way, so the reporting of adherence evidently has interactional consequences. This is a key way in and through which the importance of this issue was conveyed to the patient, and it contrasts with the low response rate from the same sample of psychiatrists to patients' reporting of certain side effects (Seale *et al*, 2007).

Some consultant responses marked the importance or problematic status of poor adherence much more clearly than others. This was done most strongly in an exchange where the consultant overtly 'pressurised' a patient to elicit a commitment from her to improve adherence (see Box 6.3). This 'pressure decision' was examined in detail in Chapter 5.

---

[29] For analyses of how 'delicate' issues are constituted in interaction, see Weijts *et al*, 1993 and Silverman, 1997.

Box 6.3: Adherence exchange (Consultation 74)

SUMMARY OF CONSULTATION

Duration = 21 minutes. Adherence exchange starts 10 seconds into the consultation. Participants = Consultant (C), Patient (P), Social Worker (SW). Duration of doctor/patient relationship = approximately 24 months

ELICITATION

Voluntary disclosure, albeit in the knowledge that a 3rd party (social worker) would probably have done so in any case

DELIVERY

P reports not taking any tablets because they doing more harm than good *[Olanzapine]*

CONSULTANT RESPONSE

C strongly problematises the report and applies direct, concerted pressure (see extract below):

1	C:	=So it'll be one tablet per day
2	P:	°Mm°
3	C:	Can I give you a pre[scription (for that)?
4	P:	[One tablet?
5	C:	Mm
6	P:	One tablet. (1.2) Okay you can give me a prescription but I

7		won't take them unless I'm (.) goin a bit (.) off [(the wall)
8	C:	[Aaah £now
9		that's [not quite what I had in mind£
10	P:	[£(Aaaah)£ that's not a good deal is it-I've (.)
11	C:	No=
12	P:	=£Aah[:::::::£
13	SW:	[(It's a better deal) (0.2) (if er)
14	P:	£(See) he's a hard man£
15	SW:	([ )
16	P:	[He is a hard man
17	C:	It's [not really quite what I had in mind
18	SW:	[( ) £he's fair he's fair he's a fair man
19		[as well£
20	P:	[Heh heh
21	C:	I'm thinking about your neighbours as well and I'm=
22	P:	=heh=
23	C:	=thinking about
24	P:	.hh £yeah I-I've improved greatly I ha-ha-have improved
25		greatly£
26	C:	Oh you ↑have↓
27	P:	Yeah [I have
28	C:	[but y-you're risking throwing that all ↑away↓
29		that's [the problem.
30	P:	[I know (.) no no I-I-I have improved greatly that way
31		yeah .hh er- since I've stopped takin all those tablets and I
32		just take .hh (every) one or two (0.2) [(and)
33	C:	[I (.) I'm not doubting
34		that for one minute.

35	P:	↑Mm↓
36	C:	(.) <u>But</u> (.) the schizophrenia does <u>not</u> come straight away.
37		(0.2) If you're gonna get schizophrenia it creeps up on you
38	P:	Does it?
39	C:	Yeah? And before you know it (.) you're under the spell of it
40		and you'll [be a changed person

The extract above was one small part of an unusually lengthy exchange about poor adherence. Elsewhere in the consultation (data not shown) C elicits P's agreement that falling over (unsteadiness) and polypharmacy are the main problems, not the Olanzapine. The discord between C and P's views on the benefits of the Olanzapine are made plain. C attends to P's overt resistance, eventually changes tack, and proposes that P tries a new medication rather than insisting on her using the one to which she is evidently so resistant. P agrees only 'weakly' to the proposal (responding that she would take it "if I had to"). This action triggers further 'bartering' and 'pressure' work from C and SW, aimed at eliciting a firm commitment from P that she will take this new medication (see fuller analysis in Chapter 5).

OUTCOME

Swap anti-psychotics (from Olanzapine to Sulpiride)

PARTICIPANTS' SUBJECTIVE RATINGS

Satisfaction with consultation: P *"Satisfied"*, C = *"Neither satisfied nor dissatisfied"*. Happiness with outcome/medication decision: P *"Very happy"*, C *"Neither happy nor unhappy"*

The importance of the issue was invoked further through consultants spending time trying to persuade the patient to try a new anti-psychotic, or doing motivational work, for example encouraging the patient to view medication more positively. Even in exchanges that culminated in the consultant accepting the reported adherence behaviour, a lot of work would still be done to communicate that poor adherence was a notable issue that cannot be overlooked.

This shows that while the consultant may agree to a proximal outcome which, on the surface, endorses non-adherence, the agreement tends to be done such that the patient knows the issue is not being taken lightly. A nice example of this is shown in Extract 6.3 below. Notice what C does *after* having marked the patient's decision as "sensible", which in everyday conversation might have marked the 'end-point' of a negotiation (line 4). First, C checks whether P will be aware if he were to become unwell again (see lines 4-10), and, by repeating the question, shows that he needs some convincing over this (see lines 17-24). And second, he seeks confirmation, *for the third and fourth time,* that P is not taking any medication: "Okay so at present you're not taking any medication" (line 1), and "And you're not taking <u>any</u> medication at all now" (line 30) (the preceding two instances were produced before the extract begins). From a psychiatric perspective this may be interpreted as an example of the doctor seeking an 'informed refusal' from the patient. But for the purposes of this analysis, it is sufficient to make the simple observation that C does not let the matter pass without doing some 'serious' interactional work; he certainly does not avoid or ignore it.

Extract 6.3 (Consultation 37)

Outcome = C acceptance of non-adherence

1	C:	Okay so at present you're not taking any medication, well
2	P:	No
3	C:	.hh obviously y- your mood is stable an- and you're obviously
4		well at present so that's that's quite sensible obviously. .hh If
5		you were to become unwell again:::
6	P:	Mm
7	C:	(0.4) like you did a couple of-few years ago more=
8	P:	=Mm=
9	C:	=more depressed and more preoccupied with those kind of
10		(0.2) thoughts .hh do you think you will be <u>aware</u> of it
11	P:	(0.2) yeah because what happened I stopped eatin::: (.)
12	C:	Yeah
13	P:	I couldn't (.) (heh) I couldn't function.
14	C:	Yeah.
15	P:	(0.2) You know what I'm sayin (0.2) I stopped eatin-I
16		couldn't concentrate (0.2) y'know what I'm [sayin
17	C:	[›But what I'm
18		thinking is would you realize‹ I mean obviously=
19	P:	=yeah=
20	C:	=you're not stupid I ›realize that‹=

21 P: =(unclear)

22 C: Would you realize then that you are not well as opposed to (.)

23 well I'm just a bit under the weather. D'you rea- d-d'you see

24 what I mean?=

25 P: =Yeah if those erm feelings came back (.) if I stopped eatin an

26 (0.2) just couldn't concentrate at work

27 C: Right=

27 P: =Then you know (.) yeah.

28 C: Okay

29 P: Definitely.

30 C: °Okay° (1.6) And you're not taking any medication at all now

31 P: Well folic acid I take

32 ((29 seconds of talk about P's non-psychiatric treatment

33 omitted))

34 C: But mentally you're obviously well

35 P: Yeah

36 (1.6 – C makes note in case record?)

37 C: Okay that's fine, er-let's keep it short and sweet (.) you know

38 where I am if you need to see me

39 P: I do

40 C: Make an appointment say (for) or make it for four months?

41 P: Four months

42 C: Is that okay?

43 P: Okay ((continues))

6.5 Communication in the context of a therapeutic relationship

These meetings were generally part of a long-term therapeutic relationship. Having recorded a small number 'follow up' consultations for the study, it is possible observe patterns of interaction by the same consultant-patient dyad being repeated over time – but resulting in different proximal outcomes. Transcripts of talk from two consultations, involving the same patient and consultant, are shown in Extracts 6.4 and 6.5[30]. The second extract was a follow-up consultation that was recorded 12 weeks after the first (Consultation 11).

Extract 6.4 (Consultation 11)

Outcome = P does not commit to improving adherence

1	C:	And do you take it at night as well (.) no?
2	P:	No I do not.
3	C:	Just (.) okay
4		(1.8)
5	P:	Yer not druggin me up docter! (0.6) I'm not stupid (me) you
6		know I'm not. (0.6) Yer not druggin me up (0.4) (like) some
7		zombie!
8	C:	And are you taking the iron tablets

[30] Extract 6.5 was also examined in Chapter 5, in the context of the analysis of how pressure is applied in negotiations about medication.

9	P:	°Yes every morning°
10		(0.2)
11	C:	(Mm)
12		(6.8 seconds) ((C makes note in case record?))
13	P:	Are you going out socially are you meeting [people
14	C:	[yes ((continues))

And then, three months later:-

Extract 6.5 (Consultation 40)

Outcome = Prescribing change to omit anti-psychotic (Olanzapine)

1	P:	The only one that agrees wi' me (.) (the two)
2		(.) Carbamaza[pine
3	C:	[(I know)=
4	P:	=they go down alright
5	C:	Yeah=
6	P:	=and the- (.) that iron tablet
7	C:	(Ye[ah)
8	P:	[But they (.) make me sick=
9	C:	=It's just while you're- because you're I mean i-it's only
10		because of the stress I realize, (.) you're in-in you're-
11		you're very stressed at present .hhhh taking a small dose
12		of Olanzapine or something a bit similar might help to (.)
13		relax a little bit:: and be less uptight and anxious

14		(1.4)
15	C:	No? You- just want to carry on your- with the Carba[mazapine
16	P:	[Aye (0.2)
17	C:	You- are you tak=
18	P:	=You want ta drug me up ain't yer!
19		(0.2 – C turns page in case record)
20	C:	And you take four hundred of that don't you
21	P:	(1.4) °(Yes)°
22	C:	°Okay°
23	P:	.hh doctor .hh with the help ( ) I pulled myself oot
24		the gutter and I'm no going back in the gutter! .hhh I've
25		got ma money the day an I'm determined I'm not gonna buy drink!
26	C:	°Yeah: okay°
27	SW:	You've done well ((P's first name))
28	P:	I know I have done I'm proud of maself

Prior to both of these sequences, C enquires about P's use of medication (data not shown), in response to which P reports having not taken her anti-psychotic (Olanzapine). After cautiously attempting to 'persuade' P to take it, C is on the receiving end of an angry 'accusation' from P that he has been trying to drug her up (line 5 in Extract 6.4 and line 18 in Extract 6.5). Though the structure of interaction is very similar in both, with C quickly 'backing off', the outcomes were different: it was only after the second exchange, three months after the first, that C decided to omit Olanzapine from P's prescription. By the second appointment it seems plausible to suggest that the resistance had become, in the eyes of this consultant at least, 'entrenched' rather than a one-off. The meaning of any contribution to interaction is thus dependent on more than just the local context of its production – it needs to be considered in context of the unfolding doctor-patient relationship.

6.6 Discussion

Communicating about the potentially difficult issue of adherence poses risks to the immediate 'here and now' interaction, and the longer-term therapeutic relationship. This chapter has explored some of the ways that patients and consultants work to minimise these risks. The loosest message of CA, according to its inventor Harvey Sacks, is that the world in which we live is much more finely organised than one might imagine (Sacks, 1995, Vol 1: 215). I hope my analyses in this and the preceding chapter have managed to communicate this message.

These psychiatrists attempted to improve adherence rates in three main ways: first, by agreeing to re-align the prescription dosage with what the patient is reportedly taking (e.g. formally ratifying a reduction); second, by changing the prescribed medication to something the patient is more likely to take (e.g. swapping anti-psychotics); and third, by encouraging the patient to view their medication more positively.[31] One implication for future research comes from the fact that a proportion of partial or non-adherence may have been ratified or endorsed by their doctor or another healthcare professional. This was the outcome negotiated in four of the 22 adherence exchanges. Could it be argued that the high rates or partial/non-adherence found in previous studies may not be as 'bad' as they first appear, because some of it will probably have been the subject of an informal agreement between the healthcare professional and service user?

This study was not designed to measure distal outcomes, so I cannot comment on whether the attempts of psychiatrists to improve adherence were ultimately successful. Rather my aim in this chapter has been to examine the dynamics of the relationship between adherence talk and the outcomes produced within the consultation (agreements, commitments etc) that are *likely* to have some influence future adherence. I recommend further studies be undertaken to understand better the three-way relationship between adherence talk, proximal outcomes and distal outcomes. Britten and colleagues' exemplary study of misunderstandings in prescribing decisions in general practice, reviewed in Chapter 3, indicates how such a study might be carried out (Britten *et al*, 2000). Undertaken in 20 general practices in England, the research involved CA of consultation

[31] Materials relating to this third method have not been presented in this chapter due to lack of space.

transcripts, combined with an analysis of interviews undertaken with participants some weeks after the consultation (the present study's post-consultation interviews were undertaken immediately after each consultation). Britten and colleagues' follow-up interviews recorded whether or not patients had cashed their prescriptions and/or whether they had been taking their medication (i.e. the distal outcomes). This made it possible to identify different categories of misunderstanding that had had adverse consequences for taking medicine, such as where patients did not mention their preferences for medication because they had wrongly assumed the doctor was already aware of them. While not without practical and methodological challenges (researchers face the same difficulties as doctors in getting to 'the truth' of adherence), this research design offers the potential for furthering our understanding of the relationship between the process and outcome of anti-psychotic prescribing.

One intriguing finding from the present study is that patients often 'disguise' requests for a change in their medication as 'honest reporting' of partial adherence. This honest reporting is generally interpreted as putting the speaker in a morally good light and as something that invokes 'trust'. From the patient's point of view, this is a sound footing on which to proceed into negotiation about medication, as examined in Chapter 5. Furthermore, the negotiation starts from the position that the prescribing decision has already been made 'unilaterally' by the patient before he or she has entered the room. Although the consultant does not *have* to ratify or endorse such decisions, in this study they mostly did – usually after checking, and some discussion. That noted, we have seen that non-adherent patients still risk a 'telling off', so adopt a number of strategies to reduce the likelihood of this happening. This emphasises that it is not simply the doctor's decision as to how s/he responds to a report of poor adherence, rather the response is shaped by how that report was produced.

As discussed in Chapter 5, these psychiatrists oriented to two main goals in these encounters: adherence to prescribing and client retention. General practitioners in a study by Britten and colleagues are claimed to have not engaged with patients' aversion talk regarding their medication (Britten *et al*, 2004). Clearly, aversion talk is not equivalent to reporting partial or non-adherence, but the present analysis suggests that these psychiatrists seem more willing than the GPs Britten and colleagues studied to engage with and respond to patients' reluctance to take medication. This, then, is a key way through which these psychiatrists orient to, and thereby invoke, their institutional role of monitoring their patients' use of medication and encouraging adherence to prescribing. This is perhaps not unexpected given the value psychiatrists reportedly place on anti-psychotic medication (Seale *et al*, 2006) and the increasing role that mental health practitioners have in assessing and managing the risks to and from service users (Davis, 1996; Alaszewski *et al*, 2000). That noted, psychiatrists in these consultations rarely invoked its importance by responding to adherence reports a 'disciplinary' manner. A more 'aggressive' approach by the psychiatrist would involve, for example, focussing more heavily on adherence, tackling the issue head on with direct questions about compliance, refusing to back off in the face of patient of resistance, and so on. This may succeed in eliciting patient commitments to improve adherence, but could these possibly be taken at face value? Also, there are limits to how far such an approach can be taken without jeopardising the long-term relationship and client engagement. Would people want to come back to see their psychiatrist if they knew they would be in for the 'third degree' on every visit? And would they want to admit to any 'lapses' in adherence in future?

Thus, there is a central tension between the psychiatrists' two main goals; of encouraging the patient to ensure they keep coming back to see them and to keep taking the tablets. It seems likely that psychiatrists are operating strategically, across consultations, in the knowledge that pushing too hard for adherence is likely to make people drop out of treatment, in which case they will have failed on both counts. Put simply, from a psychiatrist's point of view, you cannot monitor and manage adherence in people you never get to see; perhaps better, then, to make a 'tactical withdrawal' and settle for negotiating a proximal outcome that appears to endorse partial or even total non-adherence.

This analysis reveals some of the ways that psychiatrists and patients *work together* to make talking about non-compliance something that is less immediately threatening to 'face' (Goffman, 1959) and to the therapeutic alliance more generally. The apparent desire to 'preserve the relationship' across consultations by avoiding conflict is an exact parallel with general practitioners and antibiotics, where GPs often prescribe unnecessarily in order to keep patients on their side and avoid them 'shopping around' to different GPs until they find one who will give them what they want (Rollnick *et al*, 2000; see also Butler *et al*, 1998).

This means that these findings can be added the growing body of research evidence, discussed in Chapter 3, about 'non-scientific' or ostensibly 'irrational' drug prescribing which highlights the influence on non-clinical, *interactional* factors on decisions to prescribe. At one level, the non-disciplinary responses of psychiatrists to reports of poor or non-compliance can be explained by the collaborative efforts of both parties to create a safe conversational environment. However, I would argue that the avoidance of confrontation in these consultations is most likely to be related to a desire to preserve a co-operative relationship in which conditions are created for the more democratic forms of 'negotiation' about medication described in Chapter 5.

Chapter 7

The permeable institution

CONTENTS

7.1 The total institution

> "Institutions like mental hospitals are of the 'total' kind, in the sense that the inmate lives all aspects of his life on the premises in the close company of others who are similarly cut off from the wider world. These institutions tend to contain two broad and quite differently situated categories of participants, staff and inmates." (Goffman, 1961: 183-184)

Erving Goffman was one of the first sociologists to examine the experiences of patients in order to understand how mental hospitals work. Like other researchers of that time, he found those institutions to be disturbingly easy to be admitted into, extraordinarily difficult to get out of, and damaging to in-patients who were isolated from the outside world (Caudhill, 1958; Strauss *et al*, 1964; Rosenhan, 1973). Goffman's *Asylums* (1961), reviewed in Chapter 2, was particularly influential and his total institution model or metaphor remains firmly planted in the minds of sociologists, psychiatrists and service user advocates (Weinstein, 1994). Even so, some have argued that the model was out of date even at its inception (ibid). This is not my view. Rather, in this chapter I will argue that the total institution firstly needs to be understood for what it was; namely an *ideal type* against which empirical cases can be examined and compared. Using findings from previous research and my own ethnographic study of life on three acute psychiatric (admission) wards in London, I shall argue that there has been a trend over time towards an increased degree of permeability on such wards and the hospitals in which they are located. Further, I offer an alternative ideal type to the total institution, which I believe represents better the reality of everyday life in contemporary 'bricks and mortar' psychiatric institutions. I call this the "permeable institution".

7.1.1 A closed social system

In his social anthropological study of a psychiatric hospital, Caudhill (1958) argued convincingly that the old psychiatric hospitals were closed social systems that affected the behaviour of people who constituted them. He observed a formal social structure with a sharply defined status hierarchy of physicians, psychologists, social workers, administrators, clerical workers, attendants and patients, and noted that these groups developed separate values and perceptions of hospital life. By looking beyond interaction within or between social groups to transaction - the processes going on throughout the hospital - Caudhill was able to track and account for phenomena such as sudden 'mood sweeps' and collective disturbances (Caudhill, 1958). But the relationship between life in hospital and the outside world was largely unexplored.

The process of 'de-institutionalisation', discussed in Chapter 3, was well underway when Baruch and Treacher (1978) examined the workings of a general hospital psychiatric unit in a large provincial city in England. However, they found a geographically isolated institution that experienced problems due to its impermeability to the outside world:

> "Ironically, the unit was situated within a large and foreboding nineteenth-century general hospital which was geographically isolated from the community it serves. The unit's relationship with the community was so weak that many of the specific problems that psychiatric units were meant to avoid were depressingly still evident. The unit's staff members were effectively 'institutionalised' – they rarely made domiciliary visits to their patients and they were not involved in the communities from which their patients came, so they could never develop an understanding of the patients' way of life or devise methods for using community resources to help the patients." (Baruch & Treacher, 1978, p.223)

A different picture emerges when researchers have chosen to look for 'deviant cases'. Prior (1995), for example, offers a fascinating account of a single patient, 'Samuel', who managed to maintain a strong personal identity throughout his 36-year stay in a large mental hospital in Northern Ireland. For the last 10 years of his 'compulsory' hospital treatment Samuel received no treatment whatsoever and refused to be discharged on the grounds that he was happy with his life. For him, hospital functioned as a lodging house while he held down a job as a labourer and played an active role in the local church. He thus "kept his links with the outside world, through family, work and church activities, which indicates that some sections of the community ignored the 'mental patient' identity and did not engage in social distancing" (Prior, 1995, p.650). This account of a single case therefore challenges the notion of the all-pervading power of the total institution, but does not undermine the validity of the model *per se*. On the contrary it exemplifies the search for negative instances in order to contribute to theoretical debate (Seale, 1999, pp.73-86). Samuel's story reveals how some people are able to survive total institutions relatively untouched by their negative effects.

7.1.2 An outdated model?

Weinstein (1994) argues the total institution model was out of date soon after *Asylums* was published, because deinstitutionalisation was already underway and mental hospitals were experiencing changes that ameliorated the problems identified by Goffman. That noted, Weinstein concedes the metaphor's value in sensitising psychiatrists and public officials to the anti-therapeutic consequences of hospital treatment, and, crucially, he reminds us that Goffman constructed an *ideal type* - a conceptual device to be used as a tool for examining formal organisations (ibid). While the type or model was constructed from observations of reality, Goffman (1961) acknowledged that it was not intended to correspond exactly to any single case: what is distinctive about total institutions is that each exhibits *to an intense degree* many of the same general features. Criticism of the total institution model for corresponding poorly with reality therefore misses the point. However, it has to be said that this 'naïve' reading of Goffman is not helped by his cavalier use of definitions (Williams, 1988) and a prose style that encourages readers to forget his qualifiers and caveats rather quickly (Weinstein, 1994). Contemporaries spotted such literary/theoretical sleights of hand, claiming that the model was overdrawn and illusory (Levinson & Gallagher, 1964) and inmates in the various types of total institution define their situations quite differently (Lin, 1968).

So is the total institution model still relevant? Or is now the time to think about introducing a *better* ideal type that is more recognisable to the people who live or work on today's psychiatric wards? The picture emerging from recent U.K. health service research literature, reviewed in Chapter 3, suggests that this may be the case. Indicators of a much greater degree of permeability on today's wards include:

1. The comparatively short length of psychiatric in-patient stays (Rogers & Pilgrim, 2001; Thompson *et al*, 2004). This makes it questionable whether people remain in hospital long enough to fully experience the difficulties described in earlier studies.
2. The ease by which drugs and other illicit substances are finding their way onto the wards (Phillips & Johnson, 2003; Dolan & Kirwan, 2001), for example via visitors or people's regular

dealers (Phillips & Johnson, 2003). This mirrors what has been found in other ostensibly total institutions, such as prisons (e.g. Cope, 2000).

3. The extension of nurses' responsibilities beyond the boundaries of the ward's spatial environment and into the outside world. For example, community mental health professionals often call upon the knowledge of hospital nurses when dealing with patients who have been discharged into their care (Deacon, 2003).

In this chapter I will examine the nature of the modern, acute psychiatric ward, focusing on its *permeability* to the outside world. Some of the consequences of a high degree of permeability will identified, as will some of the methods used by social actors (staff and patients) to regulate or resist the level of permeability of their ward.

7.1.3 The importance of permeability

Previous authors have been aware of this permeability, though to a limited degree. Caudhill, for example, acknowledged the "question of the influence of the culture in general upon events in hospital", but for practical purposes chose to limit the scope of his analysis (1958, p.27). Goffman (1961, pp.111-114) also discussed "permeability" directly, regarding it as one of a number of dimensions of variation among total institutions. He defines permeability as the degree to which the social standards maintained within the institution and the social standards maintained in broader society have influenced one another. However, the emphasis in his account remains firmly on the impermeable aspects of the institution and minimal "role carry-over" from the outside world:

> "In examining the admission procedures of total institutions, one tends to be struck by the impermeable aspects of the establishment, since the stripping and levelling processes which occur at this time directly cut across the various social distinctions with which the recruits enter." (Goffman, 1961, p.112)

Further, Goffman argues that impermeability is necessary for morale and social stability. He notes, for example, that "the few patients of high socio-economic status in a state mental hospital can provide everyone with assurance that there is a distinctive mental-patient role"; adding - with some irony I suspect - that "the harshest total institution may be the most democratic" in that it assures inmates they are being treated no worse than anyone else (ibid, p.112). Similarly he notes that if the institution is appreciably permeable, staff members who have the same, or lower, social origins as the inmates find it difficult to maintain social distance from them, thus complicating their role and opening themselves up to inmate derision (ibid, p.113).

Research undertaken more recently indicates that there is analytic mileage left in the total institution model (for example, McKorkell 1998; McColgan, 2005). However, even when the model is assumed the analysis can nevertheless direct the reader to permeable aspects of the institution. For example, Leyser's (2003) ethnographic study of life in a U.S. mental hospital found male residents accessing masculine power in similar ways to outside populations (e.g. using sexualised talk to turn women into 'props'). Leyser concludes that gendered norms found in the larger society were very much part of life in the hospital because residents brought into the institution their experiences of a gendered world, and were exposed to the "outside world" during their stay through media stories, family visits and interactions with staff (ibid).

Previous research accounts have thus paid some attention to the relationship between the organisation and its environment, but the issue of permeability has generally been downplayed. My position, is that: (1) previous sociological accounts of psychiatric hospitals in the 1950s and 1960s portray them as comparatively closed to the outside world, which seems to be a fair representation of what they were like at the time, (2) the 'bracketing' of permeability as a side issue in those accounts has led to its importance being overlooked, (3) the subsequent trend towards a greater degree of permeability in psychiatric hospitals has made those accounts appear dated in some respects, and (4) this makes it important to turn the analytical spotlight onto the permeable membrane between the hospital and its environment.

The remainder of this chapter presents findings from the Acute Ward Ethnography, which involved me undertaking fieldwork on three acute psychiatric wards (see Chapter 4 for discussion of method). I will first describe some aspects of life on the ward and present evidence that acute psychiatric wards are 'permeable' institutions. I then describe the consequences of permeability, for patients and staff, and illustrate some of the strategies that both groups employ to regulate or cope with permeability.

7.2 Living on an acute ward

A patient's day is punctuated by scheduled activities such as medicine rounds (twice daily), optional occupational therapy sessions (weekdays only), ward rounds (once a week) and meals. Life can be boring, especially at weekends when relatively few, if any, social or group activities are organised. Even so, the ward tends to be a busy place for much of the time, characterised by a lot of comings and goings throughout the day. They are staffed by three nursing shifts per day, which often include one or more agency nurses who may be unfamiliar with patients. Each day visitors are likely to include professionals from a wide range of occupational groups, such as pharmacists, patient advocacy workers and occupational therapists, as well as the carers, family members and friends of patients.

Invariably wards in general hospital psychiatric wards offer limited access to dedicated and/or secure outside space. A quarter of London's acute wards are kept permanently locked (Bowers *et al*, 2002). The remainder, including the three wards I studied, may be locked temporarily; for example to prevent involuntary patients from absconding. When the door to the ward is open, visitors often include patients who wander in from other open wards in the psychiatric unit. Nurses and care assistants use their discretion as to whom they allow in (discussed further below).

In one of the modern wards involved in the ethnographic research, movement between rooms was restricted, as was typical of all the wards studied: there were 'staff only' areas and rooms to which patients had restricted access. For example, they were not ordinarily allowed into their bedrooms during the day (09:00 – 16:00). Aside from that patients could move relatively freely about the ward. People often hung around at the intersection of the two main corridors; one or two would wander aimlessly up and down the corridor. Some patients tended to stay in the TV room most of the time, only getting up to use the toilet or go to the canteen; others tended to spend most of their time in the smoking room, the door of which was directly opposite to the entrance to the nursing station. The canteen was open throughout the day and people could help themselves to a hot drink from the machine – it was not unusual to find approximately one third of patients in there. It is therefore a dynamic environment, notable for the large amount of intra- and inter-spatial movement occurring throughout the day (discussed further below).

7.3 The evidence for permeability

7.3.1 Ward membership is temporary or 'revolving'

The patient group includes adults of all ages (18-64), from different social groups and with very different types of problems. Patients can therefore feel that they have been 'placed among strangers' (Mental Health Act Commission, 2003), often against their will, and into situations of forced intimacy. Even so, patients tend not to stay for long so these relationships are mostly transitory. The high patient turnover means that the ward population changes rapidly: sometimes from shift to shift. These changes are largely beyond the control of ward staff who have little or no influence over decisions about admission and are sometimes prevented from discharging patients; for example because the patient is homeless. The patient group includes people who are on extended leave, sometimes to free up beds for new admissions, and who might not visit the ward from day to day, or even week to week. Discharged patients, or those from other wards or day care services in the psychiatric unit, often visit either to socialise with other patients or to use the ward facilities (see Box 6.1). These visits are often welcomed but sometimes result in conflict (discussed further below).

Box 7.1: Former in-patient does 'round-trip' of the wards
(summary of fieldnote extract from Ward B)
Deepa was discharged from Ward B and is now a 'day patient'; that is, she attends the day hospital on the ground floor of the psychiatric unit a few days per week, from 9 a.m. to 5 p.m. She is not supposed to stay behind for an evening meal in the main canteen, but usually does – none of the care assistants who supervise meal times seem to notice or mind. After having dinner with her there, she and I returned to Ward B. After ten minutes or so in the TV room, she announced to me that she found it "boring" (mainly because she did not recognise any of the patients and none of the nurses she liked were on that shift). She suggested that we visit some of the other wards in the unit. She proceeded to do a 'round trip' of them with me in tow, including a visit to the ward on the floor above in which most of the 'floating' patients congregate. While care assistants and nurses often intervene to stop unwanted visitors coming onto their ward [discussed below] on this occasion Deepa and I were able to move between wards without any trouble.

The staff group is equally fluid. The core ward nursing team changes with each shift and a nurse with whom a particular patient has formed an attachment might not be seen for days or even weeks because of rota patterns, leave or sickness. The use of agency or bank staff, and student nurses on short-term placements, means that many shifts include nurses who are strangers to the patients.

7.3.2 Contact with the outside world is maintained

Many patients have daily contact with families and friends, and the wards either are open to visitors throughout the day or at the discretion of the nurse in charge. Legitimate visitors are rarely turned away. Although there are some visitors on the ward at most times, patients tend to maintain contact with the outside world by phone and, in particular, by personal mobile phones that patients are permitted to have on most wards (Bowers *et al*, 2002). Patients use this contact to request cigarettes, food and so on, and sometimes to enlist family and friends to intervene with staff on their behalf; for example to prevent medication being given forcibly. Such communication thus has a direct influence on ward life.

Patients maintain contact with 'outside' professionals, such as social workers, who may keep in contact with clients of theirs who have been admitted. Sometimes the patient initiates 'inreach'. Once, a patient telephoned the police directly to ask them to intervene after having been assaulted by another patient, because she believed that members of staff were not taking her complaint seriously.

Contact is also maintained during periods of leave, which can range from a few hours, to days or weeks. Patients on unsupervised leave were observed leaving the ward to join a major anti-government street demonstration in Central London, to go begging or to feed the dog (see Box 7.2).

Box 7.2: Feeding the dog ***(summary of field-note entry for ward B)***
A patient on the inner-London ward was concerned about his dog, which had been placed in an animal shelter by the man's social worker. Unknown to staff on the ward, he retrieved his dog the first chance he got, took it back to his flat, and continued to feed it every afternoon during his daily leave from hospital.

7.3.3 Institutional identities are blurred

Goffman (1961) and others have documented how people are stripped of their identities on entering 'total' institutions, for example by having personal belongings removed and being forced to wear standard-issue clothing (see Chapter 2). I found, by contrast, that these processes in the settings studied are considerably diluted and that institutional identities are blurred to the point where visitors and new patients, and indeed researchers, can easily mistake staff and patients for one another (see Box 7.3). Unlike their counterparts on general wards, psychiatric patients do not wear plastic identification wristbands. Although some nurses and care assistants have name badges or keys hanging from their belt loops, they wear the same informal clothes as patients. The distinctions between nursing staff and patients in dress are subtle. For example, although both groups often wear trainers, staff rarely wore tracksuit bottoms, except during occupational therapy sports groups or more casual weekend shifts. These differences take time to learn and are sometimes not recognised by the uninitiated, and it was not unusual for a new member of staff to be mistaken for a patient. This is compounded by the fact that patients and ward staff invariably address one another by their first names.

Box 7.3: 'Agency worker' who was a patient *(summary of field-note entry for ward C)*

I was sitting with Maqbool and Danny at a table in the ward's coffee area, where people can help themselves to free hot drinks from a vending machine. A new agency worker – a care assistant I assumed – casually stood at the entrance to the room, discretely keeping an eye on what was going on. Imren and Claudia were sitting at the next table. The conversation between them escalated in seconds into a row that culminated in Claudia throwing a cup of coffee in Imren's face. I immediately looked to the care assistant, assuming she would intervene, but was truly shocked to see her stay put, looking unperturbed. It was left to Danny to intervene and de-escalate the situation,[32] while the care assistant looked on. It was only later that the penny dropped – the young woman at the doorway was not a care assistant after all, she was a new patient.

Such informality and role ambiguity palpably reduces the social distance between nursing staff and patients, and it is reduced further by the fact that the nurses and care assistants I observed broadly reflected the diversity of the patient group, with regard to race, gender, age and social class. This was not so with the consultant psychiatrists on the three wards, who were predominantly male (8 out of 9), white (9) and middle class. Their social distance from patients was routinely invoked through other people addressing them by their honorific and through their adherence to a comparatively formal dress code.

Thus, in several respects these wards exhibited the features I have labelled 'permeability': a 'revolving' membership who maintained many contacts with the outside world, and a blurring of institutional identities.

[32] De-escalation is one of a number of methods used by patients to manage risk on the wards. I discuss this further elsewhere (Quirk *et al*, 2004; 2005).

7.4 Consequences of permeability

7.4.1 New risks to patients and staff

Many service users view admission to a psychiatric ward as a moral failure rather than a medical event, and as a process that adversely affects their sense of identity and social position. However, I found little evidence of 'institutionalism' (Wing, 1962) or 'depersonalisation' (Goffman, 1961; Rosenhan, 1971). During the comparatively short hospital stays, patients typically maintain many of the obligations of personhood experienced before admission (Bowers et al, 1999). At the same time, the asylum function of a psychiatric hospital can be threatened through patients having continued responsibility for managing relationships, their housing situation, personal finances and so on.

A further consequence of increased permeability is that unwanted people can come into hospital and cause trouble. One manager described how a furious ex-patient returned to the psychiatric unit countless times to threaten staff. In the manager's view, hospital security measures, described below, functioned more to keep such people out than to keep involuntary patients in.

7.4.2 *Illicit drug use on the wards*

Drug use and drug dealing were prevalent on the wards in this study, as is the case on other psychiatric wards in England (Williams & Cohen, 2000; Phillips & Johnson, 2003; Hinscliff, 2003). This was most evident on the inner-London ward. In some cases, patients obtained drugs from the sources they had used before admission. In others, the dealers were themselves in-patients or former in-patients who visited the wards (see Box 7.3).

Box 7.3: Illicit drug use

SOCIABLE/RECREATIONAL DRUG USE *(FIELDNOTE ENTRY FOR WARD C)*

I followed Jimmy [a patient] into the reception area of the psychiatric unit where he introduced me to three other patients from different wards… When Jimmy introduced me…he said "Alan can I introduce you to some of my friends", and they were all sitting on chairs in the reception area in front of the shop that was closed at the time as it was a Sunday… Then he said, "this is Alan. He's doing some research here…finding out what it's like here"… There was only one spare seat next to them, which Jimmy offered to me. He sat opposite. While he was talking with one of the patient's daughter, who was there on a visit, one of the other patients said to him "Would you like some of this?" and passed over a spliff … Jimmy said he would have just one puff. He said to me "I don't know much about drugs, do I

Alan?" and he said he only very occasionally has this ...... A further patient in the group said that was the same for him too and that he hadn't had a spliff for two days.

DRUGS EXCHANGE ON THE WARD *(FIELDNOTE ENTRY FOR WARD B)*

Rose [a nurse] entered the room where I was interviewing a patient and called "Alan can you come?" and, minutes later, a second time with some urgency. She took me into the glass-fronted nursing station and told me I had just missed some drug dealing, which had occurred right in front of the office window, literally within about two metres of the office. I think it involved the patient who backed away when I later introduced myself.

AWARENESS OF THE ISSUE BY STAFF AND PATIENTS *(VARIOUS FIELDNOTE ENTRIES)*

(i)Fieldnote of informal interview with manager

She agrees that drug use is prevalent on the wards – said half-in-jest "the best place to score locally" – and reported finding the remains of a joint outside her door recently.

(ii) Fieldnote of informal interview with patient

He said that Derek [a patient] and him are known by staff to use drugs. He takes speed. He said that "this place is full of it [drugs]" and reckons that "half the people use drugs". He said the reason staff don't intervene much is that "the place would drive people even more mad if they stopped drugs coming in".

(iii)Fieldnote of informal interview with senior nurse

Katy [a senior nurse] said that she sometimes asks visitors to leave if she is suspicious about them (re. drugs)… When I asked her whether they would stop people visiting, she said emphatically "We cannot stop people coming onto the ward… what can we say? 'Empty your pockets'? NB She completely agreed with the emergent hypothesis, when I put it to her; namely that staff do assess the motives of people who visit or return to the ward. For example, there is a "wheeler dealer", whom they know uses drugs (his urine tested positive). People come onto the ward to see him. Sometimes they can disturb other patients, at which point she will ask them to leave.

7.5 Management of permeability

Both staff and patients manage the consequences of the permeability of their ward or psychiatric unit in the following ways.

7.5.1 Limiting unwanted movement

Nurses and care assistants are often preoccupied with the risk of patients absconding and with preventing unwanted visitors from coming onto the ward. Overt security measures are used to regulate movement of people into and out of individual wards or the psychiatric unit. These include CCTV cameras trained on entry and exit points, entry phone systems, security key-pad access on doors (the code is given to authorised staff only), use of security guards, the use of 'body blocking' techniques by care assistants or nurses,[33] and the posting of staff on the ward door in a 'bouncer' role (see Box 7.4).

An alternative way of managing the risk of patients absconding is to put individual patients under special observation. Here a nurse is assigned to keep within arm's length of the patient at all times. Special observation is not only used as a form of permeability management - patients might also be 'specialled' to reduce the risk of self-harm (see Jones *et al*, 2000). When such measures are deemed insufficient to thwart "escape attempts" (see Bowers *et al,* 1999b) staff might decide to lock the ward door or transfer the patient concerned to a locked, intensive care unit.

Box 7.4: Nurse in 'bouncer' role at the ward entrance *(fieldnote entry for Ward C)*

[A nurse] told me that nursing staff are having a meeting soon about specialling because it has become crazy, i.e. many patients are under one-on-one special observation, requiring extra nurses on each shift. In the meantime they have "posted" a member of staff who sits by

[33] For example, a member of staff might stand in the doorway to a room in order to prevent a patient or patients from leaving. Patients are thus 'contained' in the room even though a lock and key has not been used. See Ryan and Bowers (2005) for a description of how this technique is used in psychiatric intensive care units.

the front door. This was the case throughout my three-hour morning visit. The chair is a couple of metres inside the front door, its back to the laundry room. When I saw the nurse who was guarding the front door, he sometimes sat with his legs outstretched across the corridor. I saw him and another nurse challenge a patient who brought a visitor (a patient from another ward) onto the ward and stopped them before they had gone more than three metres. The visitor left without a fuss.

7.5.2 Using discretion

Staff members routinely exercise discretion in ways that directly affect permeability, either for the ward as a whole or for individual patients. Aside from making decisions about locking the door, special observation and patient transfers (discussed above), they also decide when patients are ready for discharge and the precise conditions of patients' leave. The 1983 Mental Health Act may be invoked in the process. Care assistants and nurses also assess the legitimacy of visitors: many observations were made, across the three wards, of visitors being asked to leave if they were suspected of being 'up to no good'. Discretion extends to creative approaches to managing the consequences of the infiltration of local street culture onto the ward. Examples of this, in relation to illicit drug use, are the nurse who cancelled a drug deal made by a patient using the office phone (see Box 7.5) and an incident where nurses turned a blind eye to drug dealing because they judged that the consequences of intervening would be worse.

Box 7.5: The cancelled drug deal ***(summary of fieldnote entry for Ward C)***

A patient [known by staff to have a history of crack and heroin use] stormed into the nursing station without knocking and demanded to use the office phone so that she could "talk to her mother". She phoned a person she referred to as "T" and asked him to meet her urgently in "the normal place outside the front of the hospital". The one nurse in the room was suspicious and after the call finished challenged the patient, who denied it was a drug deal. After the patient had left the nursing station, the nurse, unconvinced by her account, pressed the redial function. When the phone was answered, she said "Hello is that 'T'?; the deal is now cancelled" and put the phone down.

7.5.3 Patient input: negotiation and subversion

Staff attempts to manage permeability are subject to negotiation. For example, patients commonly negotiate more relaxed conditions of leave or an early discharge. Such negotiations can happen in formal ward rounds (discussed in the following chapter) as well as in informal discussions with doctors and nurses on the ward. Attempts at permeability management may be actively subverted. In one example patients acquired the security access code for a side-entrance to the hospital, which they used when they wanted to by-pass hospital security (see Box 7.6).

Box 7.6: Subverting security measures *(fieldnote entry for Ward B)*

After getting a coffee from the canteen, at 4pm after the 'social' [occupational therapy] group, Alex [a patient] asked me to follow him. He said he had something interesting to show me. He led me back towards the entrance to the day hospital, to the side double-door exit that leads out towards the side road. He said "watch this", entered the code to the security lock and pushed open the door. He let it swing wide open. I felt slightly awkward, as we were near the entrance to the day hospital - I didn't know how the staff would react if they saw me being shown this. I didn't know quite what to say. But Alex continued, saying that this door is meant to be used by day hospital staff only but that about 25 patients know the code. He said people use this if they want to do some "dodgy dealing" or similar, and don't want to be recorded on video leaving the psychiatric unit. He said they will probably change the code, but patients will soon get to know it again.

While patients have some input into their ward's level of permeability, this is a psychiatric setting in which nursing staff have tools that permit them to have much more control than patients ever can. Patient subversion in this context is therefore better understood as a "weapon of the weak" (Scott, 1987) rather than an equalising resistance strategy. Patient's methods of non-cooperation and resistance are the subject of the following chapter.

7.6 Discussion

There are striking differences between these three London wards and the psychiatric hospitals studied by Goffman (1961) and others in the 1950s and 1960s. The latter were geographically remote from the catchment areas from which their patients were drawn and their residents were isolated from the wider society, for lengthy periods of time. The decline of long stay institutions in many Western countries means that today's psychiatric wards are part of a system of psychiatric care whose focus is elsewhere and for which an in-patient stay is viewed as a transitory spell in a longer episode of care. In the context of community care, hospital admission has thus become a small part in the life of many mental health service users, whose management of a family, a job, social services, housing and money has to continue while they are in hospital. A key difference for today's inpatient, then, is that in many respects he or she *remains a person* while in hospital, and is much less likely to be relieved of the obligations of personhood than were inmates of the old asylums (Barnham & Hayward, 1991; Barker *et al,* 1999).

While some parts of the U.K. psychiatric system may still conform to the 'total' institution model, it seems more plausible to suggest that permeability is the norm. At any rate, institutional care in this sector might better be understood, nowadays, as representing degrees of permeability rather than degrees of totalitarianism. The extent of permeability across the U.K. and in other countries, though, remains an open empirical question: the case studies presented, like Goffman's (1961), are designed to delineate an ideal type with which it is helpful to think.

It was noted in Chapter 3 that much sociological literature on psychiatry has pointed to the blurring of the boundaries between mental hospital and the world outside in the latter half of the twentieth century. Studies have variously noted the changing role of psychiatric institutions in the control and regulation of mental health problems (Basaglia, 1987; Prior, 1993), and the new social/institutional context in which the remaining wards operate, one in which there has been a psychiatrisation of everyday worries (see Chapter 3). Further, the moves towards community psychiatry and management of risk (Castel, 1991) mean that home treatment teams can now literally take care and surveillance into people's homes with the aim of *intercepting* problems before a hospital admission is required. This idea appears to lie behind the thinking behind the section in the new Mental Health Act for compulsory community treatment (discussed in Chapter 3; see also Chapter 9).

The contribution of this analysis to the literature is a description of some of the consequences of this development for life on a modern psychiatric ward, and of some of the methods used by social actors on the wards to regulate or subvert their ward's degree of permeability, within certain parameters. Further, my 'grounded' observations have been used to construct an alternative ideal type to that of the total institution, which I believe better represents the reality of everyday life in contemporary 'bricks and mortar' psychiatric institutions. My conceptualisation is of a *continuum* of institutional permeability, with total and permeable institutions at each extreme. This is summarised below.

Figure 7.1: Continuum of institutional permeability

	INSTITUTIONAL PERMEABILITY	
Low ◁	————————	▷ **High**
TOTAL INSTITUTION		**PERMEABLE INSTITUTION**
	Inpatient stays	
Long-term (months, years)	↔	Short-term (days, weeks)
	Geographical location	
Isolated, segregated	↔	Part of local community
	Communication with outside world	
Regulated, censored	↔	Open, e.g. via use of mobiles, access to internet, relaxed

		visiting times
	Openness of ward	
Door locked 24/7 Staff posted on door to regulate access	↔	Voluntary patients come and go as they please
	Risks to patients	
Institutionalism	↔	No respite from risks faced in outside world
	Visibility of control	
Inside life is invisible to outsiders	↔	Organisational transparency, e.g. via audits, spot-checks, media stories, research
	Social structure	
Sharply defined status hierarchy with clear social distance between levels	↔	Blurred social structure and lines of authority
	Ward culture	
Values/perceptions of hospital life tied to position in hospital hierarchy	↔	Coterminous with outside world - pre-patient identities are retained and

		routinely invoked
	Staff-patient relationships	
Paternalism	↔	Concordance
Highly formalised		Informal
Patients are silenced		Patients incited to speak

In Chapter 2 I reviewed Foucault's argument that the liberation of the 'mad' from cruel treatment was simply a shift to a more subtle form of control based on self-surveillance. Under this reading, people are no more 'free' in a permeable regime than they would be in a total institution, because they are obliged to personally take responsibility for the reformulation of their self and its ongoing monitoring. Foucauldians, such as Arney and Bergen (1984) and Armstrong (1983), whose work I reviewed in Chapter 3, view patient-centred approaches and shared decision-making as a shift from the sovereign power once exercised by authoritarian, 'old-fashioned' doctors, to the more subtle but even more pervasive form of disciplinary power that patient-centredness represents. The shift from total to permeable institutions is thus an exactly parallel development, in Foucauldian terms. Viewed from this perspective, permeable and total institutions may be understood as two alternative ways of producing persons, without one being ranked as 'better' than the other.

On the face of it, permeability is a quality that is at odds with public expectation, reflected in some media coverage of adverse events (Clarke, 2004), that psychiatric wards should contain patients and protect them from themselves and protect the public from them. The culture of the old psychiatric hospitals is more in keeping with such expectations, so some commentators might be tempted to call for a reduction in the permeability of modern wards. Permeability might be reduced by, for example, locking and securing ward doors, restricting use of mobile phones, enforcing strict visiting times, searching visitors and patients as they come onto the ward and putting nurses back into uniform. As noted in Chapter 3, some argue that this is already happening to some degree. Morrall and Hazelton (2000), for example, argue that we are seeing a 're-birth of asylumdom' in the U.K. and Australia (Morrall & Hazelton, 2000), as indicated by a projected growth in the numbers of 'secure units' in the community, the growing concern with issues of security and risk management in mental health care, and new technologies for containment and surveillance in acute wards (see also Priebe & Turner, 2003).

It remains to be seen whether policy makers will see a return to 'total' regimes as a solution to present social problems. The analysis presented in this chapter shows the dimensions of the institution that will be subject to change should this solution be chosen.

Chapter 8

Patients' methods of non-cooperation and resistance in ward round decisions

---

CONTENTS

In this chapter the focus shifts from the permeability of modern acute psychiatric wards to an aspect of lay/professional interaction occurring within them; namely, patients' methods of non-cooperation and resistance in ward round decisions. The large body of research evidence reviewed in Chapter 3 indicates that relationships between lay people and professionals have changed over the last few decades (Armstrong, 1983, 1984; Arney & Bergen, 1984), and that what was once a meeting between the knowledgeable expert and ignorant lay person is now more accurately described as a 'meeting between experts': the doctor being an expert in biomedicine with patient the expert in his or her own life (Tuckett *et al*, 1985; Department of Health, 2001). Reasons for this development include that people are increasingly encouraged to take responsibility for their own health, and service users are being encouraged by professionals to exercise their choice and contribute to shared-decision-making about their care. The literature review also noted that few advocates of shared decision-making in psychiatry would argue it is appropriate in crisis situations, or that 'mutual participation' is the only acceptable type of doctor-patient relationship. Other such relationships, or interactional styles, include 'activity-passivity', where the doctor does something to the completely helpless patient, and 'guidance-cooperation', where the patient with an acute condition seeks help and is ready to cooperate (Szasz & Hollander, 1955).

Previous research suggests that that an acute psychiatric ward is probably not the best place to look for examples of 'guidance-cooperation', let alone 'mutual participation'. As described in Chapter 3, it is a healthcare context in which nursing staff are preoccupied with the management of dangerous behaviours and patient throughput; nurses are dissatisfied with the difficulty they have in forming therapeutic relationships; and patients, many of whom are being held involuntarily, dislike the centrality of pharmacological interventions at the expense of psychological approaches. Indeed patients, especially those held under the Mental Health Act, generally have less of a sense of control than they would while meeting the same mental health professional in a different setting, such as an outpatient consultation, not least because they do not know whether they will be allowed home afterwards.

Mental health professionals may choose not to initiate shared decision-making, or they may abort it, if the patient shows signs that they lack the capacity to engage in a reasoned discussion about their treatment. But what about situations in which the *patient* chooses not to cooperate with shared decision-making or play their part in producing a guidance-cooperation approach? As discussed in Chapter 5, a downside of a patient-centred approach for service users is that they are *co-implicated* in the treatment decisions that are made, and that while they are free to choose, they are also forced to choose and are held to account for the choices made (c.f. Silverman, 1987). Service users may not perceive this to be a problem if they get their preferred treatment. But if they have 'agreed' to some proximal outcome they do not actually want,[34] they must either take the unwanted treatment or risk subsequently being 'told off' by their psychiatrist for having broken the 'verbal contract'. Non-cooperation and resistance in decision-making offer a means through which patients can avoid such difficulties.

[34] For examples, see the analysis of 'pressure' decisions in Chapter 5.

The analysis of outpatient transcripts showed some of the more subtle, non-confrontational ways in which patients can minimise their accountability in the context of 'negotiated' decision-making; that is, in decision sequences with an agreed outcome. One example of this, shown in Chapter 5 (section 5.5), was where the patient orientated to the consultant's proposal to take a new anti-psychotic as *advice* which need not necessarily be followed: "Yeah (.) alright then (0.2) I [I'll take your advice" (Extract 5.7, line 72). While both participants did enough interactional work to show one another (and us) that the decision had been negotiated rather than coerced, the patient's actions reduced the risk of provoking a 'disciplinary' response from the psychiatrist, should non- or partial adherence be reported at their next meeting.[35]

In contrast to such 'negotiated' decision-making, the focus in this chapter will be on activities that communicate the patient is not cooperating with the decision-making process, or is resisting being guided or coerced into choosing the clinical team's preferred treatment option. A typology of resistance techniques will be presented, generated from an analysis of transcripts, fieldnotes and interview data relating to the six ward rounds I observed for the Acute Ward Ethnography study. These were run by five consultant psychiatrists and involved 22 patients. Analysis of these data has been broadly informed by knowledge of CA techniques (see 4.5.2 for further discussion). As in Chapter 5, I draw on the CA concept of

[35] Communication about adherence in outpatient consultations is examined in Chapter 6.

preference organisation as it is useful for understanding how we are able to make inferences about each other's preferences in decision-making.

To give a sense of the context in which ward round decisions are made, I summarise below how treatment compliance is monitored and enforced in hospital. It will be shown that nursing staff sometimes go to great lengths to exert pressure on patients who refuse to take their medication. While such efforts may be disguised in order to reduce the potential for conflict, patients typically know what they are 'up against' when contributing to decisions about their treatment; namely, that anything they agree to can potentially be enforced, in a way that it cannot be in community settings - yet.[36]

8.1 Context for decision-making

> "Truthful joke. What's the difference between a consultant [psychiatrist] and a drug pusher? A drug pusher offers you drugs and you can refuse and nothing happens – a consultant offers you drugs, you refuse, they force you." [Psychiatric inpatient, National Violence Audit Study[37]]

---

[36] I am alluding here to the Community Treatment Orders in the new Mental Health Act.

[37] The national audit of the management of violence in mental health settings was conducted in 1999/2000 by the Royal College of Psychiatrists' Research Unit (McGeorge *et al*, 2000). An analysis of free text responses, such as the comment shown here, is included in the paper: Quirk, A., Lelliott, P. & Seale, C.

An acute psychiatric ward is a healthcare context in which the threat of forced medication is very real to patients. As one informal patient put it to me, you feel "like you had to take" your medication. Another described how he felt that "there's no choice apart from compliance":

> "When I was admitted in here, you know, I knew that it was either compliance or section and er, there's no choice apart from compliance because if you choose section then they will force you to take the medication and you would be sectioned, yeah? And if you showed compliance, you'd get the same treatment anyway, so you know, you don't have any choices. It's the whole affair, it's Catch 22." [Patient, Ward C, Acute Ward Ethnography]

This did not stop patients attempting to avoid taking their medications, despite the fact that the taking of them was monitored by nurses at the medicine round. Sometimes patients flatly refused to take their meds, but more often it was done covertly, for example by hiding their tablets under their tongue during the medicine round and spitting them out later.

(2004) Service users' strategies for managing risk in the volatile environment of an acute psychiatric ward. *Social Science and Medicine,* 59: 2573-2583.

8.1.1 Monitoring and enforcement of treatment adherence

Staff responses to such covert refusals of medication included asking patients who were suspected of not swallowing their meds to stick their tongue out. Other responses involved much skilful planning and manoeuvring to keep the exercise of coercive power hidden from the patient concerned[38] (see Box 8.1).

Box 8.1: Staff response to a patient's refusal to take her medication ***[fieldnote extract from Ward C]***

Context: *Katherine, a patient, was called into the ward office so that she could be given her 10am medication. She refused to take it, and was abusive to nurse-Mary and ward manager-Carlene. She left the office and returned to her room.*

Fieldnote extract

Ward manager-Carlene rang the other wards and asked for the support of a couple of nurses. They casually wandered onto the ward, and into the nursing station, where they sat chatting with Carlene, ever-so-informally. Carlene then came out of the office and explained to nursing assistant-Joe what was going on. She said that they were worried about Katherine refusing her medication, and that they were

[38] As we shall see in the following chapter, such 'veiled coercion' is also a feature of some MHA assessments (see section 9.11).

going to try again to get her to take it. She wanted Joe to follow behind Katherine into the room once she had agreed to come along. They were going for a 'softly, softly' approach (my term).

On the ward manager's instructions, nurse-Mary went into Katherine's bedroom in order to ask her into the nursing station for her meds. While this was going on, Carlene looked in, just out of Katherine's line of sight. Joe was seated with me on the other side of the door to her room. I then saw Carlene duck back and hide in the loo to avoid being seen when Katherine came out with Mary. As those two walked the 5 metres to the nursing station, Carlene casually emerged from the loo and followed them in. She silently beckoned NA-Joe to join her, which he did.

So the result is that Katherine was escorted by N-Mary, and followed in by Joe and Carlene. Meanwhile the two nurses from the other wards were already waiting in the room, looking cool and as if they were not a part of what was going on. Katherine took her medication without much fuss after this.

Outcome: *Compliance with treatment.*

The material presented in the rest of this chapter concerns how decisions are made in ward rounds. After describing key aspects of these routine encounters, I will present a typology of methods of non-cooperation and resistance used by patients. These are: (1) refusing to participate in the decision-making process, (2) concealing clinically-relevant information, in order to mislead the clinical team into thinking the patient is better than s/he actually is, and (3) expressive discordance, where the patient explicitly rejects specific proposals for treatment and refuses to 'back down' or compromise about this (treatment discordance), or where the patient rejects his or her diagnosis, psychiatric definitions of the problem, and/or psychiatric knowledge *per se* (ideological discordance).

It will be argued that these three main types of non-cooperation can be observed in *any* psychiatric setting, including outpatient consultations and MHA assessments. However, the specific form they take in hospital results, in part, from the ability of staff to monitor and if necessary enforce the outcomes of treatment decisions. This ability can provoke a greater level of patient resistance and non-cooperation because 'verbal contracts' made in ward rounds, such as agreements and commitments, are perceived by all parties as 'binding'. Therefore patients cannot agree to, say, some change to their medication but not really mean it because they know they are in a place where compliance is policed. The analysis will demonstrate that volatility in ward round interaction cannot be explained simply by referring to an inherently antagonistic doctor-patient relationship in psychiatry or to the psychiatric condition of the patients involved. Rather, the findings indicate the value of examining very closely the specific interactional circumstances that give rise to the different forms of non-cooperation and resistance.

8.2 What is a ward round?

The ward round is the main forum in which major decisions are made about a psychiatric in-patient's treatment and management, such as decisions about discharge, changes in Mental Health Act status, conditions of leave, and medication. This is often the only time that a patient gets to see and talk to his or her consultant psychiatrist: between ward rounds, decisions tend to be made by the junior doctors on the ward or by the nurses. Individual patients are typically seen once a week or fortnight. Patients are not compelled to attend so often those who are most ‘resistant’ will not be there (though some will make a point of turning up to argue their case). In such cases, decisions are made unilaterally in the patient’s absence and reported back to him or her later. Consultant psychiatrists report that they prefer to have all of their patients on one ward, but in practice they tend to spread across different wards in the psychiatric unit resulting from patients being admitted to whichever ward had an empty bed at the time of admission. Therefore, the ward round either has to move from one ward to another, or patients and participating staff are brought in from other wards. Either way the ward tends to be very busy when a ward round is being held.

8.2.1 Intimidating for patients

Ward rounds are typically held in an interview room on the ward or in a room nearby. They begin with the patient being led or called into the room and asked to take a seat in the circle of members of his or her clinical team. The number of professionals directly involved in them varies greatly, but six was the average in the ones observed for this study. The consultant leads the questioning and facilitates the discussion, for example by inviting participants to give their opinion on how the patient has been progressing. In most cases, the other mental health professionals in the room, such as the junior psychiatrist, nurse and occupational therapist, present case-note information and their own observations about the patient. This can make for an intimidating experience for the person on the receiving end, according to a former patient:

> "Ward rounds are the most intimidating places for people to walk into a room full of strange people, and generally told to sit in such a place. And then listen to yourself being spoken about. And given very little chance to speak themselves. Decisions are then made more in spite of the person being there than for the person being there." [Research interview with patient advocacy worker and former in-patient, Ward A]

Patients also reported experiencing it as an interview or *examination* in which their talk and non-verbal behaviour were monitored closely and recorded in the case file for future use:

> "The other off putting thing is that you can say inane things, like you've missed an OT [occupational therapy] session, but

> they all suddenly start scribbling in their notes. It's bizarre!... [It's] a very artificial situation – the only other time I can think of when you go into a room of people, who are all focusing their attention on you is for a job interview".[Research interview with patient, Ward A]

Hyphen-21 has published a code of good practice for ward rounds and other meetings (available, at the time of writing, on the website of the Sainsbury Centre for Mental Health: www.scmh.org.uk). The aim of the guideline is "to set out the conditions necessary for an atmosphere of care and respect to flourish" in such meetings. Developed in close consultation with mental health service users, it can be taken to indicate patients' perceptions of some of the current problems. The guidance covers how questions should be asked by the multi-disciplinary team, thus invoking concerns about the examination-like and confessional nature of these meetings (see Box 8.1).

Box 8.1: Extract from Hyphen-21's Code of Good Practice for Meetings with Service Users

- "The service user's mental or emotional state should not be insensitively examined in public and amongst strangers with tests which lower his/her dignity"
- "Questions to which workers already know the answer should not be asked", and

❖ "Unless it is judged to be absolutely necessary, service users should not be asked questions which take them into painful or intimate areas of their lives."

Source: www.scmh.org.uk.

8.2.2 Forms of surveillance

The ward round is thus a goal-oriented encounter between the patient and mental health professionals which typically resembles an examination of the patient with confessional aspects. It is characterised by high levels of surveillance in its various forms.[39] First, there is ***covert monitoring of the patient***, in that the observations made by staff during the ward round are routinely recorded afterwards in the patient's casenotes. Second, there is ***overt monitoring of the patient***: sometimes such note-taking is done while the ward round is still in progress, in full view of the patient. This can contribute to the patient's perception of the encounter as an 'examination'. Further, the consultant and/or others in the team sometimes refer to the casenotes while the patient is speaking, such that the patient knows that the reactions of the team have been pre-determined by comments of 'disembodied others' recorded in the file. This can contribute to the patient's perception that his or her

[39] See Bloor & McIntosh (1990) for a fuller description of the different types of surveillance, both of external behaviour and of what is going on in a patient's/client's mind.

'person presentational options' are limited, and that skilful impression management can achieve only so much in these circumstances (c.f. Cahill, 1998). Third, ward rounds are characterised by ***self-reporting by the patient,*** as this is arguably *the* pre-eminent formal encounter in which psychiatric inpatients are expected to reflect and report on themselves - partly because it is often the only time their consultant gets to see them and ask about such matters directly. Finally, there is ***proxy surveillance***: reports from other professionals and lay people, such as carers, are typically referred to in a team discussion before the patient enters the room. For example, the ward nurse is likely to 'brief' others in the clinical team about how the patient has been over the past few days, and correspondence about the patient (e.g. from their GP) may be read out. Sometimes such reports are made or referred to while the patient is in the room.

I shall now discuss the three main methods of non-cooperation and resistance used by patients in ward rounds.

8.3 Types of non-cooperation and resistance

8.3.1 Refusal to participate in decision-making

Box 8.2 below shows the content of a fieldnote recording how a patient behaved in a ward round I observed. The consultant's delicate broaching of the issue of absconding risk quickly escalates, in the space of a few seconds, to the point where the patient storms out of the room and refuses to take any further part in the discussion. It is thus a comparatively overt form of non-cooperation.

Box 8.2: Patient storms out of ward round ***(fieldnote entry for Ward B)***

The patient walks into the interview room, located 15 metres down the corridor from the entrance to the ward. The consultant stands up, offers his handshake (which is accepted) and says "Hello Mr Smith" [done such that it communicated that this was their first meeting]... The consultant informs the patient that people are anxious about him leaving the ward and not coming back. The patient replied by saying that a nurse told him he had been discharged at 10.30am. The consultant paused, knowing this to be incorrect, and said, most delicately, that there must be a "misunderstanding". At this the patient shouted "Oh you're talking rubbish, forget it!" and stormed out of the room. Realising he needed an escort back to the ward, the ward manager and another professional in the room hurriedly followed after him.

The patient in this example had been described in the clinical team discussion before he entered the room as being someone who was a "high absconding risk". The ward manager explained to the others that nursing staff always make sure the front door is locked when he uses the disabled toilet (which is next to the ward's entrance/exit door), for fear that he might try to abscond, and reported that he is "always looking to escape" at night. On hearing this, the consultant signalled that non-cooperation was a real possibility ("Oh dear oh dear, he may refuse to come into the ward round"); it probably also accounts for the sardonic tone used in his phone call to the ward: "Will you cordially invite Mervyn to the ward round?" This individual therefore already had a 'resistant patient' identity hung upon him before he entered the room. Further, as the ward round progressed there seemed to be no obvious aim to the encounter, from the clinical team's point of view, other than to avoid confrontation. Medication was discussed, but only after the patient had left the room, at which point the team made the prescribing decision unilaterally (see Box 8.3). A 'shared' decision this most definitely was not.

Box 8.3: Unilateral decision made by the clinical team in the absence of the patient *(field-note entry for ward C)*

[After the patient had stormed out of the room] the consultant asked the group, "So what shall we give him?" He said that the patient had tolerated Acuphase well; the team discussed his medication. The consultant summarising the decision they had made: "So stopping his Olanzapine, and we're going to give him Zuclopenthixol." He enters this on the prescription sheet, and the registrar fills out the casenotes, presumably recording information about the ward round.

As well as withdrawing from the ward round once it has begun, patients sometimes flatly refuse to attend. Either way, refusing to participate involves *overt* action by the patient. This has the effect of making shared decision-making impossible, by virtue of the simple fact that the patient was not involved.[40]

8.3.2 Concealment of clinically-relevant information

In *The Presentation of Self in Everyday Life,* reviewed in Chapter 2, Goffman (1959) argues that when an individual enters into the presence of others, they commonly attempt to find out information about that person (e.g. their competence and trustworthiness), and this can be indicated by the smallest detail of speech, tone, posture or dress. Such information, and what is known beforehand about the individual, helps to define the situation, enabling others to know in advance what this individual will expect of them (ibid, p.1). So when a person projects a definition of the situation and therefore makes a

[40] Excluded from this category, for lack of first-hand evidence in this particular study, are the other methods used by patients for not turning up to the ward round, such as staying in bed and pretending to be asleep, or hiding in 'free space' away from the ward. Such activities may be better categorised as 'avoidance' of the decision-making process rather than the more confrontational 'refusal to participate' discussed here. Avoidance seems to be more commonly practiced in other psychiatric settings where the patient is not confined in the institution, such as outpatient consultations (a proportion of the 'non attenders') and MHA assessments (candidate patients sometimes hide from the assessment team or refuse to open the door to them – see section 9.3.5 in the following chapter).

claim to be a particular kind of person within it, a moral demand is made of others, obliging them to value and treat him or her in the manner persons of that kind have a right to expect. Such information is thus the "raw material" of person production (Cahill, 1998), and our ability to control it - especially being able to conceal things that we do not want other people to know - is crucial in defining the type of person we would like others to take us to be.

Also noted in Chapter 2, was that file-persons or 'cases' tend to be built up intensively during an inmate's stay in a total or carceral institution (before persons can be changed, faulty persons who require changing must first be produced), and this pre-determines how staff members will react to the individual concerned. Cahill (1998) nicely summarises how this limits an inmate's ability to define who they are:

> "... the individual who encounters someone who is in possession of her file also encounters a chorus of others who have left their marks in the file. Those disembodied others communicate with the possessor of the file, but not with the individual, throughout the interaction between the two. And because much of what they communicate through the file has been subjected to rituals of truth, it tends to carry more weight than anything she might say to the possessor of the file... Her person presentational options are clearly limited." (Cahill, 1998, p.143)

One method patients have for controlling information is concealing some of their activities, thoughts and beliefs from the people around them. Previous studies, reviewed in Chapter 3, indicate that concealment is possibly the most common form of client resistance to surveillance and disciplinary power (Bloor & McIntosh, 1990; see also Peckover, 2002). However it has been argued (Cahill, 1998) that concealment is particularly difficult in total institutions because almost all aspects of an inmate's life are monitored by staff.

The present study provides evidence for patient concealment in a more permeable institution than that studied by Goffman – although whether it achieves what the patient wants is another matter. Below is an extract of an interview I had with a patient, in which she talked about how she communicated with staff on the ward. She describes how she deliberately kept her thoughts to herself - in ward rounds and in everyday conversations with nursing staff – in order to mislead them into thinking that she was better than she actually was.

> *{Did you ever try and convince them [psychiatrists etc on the ward] that you were better than you actually were?}* "I did yeah… I was just telling them that I wasn't having thoughts of microphones inside me and bombs - because I thought there was bombs all around the place in the flats and the video and everything at home. And I was telling them that I haven't got

> any of these thoughts any more, but really I did have." *{Did they believe you?}* "I think they did". [Research interview with patient, Ward A]

This is a *covert* form of resistance in that it does not involve an explicit rejection of the clinical teams' definition of the situation or proposals for treatment (discussed in the following section). Bloor and McIntosh identify a crucial advantage of this technique; namely, that it neutralises the potential for the exercise of power without explicitly challenging it in ways that would lead to penalties (Bloor & McIntosh, 1990). An exception to this is where professionals perceive an individual to be concealing things from them, and interpret this concealment *as* non-cooperation or resistance. For example, it would be counter-productive if it resulted in a deferred discharge, in cases where the clinical team first require some evidence that the patient has improved. The patient is in a classic 'no win' situation, in that if she reveals her thoughts and beliefs, the psychiatrist may not discharge her (because she is not yet well enough), yet if she does not, then it may be perceived as 'resistance'. This makes the incitement to talk very strong in this context. Knowledge of this leaves patients with little option other than to "play the game" and say what they think staff want to hear (for example, see Box 8.4).

Example of concealment

An example of concealment is shown in Extract 8.1 below. Those present in the ward round included the patient (P), a consultant psychiatrist (C) and a nurse (N). While reading the transcript, please bear in mind that it is based on detailed notes I took at the time, because tape recording was not possible. Conventional CA transcribing notations have not been used.

Extract 8.1: Example of concealment

Proximal outcome = treatment is unchanged: P remains held involuntarily in hospital under the Mental Health Act

Note: This was one of the shortest ward rounds observed, lasting approximately 3 minutes.

1	C:	How are you?
2	P:	Okay
3		((Consultant rapidly asks a series of questions about P's
4		family for about 90 seconds, to which P proffers only minimal 'yes/no' responses))
5	C:	Do you have any concerns about voices
6	P:	No
7	C:	Are you concerned about harming yourself?
8	P:	No

9	C:	Are you okay to be on the ward?
10	P:	I'd just rather be home.
11	C:	We have to be sure you are okay because last time you were
12		in hospital for long time, and then you had to come back in
13		again soon after you were discharged.
14		((They quickly discuss referrals etc))
15	C:	Do you have any questions?
16	P:	When can I leave?
17	C:	It's difficult to say, we were hoping you would tell us more...
18		Okay thank you.
19	P:	Thank you. ((P leaves the room))
20		Staff interaction after the patient has left the room
21		C said to N and others, it's difficult because "she is not
22		communicating with us" ((the team continue talking))

In the transcript above the patient invokes her preference for being discharged at line 10 ("I'd just rather be home") and in and through her response to the consultant's preceding 'final concern' inquiry (Robinson, 2001), at line 16: "When can I leave?" The goal of the team[41] is invoked by C, on lines 11-13; namely that they have to be

[41] Team opinions may be less stable and unitary than this implies. Bridget Hamilton, who was a PhD student at the University of Melbourne studying the language used by nurses in acute psychiatric in-patient services, commented on the abstract of an earlier version of this chapter. She noted that there is often not a single team view in such meetings, and that there is a difference between nursing sense/solutions and psychiatric ones. In her study, she found that nurses were primarily disciplining/civilising patient behaviours towards fitness for discharge, rather than probing their thoughts, and were thus positively *inclined* towards patient concealment/acting normal. In this sense there was collusion between nurses and patients against 'psy' so that beds could be turned around quickly (see Hamilton & Manias, 2006

sure the patient is well enough ("okay") before they can discharge her, on account of her previous experience of being re-admitted to hospital soon after being discharged.

Note that in using at line 17-18, "It's difficult to say, we were hoping that you would tell us more" - to parry the patient's question about when she will be allowed to leave - the consultant orients to, and thereby locally constructs, the patient's actions as concealment. That this is also hearable as a 'telling off', rather than a 'lever' to elicit more information from the patient (as in 'if you tell us more we may be able to discharge you'), is evidenced by the fact that (a) the consultant initiates closure of the encounter very soon afterwards, with "Okay thank you" on line 18 (rather than, say, 'fishing' for further information), and (b) the consultant comments, after the patient has left the room, that the patient is "not communicating with us" which makes it difficult. The proximal outcome is that the patient is kept in hospital and her treatment is unchanged. This is evidently the patient's dispreferred option, so 'concealment' was counter-productive on this occasion.

Concealment is a clear obstacle to shared decision-making, in the sense that by choosing not to open up to staff, the patient withholds clinically relevant information. This makes it difficult if not impossible for a 'text-book' shared decision to be made.

---

for a review of related literature). No data are available to back up this claim with regard to the ward rounds I observed, but it seems very plausible.

8.3.3 Expressive discordance

Expressive discordance may be defined as a form of resistance that involves the patient explicitly rejecting his or her diagnosis, psychiatric definitions of the problem, or specific proposals for treatment. Staff attempts at attaining concordance are *explicitly* rejected by the patient, so the resistance is overt. This category therefore does not include covert resistance where patients 'play the game' and tell staff what they want to hear. Resistance of staff proposals for treatment can initiate a process of negotiation, but even that may result in 'stalemate' where staff and patient perspectives and goals remain diametrically opposed. This, then, is the obverse to concordance, which is an agreement reached after negotiation between a patient and a health care professional that respects the beliefs and wishes of the patient in determining whether, when and how medicines are to be taken. As discussed in Chapter 3, this approach recognises that consultations between doctors and patients are most often concerned with two contrasting sets of health beliefs, and that those of the patient are no less cogent or important than those of the health professionals in deciding the best treatment approach for that individual (see section 3.1).

Goal discordance between staff and patients on psychiatric units is well documented (for example, Dimsdale *et al*, 1979), but little is known about whether or how such discordance is *expressed* in key decision-making forums such as the ward round. My analysis has identified two types of expressive discordance. The first is what I have called ***treatment discordance***, which is where the patient stays within psychiatric discourse, to argue against specific treatment proposals or suggestions from the clinical team. The second may be termed ***ideological discordance***, which expresses a more fundamental disagreement. In this 'higher' level of resistance the patient challenges the whole system of psychiatric knowledge and the psychiatrist's authority, creating a situation where their respective health beliefs appear irreconcilable.

In this psychiatric setting, where the patient's capacity to make rational decisions is in question, his or her contribution to ideological discordance is particularly vulnerable to being heard as some irrational, anti-psychiatry "rant", and as symptomatic of some psychiatric disorder. It is therefore unlikely to be effective as a technique of resistance; if patient's aim for this resistance is to get the treatment he or she wants. For this reason, patients may choose to keep such views to themselves and *disguise* this more fundamental disagreement by expressing it as treatment discordance. In other words, they play the game, speaking in a language they think the professionals want to hear, but resist at the level of specific treatment decisions.[42]

---

[42] This makes it close to, but analytically distinct from, the 'concealment' discussed in section 8.3.2.

My general impression, from interviewing patients and sitting in on conversations between them when staff members were not present, was that this form of disguised resistance is probably quite common on acute psychiatric wards. I observed that the antagonism expressed in these 'private' conversations towards the psychiatric system and the legitimacy of psychiatric knowledge did not square with what was said when these same patients met their consultant. Rational arguments against 'psy' tended to remain unspoken in such situations (see Box 8.4).

Box 8.4: Keeping ideological discordance to yourself *(summary of field-note entry for ward C)*

Mid-afternoon in the large, empty pool/games room, I had a long conversation with Martin (a patient with a long treatment history). He is clearly very knowledgeable about the 'anti-psychiatry' literature – Laing, Goffman etc. He told me, very articulately, about how he disagrees with psychiatric classifications in general and his diagnosis of schizophrenia in particular, and about his fundamental opposition to using drugs to treat his condition. I have observed him expressing such views to nursing staff in everyday situations on the ward. However, when it comes to ward rounds he told me that his strategy for avoiding confrontation is to say as little as possible, but ensure he says "Yes, the medication is doing me good", even though he does not believe this.

Example of treatment discordance

The ward round in question (Extract 8.2 below) was conducted shortly before the patient, who had voluntarily admitted himself to hospital, was due to go on leave for a week. To summarise, the consultant proposed that the patient should have had his medication administered by injection beforehand. The patient's rejection of this proposal triggered three or four minutes of negotiation, during which the consultant and others in the clinical team tried everything they could to persuade him to take his tablets while he is on leave. My general observation was that the interaction was good-natured throughout, and it did not look or sound like conflict, but the patient was not having any of it, stood his ground, and did everything he could to maintain his position that he no longer needed medication. Eventually they reached stalemate; which the team resolved by deciding to prescribe him tablets at a lower dose, but which they were sure he was not going to take while away from their direct supervision.

Those present in the ward round included the patient (P), a consultant psychiatrist (C), social worker (SW), occupational therapist (OT) and junior psychiatrist (JDr). Again, please note that the transcript is based on detailed notes rather than a tape recording.

Extract 8.2: Example of treatment discordance

Proximal outcome of ward round = P is prescribed anti-psychotic tablets to take while on leave, even though the clinical team evidently suspect he is unlikely to take them

1	P:	I'm okay, okay, I want to come off medication.
2	C:	Things might be okay, okay now, but only because of the
3		medication you've been taking.
4	P:	To tell you the truth, I used to spit them out.
5	C:	Would you be happier on an injection[43]?
6	P:	Not really.
7		((P changes topic. There follows a discussion about his
8		"delusions" and living circumstances. Medication is not
9		mentioned in these exchanges.))
10	C:	What I'm concerned about now, is that you're doing well now
11		because you are in hospital. I do believe you need to have
12		some medication.
13	P:	But doctor, I'm okay.
14	C:	But when you are not on medication, things haven't been
15		okay... You can be on leave but you need to keep taking your
16		medication.
17		((P talks to the group, telling them that he does not hear
18		voices))

[43] 'Depot' injections were introduced in the late-1950s to overcome non-compliance with psychotropic medication taken orally.

19	C:	What about having either an injection or tablets?
20	P:	Tablets.
21	C:	But will you spit them out?... You seemed better on
22		Olanzapine.
23	P:	But I wasn't taking it.
24	C:	No, what I'd like is for you to go on leave, but take the 7.5mg
25		tablets... You're only okay because the injection is still
26		influencing you and keeping you well.
27		((Talk unrecorded))
28	P:	When on medication I get side effects, headaches... I have to
29		face life without medication.
30	C:	Can we compromise? You go on leave, come off the
31		injection, and have 7.5mg tablets. It's a very small dose. And
32		see how we go.
33	P:	I don't want to get headaches.
34	C:	It's a small dose. If we agreed, will you take them?
35		((P talks about his addiction to valium and that they are all he
36		wants to take)
37	P:	Do you think I'll ever come off medication?
38	C:	Not for at least another couple of years.
39	P:	If I go to college and surprise you, and write a book. But if I
40		came off medication, no-one in psychiatry would believe me -
41	C:	((- Interjection-)) We want you to get better.
42	OT:	Can I tell what I observed when you were with me in OT?
43		You are much more settled once you are on medication.
44	P:	I'm feeling better.

45 ((SW tells P that one of the conditions of living in a group
46 home, as P does, is that residents must take their medication.[44]
47 P's reply was not recorded. In answer to SW's question about
48 where he would like to be living a year from now, P says he
49 would like to be with his mother in Sussex))
50 C: But it's also in the interests of your parents that you stay
51 well... We can give you an injection so you don't have to
52 bother to take tablets.
53 P: I don't want an injection
54 C: Okay so we'll give you medication to take with you and have
55 a CPA meeting next week.
56 ((OT asks P whether he can attend at least 2 or 3 OT sessions
57 at the hospital over the coming week. P and OT then
58 'negotiate' how many, ending with P finally agreeing to
59 coming in for two sessions))
60 ((Closure. P leaves the room))
61 Staff interaction after the patient has left the room
62 C announces to the team "I think he's well because he's had
63 an injection." JDr checks with C whether he should prescribe
64 tablets or dispersibles[45] C replies "TABLETS, BUT I DON'T
65 THINK HE'LL TAKE THEM". ((emphasis added))

---

[44] A service user discussed in the following chapter was living under these conditions when she was assessed under the Mental Health Act (see Box 9.3). Her care plan stipulated that she had to take her medication as prescribed if she wanted to keep her flat in supported accommodation.

[45] 'Dispersibles' are drugs that melt instantly in the mouth. These may be given to patients in hospital who are known to hide the tablets under their tongue at the medicine round and spit them out later. They would be useless in the situation described here, where the patient is about to go on leave, because compliance can only be achieved if a member of staff stands over the patient.

Overt resistance to pressure from the clinical team

While not aiming to offer a detailed conversation analysis of the transcript above, I will build on my earlier analysis of how pressure is applied in decision-making, presented in Chapter 5, to identify some of its key features. The first is that the decision sequence is constituted of various proposals, rejections, revised proposals, and counter proposals. The patient uses various techniques to resist the clinical team's proposals for him to take medication, in some form or other, while he is on leave. These include: proposing to come off his medication because he is now "okay" (line 1); claiming that his current wellbeing has had nothing to do with taking tablets because he used to "spit them out" (line 4); repeating, on line 23, that he was not taking his Olanzapine tablets; justifying his proposal to not take his medication by claiming that he does not hear voices (lines 17-18) - that is, denying suffering from hallucinations, which is one of the major 'positive' symptoms of schizophrenia for which antipsychotic medication is prescribed (Healy, 2002); claiming to experience "side effects, headaches" from his medication (line 28) which he does not want to get (line 33), and that he has to "face life without medication" (lines 28-29); and rejecting staff proposals outright, at various points in the encounter, even though this was evidently the dispreferred response as far as the clinical team were concerned.

With regard to its position on the 'spectrum of pressure' in negotiated decision making (see Chapter 5), this decision sequence may be categorised as a *pressure decision* – one in which the clinical team eventually 'gives up' in the face of implacable resistance.[46] There is a negotiated outcome to the decision-making of sorts, but it is evidently not the one the consultant would have preferred. Her comment after the patient has left the room - that she does not think the patient will take the tablets they have just decided to prescribe (lines 64-65) – leaves little doubt about this. This, then, is far from a text-book example of 'shared' decision making. Rather, the negotiation over medication is a response to, and partly constituted of, the patient's continued resistance to the various treatment proposals made by the consultant.

Patient resistance in the context of treatment discordance (as distinct from ideological discordance) can take various forms, briefly summarised here. Patients may resist psychiatric treatment by denying that they are experiencing any symptoms of mental illness, reporting that their medication is causing side effects, or claiming to have not taken the very medication to which health professionals attribute their improvement. In addition patients may accept having been deluded once, but not now (e.g. Question: "Looking back, do you think you were ill?"; Answer: "Yes, but I shouldn't have been sectioned and I'm alright now."). They may also argue that their "delusions" were actually real events but that the real problem has

[46] None of the consultants in the outpatient consultations responded to patient resistance in this way. They either quickly 'backed off' at the first sign of resistance (section 5.5.1) or continued applying pressure until the patient finally accepted the consultant's proposal (sections 5.5.2 and 5.5.3).

now been resolved (e.g. people really were calling out to them but are not doing so now). Finally, they may challenge or deny reported observations made by staff (e.g. "They said I hit a nurse but I didn't").

Oracular reasoning

Extending the analysis of Extract 8.2, I would argue that the participants are demonstrating what Mehan has termed 'oracular reasoning': a process of arguing from, and defending, a basic belief by denying or repelling contradictory evidence (Mehan, 1990). Mehan examined the interaction between a board of psychiatrists and a patient in a 'psychiatric out-take interview'. [47] Mehan classifies it as a 'gate-keeping encounter' in the sense that it involved psychiatrists (gatekeepers) deciding on whether an involuntarily-committed patient could leave hospital (ibid). The meeting began with the head psychiatrist questioning the patient, but the interrogation quickly broke down into an argument about the quantity and quality of the patient's treatment. A major source of conflict was the different attitudes adopted by the doctors and patient towards medicine. The latter's attitude was that medicine is for sick people, and that since he was healthy, he did not need it – in fact, to take the medicine would be to admit he *is* sick, which he was not. The expressed attitude of the doctors, in contrast, was that medicine is part of the rehabilitation

[47] The encounter was originally filmed for a documentary about a U.S. mental hospital. Mehan's analysis is based on a transcript he made of it.

process, so the patient's admitted reticence to take medicine is taken as a sign that he is both sick and unwilling to help himself. The conflict was resolved by the head psychiatrist abruptly ordering the patient to be taken away, after which the board made a 'unilateral' decision in which their definition of the situation prevailed.[48]

There are striking parallels between the interaction examined by Mehan and the decision-making considered here (Extract 8.2). Practices of oracular reasoning in the present example include:

1. A basic premise or a fundamental proposition is presented which forms the basis of an argument:

   Patient – *I'm well, so I would now like to stop taking my medication*
   Consultant – *You are well but it's only because you are taking your medication*

2. When confronted with evidence that is potentially contradictory to a basic position, the evidence is ignored, repelled or denied:

[48] Mehan derives the term 'oracular' from the reasoning of an African tribe who consult an oracle when faced with an important decision. They continue to believe in the oracle, even though it sometimes contradicts itself, through denying or repelling contradictory evidence. Mehan's central point is that both well-educated and poorly-educated people reason in this way when defending a basic belief (Mehan, 1990).

Patient – *I haven't been taking the medication, so my present well-being can't be attributed to it*
Occupational therapist – *You were much more settled on medication*

3. The presence of evidence that opposes a basic position is used reflexively as further support of the efficacy of the basic position.

Consultant – *You seemed better when you were on Olanzapine*
Patient – *But I wasn't taking it, that's why I seemed better to you*

In other words, the clinical team and the patient agree with the proposition that the patient is well, but they interpret the same evidence in completely opposing ways, and use it to support and stick to their arguments, despite evidence being presented to the contrary. Whilst sharing an understanding that the patient is doing well, they diverged over the role that medication has had in this.[49]

As noted, the patient is arguing from *within* psychiatric discourse (hence its categorisation as treatment discordance rather than ideological discordance). He rationally argues against the need for

[49] I cannot quantify it, but my impression was that this was a very common disagreement between mental health professionals and patients in this setting. Further analysis of the outpatient data (Chapters 5 & 6) is likely to reveal examples of such disagreement; albeit probably expressed with more subtlety than in the example presented here. Mehan's (1990) research shows that this fundamental disagreement was evident decades ago, suggesting that this potential source of conflict is endemic to psychiatric encounters.

medication in his particular case, but does not challenge the legitimacy of medication as a form of treatment for some people, for example by invoking some anti-psychiatry counter discourse that argues against psychotropic medication. Instead it is *overt resistance* to the specific form of treatment proposed for him rather than to the system of psychiatric knowledge *per se*.

An uphill struggle for the patient

Continuing with the analysis of Extract 8.2, we can observe that the patient faced an uphill struggle to get what he wanted. Before he had even entered the room, the clinical team had agreed that the locus of his problem was located in his mental state and not in the social context, and that he was not accepting treatment. The team's discussion is summarised in Box 8.5.

Box 8.5: Events immediately before the 'discordant' ward round *(field-note entry for ward C)*

They [the clinical team] negotiated in advance - in their 'backstage' discussion before the patient entered the room - that this was to be an "informal" chat with this patient. They agreed that the problem was that he was "not accepting treatment". Referring to the patient's case notes, the consultant informed the others that he has a diagnosis of schizophrenia, and before being admitted he had thought neighbours were pumping gas into his flat and spying on him. The consultant also informed them that the patient will be referred to the Community

Support Team so that he can be supported by them after discharge. The social worker and consultant chatted about the patient's neighbours. The team agreed that when the patient does not take his medication he continues to have symptoms; the consultant saying "He's taking his symptoms with him wherever he goes" and that the delusions will continue regardless of where he is living.

This analysis should not be taken to imply that the perspectives of the patient and members of the clinical team are equivalent. Mehan (1990) found that where there was discordance in the encounter he examined, conflict was resolved by the imposition of an institutional definition of the problem, and the patient's experience was over-ridden. Similarly, Gwyn and Elwyn's (1999) research, reviewed in Chapter 3, shows how shared decision-making can come unstuck when doctors and patients have conflicting preferences. Without a situation of "equipoise" (i.e. an equally poised or balanced context for decision-making), shared decision-making is a misnomer and is better understood as an "informed decision engineered according to doctor preference" (ibid). But this was not the outcome of the decision sequence examined here. How could this be so?

How come the patient won?

At one level it is clear that the patient got what he wanted – and emerged 'victorious' from the cycle of pressure/resistance - in and through his unwavering resistance to what was being proposed.

Clearly this approach will not always work in a healthcare setting such as this, where staff members are able to invoke powers of coercion. So why did the patient come out on top on this occasion, unlike the patient in Mehan's (1990) study? Part of what made the ward round unusual was that the team were not in a position to enforce treatment, because the patient was in hospital voluntarily, was already set to go on leave, and would thus soon no longer be under their 24-hour supervision. The team did their best to persuade him to accept medication in a form that does not depend on such surveillance to ensure compliance (a long lasting injection administered before he left hospital) but this was rejected outright.

In this example, the proximal outcome (tablets prescribed in a lower dose, to be taken by the patient while on leave) ultimately offered the consultant and others in the clinical team *an escape from conflict or contest* with the patient – one that allowed them to save face (Goffman, 1959). Indeed they could hardly have gone along with the patient's wish to stop taking anti-psychotic medication altogether after having tried so hard to persuade him otherwise and, in so doing, making their own preferences so explicit.

Proximal outcome: an 'irrational' prescribing decision

To summarise, we have been examining an example of treatment discordance, which I have defined as such because the patient argued against the need for medication in his particular case, but never challenged the premise that medication is a legitimate form of treatment for some people. The response of the clinical team was to prescribe anti-psychotic tablets that they strongly suspected the patient would not take. On the face of it an 'irrational decision', it is evidently not so irrational after all because it gave the team a way out of the impasse caused, in part, by the patient's refusal to concede any ground to them whatsoever. This is further evidence that can be added to the body of knowledge about how and why 'non-scientific' or 'irrational' prescribing decisions are made (see Chapters 3 and 5 for further discussion).

8.4 Discussion

In their classic paper on doctor-patient relationships, Szasz and Hollander (1955) describe the 'guidance-cooperation' model, where the patient with an acute condition seeks help and is ready to cooperate with the doctor. This chapter has considered methods used by patients to resist such an approach. In ward round decisions, methods were found to include refusing to take part in decision-making, concealing clinically-relevant information and expressing discordance. All are risky for the patient, because in an institution for the 'acutely unwell' they are vulnerable to being interpreted as symptomatic of some kind of psychiatric disorder. Overt patient resistance can thus be counter-productive, for example when it provokes staff into delaying the discharge a patient may so desperately want. Concealment of thoughts and beliefs is probably the least risky option, and for this reason I suspect it is the most common form of non-cooperation or resistance in this setting.[50] However, it is likely to fail when knowledgeable proxy supervisors such as nurses are in the room, because they are often in a position to reveal what the patient is attempting to conceal. Crucially, knowledge that this will happen can induce the patient into confessing what they have been thinking and doing while in hospital.

Ward rounds were examined for three reasons. First, they are an important forum in which key treatment decisions are made, but the existing research literature has surprisingly little to say about what goes on in them. The findings presented in this chapter have shone some light into this black box. Second, the ward round is the main opportunity people admitted to hospital have for communicating directly with their consultant, and vice versa. In other words, if one wants to examine doctor-patient interaction, and multi-disciplinary team working, this is a good place to start. And third, ward rounds can be intimidating for patients; partly because of the large number of people in the room, and partly because it is a situation of heightened surveillance, in which everything you say or do is under close scrutiny and open to misinterpretation, due to the artificiality of this stressful, interview-like situation.

[50] Bloor & McIntosh (1990) make a similar point about client resistance in therapeutic communities and health visiting.

Clearly, patient non-cooperation and resistance is not confined to the ward round. Concealment features elsewhere in hospital, such as when patients choose not to 'open up' in informal chats with nurses. I have yet to examine the outpatient consultation data for instances of concealment, however my impression from listening to the tapes and reading the transcripts is that it features in those interactions too. Non-cooperation/resistance is a prominent aspect of Mental Health Act assessments, as we shall see in the following chapter. In those encounters, the candidate patient's first line of resistance is typically avoidance of the assessment team (e.g. refusing to open the door to them) followed by concealment ('holding it together' for the duration of the assessment) (see section 9.3.5).

While methods of non-cooperation and resistance are evidently used in various types of psychiatric encounter, it seems that service users *adapt* their use of them according to the particular situation in which they find themselves. For instance, avoidance in the context of outpatient consultations (a proportion of the 'did not attends') is different from the forms avoidance takes in MHA assessments. Ethnographic research cannot tell us much about the frequency of use of these techniques, but it seems likely that this is where differences between psychiatric settings will show themselves. For example, ward rounds are characterised by a higher level of turbulence and non-cooperation than is typically found in an outpatient consultation. And, while avoidance is a common form of resistance in MHA assessments, it is rarely an option for service users who are confined to hospital. The categories of resistance presented in this chapter could therefore be used in future research aiming to *quantify* these activities in a way I have been unable to do, allowing comparisons to be made between their frequency of use in different psychiatric settings.

For me, an intriguing question is why is there is not *more* overt resistance in ward rounds, given that a significant proportion of patients are detained against their will. This can be addressed at different levels.

At the ***interactional level,*** these findings indicate that patients *know* resistance can be counter-productive and so on occasion choose to express disagreement such that it does not jeopardize their chances of getting what they want. One way of 'playing the game' and avoiding confrontation with staff is to keep secret one's ideological differences. Another is to disguise ideological discordance as treatment discordance. The example of treatment discordance presented involved a patient claiming to have not taken the very medication to which staff attributed his improvement and which they wanted him to continue taking. In other words he voluntarily revealed non-adherence to prescribing as 'proof' that he did not need medication they wanted him to take.

At the ***macro/historical level***, the indications are that there has been a trend towards a convergence of lay and professional perspectives in mental health care over the last few decades. At one level we have seen the 'psychiatrisation' of everyday life (Castel *et al,* 1982), in which 'psy' categories are routinely invoked in mundane situations. At another, one can observe how service users' views on treatment and care are increasingly influential locally and nationally, and that the user movement is now a key player in NHS policy development. These developments have created a favourable environment in which to try to achieve consensus in psychiatric encounters, and it seems plausible to suggest that shared decision-making is generally much easier to achieve in a modern, permeable institution than it would have been in one of the old, total institutions.

Having considered in this chapter the ***institutional context*** in which treatment decisions are made, it becomes clear that two substantial obstacles to shared decision-making in inpatient care remain. The first is that psychiatric hospital is a place in which the patient's capacity to make rational decisions is in question, so any discordance in decision-making is easily attributable to their lack of insight. This hardly constitutes the situation of "equipoise" thought necessary for shared decision-making (Gwyn & Elwyn, 1999). The second obstacle arises from the close monitoring of compliance in hospital, as it increases the likelihood of non-cooperation and resistance. This is because commitments made and agreements reached in ward rounds are enforceable, meaning that if an inpatient 'agrees' to some treatment they do not want, they will probably have to take it – unless, that is, he or she is prepared to refuse their medications at the medicine round. Such an action is risky, however, because it can trigger the type of coercive response described in section 8.1. Resisting an unwanted treatment during negotiations about it, rather than at the point when it is delivered, can therefore seem like the more sensible option in this context. In Outpatients, the context for decision-making is markedly different in this regard, and I would argue that that this partly explains why those interactions typically produce negotiated agreements (see section 5.2).

I conclude with a note about my choice of topic for this chapter. Having decided to analyse lay/professional interaction in a 'permeable' institution, I had a choice about what to focus on and how best to depict it. Rather than portray ward rounds as I have done, as sites of contest in which there are 'winners' and 'losers', I might instead have chosen to focus on their negotiated aspects. My decision to examine non-cooperation and resistance should not be taken to imply that all mental health service users are ideologically opposed to psychiatry and seek to 'fight the system' at every turn. Unlike the romantic character R.P. McMurphy in *One Flew Over the Cuckoo's Nest* (Kesey, 1962), many of the service users I spoke to agreed that they were mentally ill, that the drugs were helping and that they were better off in hospital for the time being. On balance, though, I believe my account better represents what goes on in ward rounds than would a story of how consensus is achieved. I like to think that the majority of service users with first-hand experience of these encounters would agree with me.

Chapter 9

Doing the 'dirty work'?: the multiple roles of the Approved Social Worker

---

CONTENTS

This final chapter of findings examines the process of assessment for compulsory admission to psychiatric hospital. Previous research, reviewed in Chapter 3, indicates that the outcome of such assessments is likely to be influenced by a number of contextual factors. These include, for example, a 'breakdown of tolerance' towards to an individual's behaviour, and a lack of the resources needed to create a 'tenable situation' in the community as an alternative to hospital admission. Earlier research also suggests that this work has traditionally been seen as the 'dirty work' of the mental health professions. While the Approved Social Worker (ASW) had a central coordinating role in applying the Mental Health Act (1983), it had been underrepresented in the research literature (see Chapter 3).

This chapter presents findings from the MHA Study, which is, I believe, the only major observational research study that was conducted into how assessments are made under the 1983 Act.[51] It involved me shadowing ASWs in two London boroughs, in order to investigate how MHA assessments were organised, undertaken and experienced (see Chapter 4 for discussion of method). The focus of the analysis presented here is the ASW's multiple roles in these assessments and the related question of whether this is seen as 'dirty work' in the context of de-institutionalised mental health care. The experiences of those on the receiving end of a MHA assessment – the candidate patients – will also be considered, and it will be argued that these episodes of coercion often represent, for service users, their defining moments in their relationships with mental health professionals. These contrast with the defining moments for psychiatrists, who perhaps view moments when trust is achieved to be more important (see Chapter 5). This, I aim to show, partly explains why psychiatrists can maintain a self-image of 'patient-centredness', while simultaneously being perceived by a proportion of their patients as implementing a non-democratic treatment regime (Seale *et al*, 2006). Some of the practices observed, such as 'veiled coercion' (involving the use of deceptive methods by the assessment team), are potentially damaging future therapeutic relationships. This supports the case for using observational research methods in studies of this type, which in this case allow us to examine very closely *how* 'coercion' is actually done in naturally-occurring situations. Just as negotiated or shared decision-making is characterised by different

[51] Philip Bean's comprehensive study was about compulsory admissions made under the previous Act (Bean, 1980).

levels of pressure and resistance (see Chapter 5), so too are these more coercive encounters.

Before presenting the findings I shall briefly describe aspects of the 1983 Act. The Mental Health Act (2007) removed the central ASW role and replaced it with that of the 'Approved Mental Health Practitioner'. The findings are still relevant to these practitioners, however, because they are likely to face similar challenges and role tensions to those experienced by ASWs.

9.1 Application of the UK Mental Health Act (1983)

The MHA assessment was the focus of decision-making for Section 2 (admission for assessment), Section 3 (admission for treatment) and Section 4 (emergency admission for assessment) of the 1983 Act. The assessment involved a multi-professional 'team' which always included one or more doctors and an Approved Social Worker (ASW). Sometimes it also involved a mental health nurse, a member of the primary care team, housing worker, workers from the ambulance services and the police. Invariably these 'teams' were ad-hoc in that they are only brought into being for the sake of a single assessment.

Assessments occurred in a variety of settings including the person's home, police stations, accident and emergency departments and on psychiatric wards. They could be initiated by a general practitioner, psychiatrist or other member of the community mental health team (CMHT), social worker, the police (through the use of Section 136) or the person's family. However initiated, they were usually co-ordinated by an ASW, who was central to the process, being responsible for ensuring that the assessment involved the necessary staff and then often managing the consequences of the resulting decision.

An ASW is a qualified social worker who had undergone additional training and had been approved by the local authority to carry out various designated functions within the Mental Health Act (Sheppard, 1990). In MHA assessments the ASW had a responsibility to liaise with the nearest relative, who was clearly defined in the Act (they may not be the same person as the next of kin), has legal rights and who should act in the best interests of the patient. The ASW should also consider alternatives to hospital when undertaking a statutory mental health assessment. The MHA Code of Practice for the 1983 Act outlined the ASW's individual responsibilities in MHA assessments (Department of Health and Welsh Office, 1999: pp. 12-15). These included: taking overall responsibility for co-ordinating the assessment process; ensuring that the patient is interviewed in a 'suitable manner', for example not through a closed door or window; making the application for admission under the Act; and implementing the decision, for example, arranging for the person to be transported to hospital.

The Code of Practice specified as a guiding principle that all staff involved in the assessment should be responsible for overcoming barriers to communication with the patient:

> "As a general principle, it is the responsibility of staff to ensure that effective communication takes place between themselves and patients. All those involved in the assessment, treatment and care of patients should ensure that everything possible is done to overcome any barriers to communication that may exist." [Guiding principle 1.3, MHA 1983 Code of Practice (1999): p. 4]

The remainder of this chapter presents findings from the MHA study in order to shed some light on such communication, focusing on the ASW's experience. The focus will be on the multiple roles of the ASW that were invoked during the course of this work, as well as tensions between some of these roles. Consideration will be given as to whether this may be considered the 'dirty work' of the mental health professions, as had been found in research reviewed in Chapter 3 (e.g. Emerson & Pollner, 1975; Bean, 1980). The focus is thus very much on deviations from the norm (or at least ideal) of shared decision-making in psychiatric practice and on what happens when this breaks down.

9.2 Complexity and ambiguity

Formal MHA assessment interviews, involving face to face contact with the candidate patient, are part of a much longer and more complex process. From an ASW perspective, the build-up to them can include an initial referral, planning of the assessment, information gathering and formal or informal team discussions about how best to proceed. Some assessments involve many weeks' preparation and/or 'cat and mouse' manoeuvring, for example where the candidate patient hides because they suspect arrangements are being made to have them sectioned. Once assessed and the required medical recommendations have been signed, the person will require transportation to hospital, often by ambulance or in a police vehicle. On the day, even the most straightforward of community assessments – from the arrival of the assessment team to the person's admission to hospital - can take many hours to complete.

MHA assessments are undertaken in the context of professionals' other work and are by no means always perceived as a priority or emergency to them. This means that they typically have to be 'fitted in' or juggled with other work:

> "Yeah, that [assessment you've just observed] did go smoothly, with the police turning up quickly. But it's not always like that... If a bomb went off in town, like the other

day, you wouldn't be able to get anyone at all." [CPN, inner London]

In Chapter 3, I reviewed Lawson's model of compulsory admission to hospital as a two-stage process, made up of the events leading up to the request for help and the assessment referral (the 'breakdown' stage), followed by assessment and decision-making about admission to hospital (Lawson, 1966). However, this characterisation risks oversimplifying the everyday ambiguities and complexities of MHA assessments, which are commonly subject to false starts, disruptions, delays and no-shows. For example, there can be ambiguity surrounding their formal 'starting point', with events only being seen as such in retrospect. Indeed, the nature of the assessment is often deliberately kept 'open' by practitioners. This is illustrated by the fieldnote extract below.

Box 9.1: A possible MHA assessment ***(fieldnote extract, inner London)***

I walked into the duty office first thing. Straight away, the 'Duty Senior' asked if I wanted to observe a MHA assessment today. (Yes please.) She said there might be one this morning, which an ASW and a Section 12-approved (S12) doctor [a doctor with experience of psychiatry and approved to make medical recommendations under the Act] would be doing. The Duty Senior said it was a "complicated" one - difficult family dynamics etc… The referral agency requested a MHA assessment. And this is how it is recorded on the duty team whiteboard in the office (i.e. "MHA, 10 am") as one of the tasks that the ASW on duty must do today.

While all this pointed towards it being an "*MHA*" assessment, the ASW told me it was too soon to regard it as such. Indeed, the ASW said that if the candidate patient was at home, he and the doctor would visit, but that it's premature to book the second doctor [for the second medical recommendation], police and ambulance. They would do some sort of mental state examination, after which the doctor might sign the section form... So, for the ASW, it was too soon to view this as a MHA assessment - even though the first of the two "med recs" [medical recommendations] might be signed at the end of it.

Confusion sometimes arises over whether an 'MHA assessment' has actually taken place; certainly for clients in some cases, but also occasionally from the point of view of staff. One example of this is where the candidate patient agrees to a voluntary admission after the first medical recommendation has been signed, but before the necessary second medical examination could be organised (the two medical examinations are not always performed concurrently). Indeed, practitioners reportedly feel compelled sometimes to deviate from Code of Practice guidelines and deliberately sustain ambiguity about what is going on; that is, they do not tell the person at the outset that they are being assessed under the MHA. This is sometimes done in order to minimise client agitation and promote a smoother and safer assessment (see 9.9 below).

Crucially, much informal assessment and case construction can occur during the planning of the assessment, particularly when existing users of mental health services are involved. This can be done to such an extent that professionals carry into the assessment a clear expectation of the likelihood of compulsory admission (see 9.3.4 below). Furthermore, professionals often believe that they are in the 'build-up' to a MHA assessment, only to find that the 'assessment' is aborted or only partially completed. This was evidently a common occurrence, resulting from (a) information gathered in the build-up indicating that a MHA assessment is not required, (b) the candidate patient admitting to hospital voluntarily, (c) the candidate patient disappearing/hiding after the first medical examination, so that the second one cannot be undertaken (d) the person is not in when the team turns up for a community assessment, or (e) the team is refused access, for example by the candidate patient simply refusing to open the door to them.

9.3 The process of assessment

9.3.1 How the build-up is 'triggered'

As noted, the formal starting point to a MHA assessment is often difficult to unravel - for participants and research observers alike.

However, it is possible to identify a number of ways in which the process may be 'triggered'. These include: (1) a home visit, outpatient appointment,[52] crisis team visit (in the outer London local authority) or phone call with an existing client which unexpectedly triggers an assessment, for example where there is evidence of deterioration in the client's mental condition; (2) as above, but where the professionals already had good reason to believe that a MHA assessment would be a likely outcome (i.e. where they had received information to this effect in advance); (3) a request by a referral agency (e.g. GP, A&E department, housing or other social services department) that is treated with scepticism by the mental health professional(s) concerned, but which leads to a MHA assessment following their direct contact with the client; (4) as above, but where information gathering and case construction, rather than direct contact with the client, confirms the need for a section assessment; and (5) a request for a MHA assessment which is taken at face value and acted upon immediately, for example where the request comes from a 'trusted' referral agency.

9.3.2 Control of information

It is common for professionals to share information about the client in the build-up to an assessment. Information about existing users of

[52] Only two out of the 92 outpatient consultations recorded for the Prescribing Decisions Project (Chapters 5 & 6) resulted in the patient being admitted to hospital; in both cases voluntarily.

mental health services who have a case history, commonly flows from their care coordinator to the ASW. Such information sharing sometimes resembles 'lobbying', with the Community Psychiatric Nurse (CPN), responsible for the ongoing care, monitoring and supervision of the person, exerting an informal but potentially decisive influence on decision-making. Information sharing can occur in formal contexts, such as timetabled multi-disciplinary team meetings, where upcoming assessments are discussed, or informally, for example via telephone calls before the assessment. Such conversations may be fleeting (e.g. "Don't forget, she knows the score, she can present quite normally") or prolonged. Information on current or former clients can also be derived from case notes which hold data on the person's last stay in hospital and previous referrals. This may reveal patterns in the client's previous admissions to hospital which may lead professionals to believe that a compulsory admission will probably be required.

Information is likely to flow between various participants as part of the planning for the assessment. First, it may flow within the same professional group in the same area or locality, for example from an existing client's social worker/care manager to the duty ASW, or at handover of the case. Second, it may be communicated between different professional groups in the same area or locality, for example from the client's CPN to the co-ordinating ASW, or from the client's GP to the consultant psychiatrist. Third, it might flow between the same professional group but in different areas, for example from the candidate patient's former social worker/care manager to the ASW who is now co-ordinating the assessment. Fourth, it sometimes flows between different professional groups in different areas, for example from the candidate patient's former GP to the co-ordinating ASW. And finally, information is passed to and from the client's relatives, carers, friends or associates.

The quality and amount of information available for each assessment/case varies tremendously. Social workers in Emergency Duty Teams are more likely to be poorly served by information technology because they work out-of-hours, are not office based, and have comparatively little administrative back-up. ASWs in these circumstances have to depend more on techniques of examination/assessment and on the reports of individuals immediately caught up in the crisis situation, such as the individual who made the referral and the candidate patient.

As noted above, the extent to which a candidate patient can influence the outcome of assessment by skilful impression management, including the concealment of clinically and legally relevant information, depends heavily on the quality and amount of information that the assessment team already has at its disposal. In other words, in these encounters the balance between ceremonial and technological aspects of person production varies considerably (c.f. Cahill, 1998, reviewed in Chapter 2).

9.3.3 A typical community assessment

A typical community assessment for Section 2 admission is structured as follows. First, the team of the psychiatrist, GP and ASW turn up unexpectedly at the person's flat and do the assessment together, in the sitting room. Second, they retire to the hallway to decide on the outcome. Third, the candidate patient is told of the outcome by the social worker. And finally, the ASW signs the application form, based on the doctors' written medical recommendations, and arranges to transport the patient to hospital by ambulance.

9.3.4 Expectation of outcome

Professionals generally carry into MHA assessments an expectation of the likelihood of compulsory admission, particularly when dealing with 'known' clients with a case history. It is difficult, if not impossible, for professionals to come with a 'blank slate': as one ASW told me, they are much more likely to "run with a hypothesis" which is constantly tested throughout the assessment. Occasionally, professionals have good reason to believe that the person will almost certainly be sectioned, especially those 'deteriorating' patients who, according to the revised Code of Practice guidelines, can be sectioned on the basis of known history (pages 11-12). In such circumstances, the formal assessment interview(s) may be viewed by the ASW as "giving the client another chance".

The reliance upon the candidate patient's report depends, in large part, on the amount of other information that the assessment team has at its disposal. For example, in some Emergency Duty Team assessments, conducted out of hours, all the team have to go on is what the individual says and how s/he presents. This is certainly not always taken at face value (see below).

While compulsory admission is sometimes seen as a foregone conclusion in some assessments - in light of the case file already constructed - those on the receiving end may still feel that they had been able to sway the decision:

> "It was up for grabs to a certain extent, depending on how the assessment went… I thought I had a chance, yeah [of persuading people that I was okay]." [Candidate patient, interviewee 2, outer London]

9.3.5 "I knew that resistance was futile"

In MHA assessments the candidate patient's first line of defence is typically to keep the assessment team at arm's length: a form of non-cooperation (see Chapter 8). Some people, typically those who have 'been through the system', may suspect that arrangements are being made to have them sectioned, so actively seek to *escape* from the process. This can be done by hiding locally, leaving the area or even leaving the country. Some clients come to be known in social work teams as 'runners':

> "There's very few clients who try really hard to avoid being hospitalised, normally they know it's inevitable. But she's one of them [a "runner"]. One time we went to do an assessment and she ran off shouting "there's three men come to rape me!" [ASW, inner London]

More commonly, existing users of mental health services avoid contact with mental health professionals (e.g. by missing outpatient appointments, or avoiding home visits), although relatives, carers or friends may seek help on their behalf, possibly triggering an assessment. Once 'caught up with', the person may be resigned to their fate, knowing that further resistance is futile. This particularly applies when the police are involved:

> "I was reconciled… I knew that resistance was futile. *{Does it make a difference having the police there?}* Yeah…it's symbolic in a way because if the police are against you, for want of a better word, then what's the point of trying to live in the community, because they regulate the community. So you

can't resist the police." [Candidate patient, interviewee 2, outer London]

If avoiding the assessment team is the candidate patient's first line of defence, or resistance, then trying to 'hold it together' for the duration of the assessment is generally the next. This typically involves concealing clinically and legally relevant information, such as delusional thoughts or thoughts of harming other people. As we saw in the previous chapter, this method is also used in ward round decisions (see 8.3.2). In the context of assessment for compulsory admission, such concealment is particularly vulnerable to being perceived *as* resistance (see 9.3.6 below).

9.3.6 Evaluating the candidate patient's account

Knowledge that such concealment is very prevalent means that a key skill for the ASW and others in the team involves knowing when to take interviewees' accounts at face value and when to treat them with scepticism. For example, people are sometimes sectioned even though they have 'volunteered' to come into hospital. This is because, as one ASW put it to me, "sometimes you know they are only saying things to get you off their back and you know they don't mean it". Given that, according to the MHA Code of Practice, nurses on admission wards must tell informal (voluntary) in-patients that they may leave on request at any time (Department of Health &

Welsh Office, 1999: page 99), this is clearly an important consideration. Furthermore, skilful interviewing techniques are required to determine whether someone is merely "holding it together" or whether they really are well enough not to need of further assessment or treatment.

Sometimes the patient's account is disregarded entirely if concealment is suspected. This occurred in a team discussion I observed, concerning a patient whom the team had good reason to believe had been 'deteriorating' fast. As a 'deteriorating patient', he could be sectioned on the basis of known history, so the assessment might have been regarded by the team as giving the patient "another chance" (see above). However, while he 'held it together' in the assessment interview he still ended up being sectioned. The crucial turning point in the deliberations is represented in Box 9.2 below. To get around the 'problem' of how to section someone who had presented normally, notice how the CPN, who knew the patient well, argues that "There's a difference between what he says and what he means", which the team accepted. This was a key moment because the CPN's intervention effectively undermined everything the patient had said in the interview. Clearly, the art of impression management can achieve very little in such circumstances.

Box 9.2: Candidate patient's report is disregarded in deliberations by the assessment team *[Assessment 9; outer London]*

<u>Context:</u> *This was an out-of-hours assessment (a "dawn swoop"), characterised by an exceptionally high level of planning by the ASW. It had a very complicated build-up: the patient – a white, middle class man in his early forties – was receiving compulsory treatment in the community (under Section 25 of the MHA) but was not complying. Indeed he had managed to avoid contact with mental health services throughout the preceding three months. Previous attempts at assessment, made during daytime hours, had failed - either because the candidate patient was not at home or had chosen not to answer the door. The ASW and the patient's CPN-keyworker suspected the latter, so the decision was made to turn up at his house at 4 a.m. Fearing that the team would not be allowed in, the ASW went to court to obtain Section 135 warrant which gives powers of entry. The police (n=2) knocked on the candidate patient's door but gained entry without needing to use overt force. They kept a low profile thereafter.*

<u>Fieldnote extract</u>

The candidate patient presented comparatively normally to my eyes, and on the basis of the assessment interview I thought he'd 'got away with it' and would not need to be sectioned… [The assessment team left the candidate patient in the sitting room with the two police officers and retired to a room across the corridor to deliberate over what should be done.] A crucial turning point in the discussion was when the team brought in facts about his past behaviour and treatment history. The factual status of the candidate patient's account was undermined when the others agreed with his CPN-keyworker's statement: *"There's a difference between what he says and what he means*". Once this has been accomplished the team could legitimately disregard the candidate patient's report, focussing instead on what they already knew about him. It could be speculated that had an 'unknown' candidate patient presented in this way, s/he would not have been sectioned. Indeed the ASW involved later agreed with me when I put this to him.

<u>Outcome:</u> *The patient was taken to hospital by police car and admitted under Section 3 of the Act.*

9.4 Profile of observed assessments

This section summarises the profile of the assessments I observed, including information about the people involved. As discussed in Chapter 4, sampling decisions were not oriented towards attaining a 'representative' sample, but were instead driven by 'grounded theory' considerations (see section 4.4.3).

Assessment types: Assessments were for Section 2 (11 out of 20) or Section 3 admission (n = 9). One Section 4 assessment was observed as part of the 'build-up' to a Section 3 admission. Two instances of use of a Section 135 warrant to gain entry to the person's property were observed. Two candidate patients had been detained in a police station under Section 136 of the Act prior to the arrival of the assessment team. Five assessments were partially completed, for example where voluntary admission pre-empted the need for a second medical recommendation

Settings: Assessments were undertaken in a mixture of community and institutional settings. These included the person's home (9/20), a friend's house (1), a flat in a supported housing project (1), warden-assisted accommodation for the elderly (1), a hotel room (1), a police station (2), in a CMHT's back garden (1) and interview room (1), an outpatients department at a psychiatric unit (2) and a geriatric ward (1).

Time of day: The large majority of assessments (17/20) commenced 'during hours' (09.00 – 17.00, Monday to Friday). Of these, six continued beyond 17.00. While only three out-of-hours assessments were observed, other theoretically useful data were gathered at such times (e.g. observation of 'failed' assessment attempts).

Duration: About one third (6/20) of assessments were completed on the day the ASW received the referral: most (14) tended to be prolonged over a few days or longer.

Participants (professionals): The number and type of professionals involved is largely determined by the type of assessment being undertaken (e.g. more tend to be required for an S3 than an S4). It is also influenced by whether the assessment is prolonged, for example requiring repeated assessment attempts by different teams. Defining how many professionals were involved is therefore difficult: for example, should this include only those who actually engaged with the client or all those working behind the scenes? For simplicity's sake I have limited the definition to cover only those who came within the candidate patient's response presence (Goffman, 1983) during the final assessment attempt. (This excludes those who were involved in earlier efforts to assess the person.) In any given assessment this will include professionals such as the ASW (or in some cases, ASWs), doctors, CPNs, police officers and ambulance workers, trainee-ASWs and trainee-CPNs, and student doctors. Using this definition, the mean number of professionals in the completed assessments was five (excluding the research-observer). In assessments where a second medical recommendation was made, similar numbers of GPs and 'approved' doctors were used (7 and 8 respectively). Also involved in assessments were ambulance workers (9 times) and the police (14 times). In prolonged assessments it was quite common for more than one ASW to be directly involved, as happened during seven assessment episodes.

Participants (candidate patients/relatives): Equal numbers of men and women were assessed (10 of each). The large majority were either white UK (12/20) or northern white European (2). Other candidate patients were of Afro-Caribbean (2), Asian (2), Greek-Cypriot (1) or Turkish-Cypriot (1) origin. Accurate ages of candidate patients were not always obtained but half (9/18) were in their 30s or 40s, four were in their 50s, and three were aged over 65, while two were in their 20s and one was in his teens. Half of those who were formally admitted (7/14) were first admissions. Relatives were directly involved in more than half of the assessments (11/20).

9.4.1 Example of an assessment

The following Section 4 assessment was observed as part of the 'build-up' to a Section 3 admission. In other words while the candidate patient escaped from being sectioned on this occasion, she was assessed and compulsorily admitted to hospital the following day.

Box 9.3: Example of a Section 4 assessment *[Assessment 19, inner London]*

Context: *The candidate patient lived in central London, in a top floor flat in supported accommodation. These are flats for people who are not suited to living in hostel accommodation, where there is a requirement for residents to get involved in communal living, sharing the kitchen, and so on. It is 'accommodation for life' (e.g. the flat is kept open for people while they are in hospital) but there are strings attached. For example, the candidate patient in this instance was contractually obliged to see her social worker/keyworker twice weekly and had signed up to a care plan stipulating that she must take her medication as prescribed. The candidate patient had not kept to this, and her CPN was concerned that she was deteriorating. On the day the assessment team called, the candidate patient was not at home. As they were preparing to leave, the candidate patient entered the front door and proceeded to make her way up stairs, where she was met by members of the team.*

Fieldnote extract

The GP sees and recognises the candidate patient first, and says "Hello Maureen we've come to have a chat with you". Maureen asks "What are you doing here?". The GP walks down one flight of stairs to meet her on the landing below. She starts attempting to engage with Maureen, saying things such as "We've been worried about you"... Maureen says things including "I'm okay, what are you here for?", then pushes past the GP to get to her flat... As she passes, I get out of the way and go down to the next landing and wait there with the two police officers...

As Maureen gets to the top floor, outside her door, the ASW asks if they can come into her flat. Maureen replies, emphatically and loudly, "No you cannot!". The GP says "We've come to see how you are"; Maureen replying "I've got bad dandruff, I want to wash my hair and have a shower!". Maureen says that she has an appointment with the GP for the next day [GP checks the case file she had brought with her, and acknowledged that that is correct]. Maureen asks, quizzically, "So why have you come to see me today?"

Maureen then asks if they can talk downstairs (apparently looking to make an escape through the front door), but GP/ASW say it would be better if they could talk somewhere privately, away from the other residents. Maureen refuses, so ASW says "Well let's talk here" and Maureen sits on the top stair with ASW and GP a couple of steps below her, at about M's eye-level...

The 'interview' commenced, although there was little done to mark it as an assessment; for example there was no formal announcement that they were assessing her for an S4 [Section 4 emergency assessment for admission, requiring only one medical recommendation, by the GP]. Basically they continued to ask her questions. Maureen showed her 'agitation', but never actually shouted – she just spoke loudly in responding to their questions. As in Chapter 8, the following exchange is based on detailed notes taken at the time rather than a tape recording.

GP: So how are you in yourself?

M: I've got bad dandruff, are you gonna help me with my dandruff?

GP: Well yes. Do you know what time of year it is?

M: Is it March or April? I can't remember which.
((Approximately 20 seconds of unrecorded talk))

M: So I come and see you tomorrow. ((Starts to look in her handbag for the keys to her flat))

ASW: Maureen, how do you feel in yourself regarding your mental health?

M: Okay.

ASW: Are you taking your medication?

M: ((Pause)) That's a secret. I want to go in now. ((She takes out her keys from her handbag))

GP: Maureen if you don't speak to me, I won't have a choice.

M: I've got bad dandruff, let's talk tomorrow!

At this, the candidate patient stands up, enters her flat and slams the door behind her. The team go downstairs and have a short discussion just inside the entrance to the block of flats. The GP comments that in her view the candidate patient is "borderline" and had entered the premises quite normally. The GP then checks her records, and counts out aloud the number of times she had been involved in assessing this patient under the MHA. On the basis of this she comments to the ASW: "But I can guarantee you that within a month, at the outside, she will be in hospital". The ASW responds that this feels very familiar, that she's "got the feeling we've been here before". The ASW adds that while this candidate patient is able to "hold it together" for long enough to get through an assessment she agrees she is not really sectionable - yet. They left it that the GP would phone the ASW the following day to report on the outcome of the candidate patient's scheduled appointment.

Outcome: *The candidate patient was not sectioned on this occasion. However, following complaints from her neighbours that evening, arrangements were made to have her assessed again the following day. This resulted in her being sectioned and admitted to hospital, onto a ward in the inner-London psychiatric unit that was researched for the Acute Ward Ethnography (reported in Chapters 7 & 8).*

9.5 The multiple roles of the ASW

The ASW is perceived, by professionals and people being assessed, to have a multitude of roles which are variously deployed and understood in these encounters. Summarised below are some of the main roles of the ASW that are constituted in interaction. Typically, a number of these roles will be invoked during the course of a single MHA assessment.

'Applicant'

This official role of the ASW is routinely invoked when s/he signs the application. This is not always done in the presence or view of the candidate patient, so this role is sometimes obscured.

'Social worker'

This role may be invoked when candidate patients are asked by the ASW about their social circumstances. It is also evident when the ASW brings such considerations into the team's assessment decision, for example drawing attention to the person's level of social support and in helping to construct a 'tenable' situation as an alternative to a hospital admission. If the ASW follows up the case, the client may perceive this role when they are being "helped to come to terms with what's happened and get on with normal life again (benefits, housing etc)" (discussed further in section 9.6 below).

'Care manager'

ASWs are sometimes the candidate patient's former or current care manager. In such cases, the person's role as ASW is adopted in the context of an existing professional-client relationship. While this means that people are assessed in the context of up-to-date knowledge about the client, it may also cause conflict and feelings of betrayal on the part of the patient. This is because the care manager/ASW will be going against their client's immediate expressed wishes, despite acting in their best interests. This is likely to require follow-up work to repair any damage to trust in the relationship.

'Advocate'

This role may be invoked when the ASW represents the view of the person being assessed, such as in a team discussion where the ASW argues a tenable situation can be created to allow the candidate patient to continue living in the community. ASWs are sometimes expected to represent the views of professionals not directly involved in the assessment decision, but who have a vested interest in the outcome, such as CPNs, GPs or housing project workers.

'Hate figure'

ASWs may unwittingly find themselves cast in this role by candidate patients and their relatives. While this typically involves bearing the brunt of people's anger, it is not always resisted: "As long as it helps them get in the ambulance, I don't mind".

'Supervisor/trainer'

Qualified ASWs are commonly accompanied by trainee ASWs, who sometimes "front" the assessment as part of their training. They may also adopt this role with GPs who have had little experience in undertaking this type of work.

'Therapist'

Many social workers derive satisfaction from the therapeutic dimension of their work, with a proportion having formal qualifications in this. Some believe that such training comes in helpful when informing the client of their right to appeal.

If done in a particular way, this was perceived to offer an opportunity to facilitate client control and involvement in the process and to pre-empt the damaging effects of an episode of coercion on future professional-client relationships (discussed further in section 9.6 below).

'Policeman/jailer'

Not surprisingly, candidate patients may come to see the ASW in punitive terms, as "locking people up against their will".

'Bureaucrat'

This is where the ASW is seen to be 'following the rules (law)' and where the section is presented to the candidate patient as 'nothing personal'. In some situations this functions to minimise the harmful effects of an episode of coercion on an existing professional-client relationship. Linked with this, it may also be adopted to counter perceptions of the 'policeman/jailer' role. Often the ASW will invoke bureaucratic rules to control the actions of other actors, such as doctors and the police.

'Planner/impresario'

The ASW has a central, coordinating role in MHA assessment, being responsible for ensuring that the assessment involves the necessary staff, and so on. One ASW described a key role of his as being to successfully "stage manage" the assessment; setting everything up and making sure the event runs smoothly (discussed further in section 9.6 below).

'Contingency manager'

This is often the core role for the ASW. MHA assessments are commonly subject to unexpected turns of events to which the ASW must respond (discussed further in 9.5.2 below).

This is not an exhaustive list of ASW roles, and it should be emphasised that, first, they are not mutually exclusive, and second, they are situationally adopted or invoked. This means that the roles identified may overlap, at times leading to tensions between them (discussed below). For example, there may be a quick transition from the ASW's perceived role as 'social worker' to that of 'hate figure' once the candidate patient is told they are going to be compulsorily detained. This can occur even though the ASW had represented the candidate patient's view in the preceding team discussion; that is, as their 'advocate'.

I shall now examine two closely related roles in more depth; namely those of 'planner/impresario' and 'contingency manager'. I will then look at constraints on the deployment of social work or therapy roles, and describe some of the tensions between these and other roles of the ASW. This will help to explain why this work is so difficult to do.

9.5.1 'Planner/impresario'

Organising activities in advance, and gathering together relevant information (see section 9.3.2 above), is a central role for the ASW. It is closely associated with their contingency manager role (below), because well-laid plans very often have to be changed, or new ones made, in response to unexpected events. The degree of planning varies by team, by how the assessment was triggered and by its perceived urgency. "Borderline" cases were sometimes allowed to "drag on", with little planning for an assessment ("If we were really that bothered by him, we'd have got him in by now").

One of their formal responsibilities is organising the transportation of sectioned individuals to hospital (known as "shipping the body" in some social work teams). Observed methods of transportation included: (a) the candidate patient (P) was taken to hospital in the back of an ambulance, accompanied by the ASW and ambulance officer, (b) P was handcuffed and locked in the 'cage' part of a police Transit van, with the ASW following by car, (c) P was "given a lift" in back of a police car, with the ASW following by car, (d) P was in the back of an ambulance with the ASW, with the ambulance officers in the front seats, (e) P was handcuffed in back of the ambulance with a police officer and an ambulance officer, with the ASW following by car, and (f) P was taken in the back of a police van with a police officer, with the ASW map-reading in front passenger seat (in a case where the candidate patient was taken to a hospital outside of the borough).

The patient's experience of being sectioned is very likely to be coloured by the way they are taken to hospital. However, it is often difficult, if not impossible, for professionals to predict the form of transport, and associated level of coercion, that will be needed. This is the case even when the assessment is well under way or has been completed:

Box 9.4: Fieldnote for Assessment 13; inner London

While waiting with the police officer and the ASW in the hotel corridor, after the assessment had been completed, I asked if the person was going to be taken to hospital by police van rather than by ambulance. *((She was in the adjoining room with a WPC, gathering some possessions to take with her to hospital.))* The ASW replied "I don't know', the police officer adding "Yeah, these things are fluid, we'll see how things go".

The extent to which transport is planned during the build-up depends largely on professional expectations of the assessment outcome. While there is the clear danger of such planning prejudicing the decision-making, waiting until the assessment decision has been made will almost certainly extend the overall process. A lengthy wait for an ambulance or police car can be very uncomfortable and stressful for all concerned; small talk is not easy.

Relatives/carers may find themselves in an awkward position if they are directly involved in the build-up. Concerned to avoid complicity, and perhaps future accusations of betrayal, they may be tempted to warn their loved-one about the upcoming assessment. One ASW told me how this could be done with subtlety, such that it gave the candidate patient the opportunity to de-rail the planned assessment, for example by hiding from the team.

Box 9.5: Fieldnote for Assessment 9; outer London

The ASW had to tell the nearest relative (the candidate patient's father) that they would be doing the assessment, and checked that he would be around to support the application. One worry the ASW had, was of the father warning his son - in a subtle way. E.g. "They are coming round so you might want to get some things together for hospital". The ASW kept acknowledging to me the difficult position they are in - wanting to protect their son."

9.5.2 'Contingency manager'

The smooth-running of assessments can come under threat from numerous, unexpected sources. 'Cock ups' observed during the fieldwork included the interpreter who could not speak the language requested when booked; the 'lost' medical recommendation, signed beforehand by the GP and taken to the assessment by the ASW, which was 'fortuitously' found (from the ASW's perspective) only when the candidate patient violently smashed the ASW's briefcase onto the floor; and flat batteries or poor reception for the ASW's mobile phone, causing difficulties in booking the ambulance. ASWs were continually responding to unexpected events, so they require skills in ongoing contingency management to organise MHA assessments successfully. Task-juggling and improvisation, cajoling and persuasion, were typically required to get various busy professionals to the same place at the same time. This is illustrated by the fieldnote extract below.

Box 9.6: Fieldnote for Assessment 13, inner London

Barbara [an ASW] was on the office phone virtually non-stop in the three hours leading up to the first assessment attempt. She did not have time to stop for lunch, only a banana which she ate as she went along… She had to persuade the police to attend and was on the phone to them for over 20 minutes… Throughout she gave me a real sense of having to keep tabs on various participants. John [another ASW] said the same. For example, "just cos the ambulance service say they'll be there is not enough - chase up beforehand".

Contingency management pervades the whole of the assessment and admission process, including the build-up to it. Threats to the successful completion of MHA assessments emanated mainly from a lack of available professionals; the timing of assessments often appearing to depend upon the 'good will' of participants, such as the candidate patient's GP, whose sense of obligation to attend could vary greatly. Indeed, some individuals, notably the consultant psychiatrist in charge of the patient's care (the Responsible Medical Officer), can stop the build-up to an assessment in its tracks. A psychiatrist in inner London commented: "If [the consultant psychiatrist]… doesn't want to sign the first medical recommendation, the care manager can't really start the process off."

The difficulties of finding 'approved' doctors for the second medical recommendation was a common problem for ASWs in both the inner- and outer-London local authorities. This arose largely because they were not always able to organise the person's GP to do this. This occurred when: (a) it was an emergency situation where there was insufficient time for the GP's involvement to be arranged, (b) the GP could not be reached, (c) the person was not registered with a GP (this was a particular problem in inner-London), or (d) the GP was reluctant to get involved. The scarcity of 'approved' doctors may partly be explained by the lack of financial incentive for them to get involved:

> "It's not surprising it's hard to get ['approved'] Section 12 doctors when you only get thirty pounds or so after tax. I can only do it today because I don't have any appointments." ['Approved' second doctor attending an assessment in inner London]

In the absence of any form of rota, approved doctors were particularly scarce in the inner London borough after 23.00. But difficulties throughout the evening were reported:

> "The biggest problem we [social workers in the out-of-hours Emergency Duty Team] have is getting ['approved'] Section 12 doctors between 11 p.m. and 9 a.m.... Earlier in the evening

can be difficult too – they're on their way home, they're hungry and want to put the kids to bed… The main difference these days is that they've got answerphones and they field calls, whereas before you could speak to them and twist their arms." [ASW in Emergency Duty Team, inner London]

9.6 Deployment of 'social worker' and 'therapist' roles

9.6.1 When theory informs practice: outer London Borough

At the time when the fieldwork was undertaken, practice in the outer London borough, specifically the operation of the 24-hour crisis teams, was underpinned by a long-established treatment philosophy or culture, which strongly encourages professionals to consider alternatives to hospital admission. These commonly-held ideas and beliefs make ASWs, in particular, inclined to view compulsory admission as the option of 'last resort'.

The underlying crisis intervention theory holds that the crisis visit (which may or may not turn into a MHA assessment) is an intervention in itself which may obviate the need for compulsory detention. Emphasis is placed on seeking alternatives to hospital care by creating tenable situations in the community. For those who are admitted, the social worker follows them up in order to ensure some continuity of care. The theory also holds that relatives should be involved in the process from the outset.

This theoretical approach and associated service structure combine to encourage practitioners to delay triggering MHA assessments until other alternatives have been fully explored. Indeed, the designation "a good piece of (crisis) work" tended to be reserved in the outer London borough for interventions that averted a potential admission, a perspective that is very commonly shared by service users (see section 9.10.1 below). This resource-intensive approach was generally much valued by practitioners, particularly its 'therapeutic' orientation.

9.6.2 Pragmatism: inner London Borough

In contrast, the view of compulsory admission as the option of last-resort appeared to be much less prevalent among the ASWs in inner-London (in CMHT A particularly). This can be explained partly by the different local service context in which they were operating and the much greater demand for their services. This was said to have contributed to a more "pragmatic" approach to MHA assessments. Hard-pressed social workers in inner London, struggling to manage heavy case loads, were less likely to portray compulsory admission as having been a 'bad outcome'. The general view of practitioners was that, when making assessment decisions, they felt unable to rely on a comprehensive system of community resources. This made creating a tenable community situation for a "borderline" client a perceptibly more risky option than it would be in less pressurised and better resourced areas. Under such circumstances it is perhaps unsurprising that the psychiatrist's refusal to make the requisite medical recommendation could generate a sense of *frustration*:

> "Unlike what you told me about [the situation in the outer London local authority] you get the impression that social workers here think a good outcome is when the person is sectioned [if all other alternatives have been explored]... You get a sense of frustration from ASWs when the person's not sectioned, and that they think it's easier or less risky to sort them out in hospital." [Psychiatrist, inner London]

The relationship between treatment ideology or philosophy and resource levels is complex, and is best characterised as a 'chicken and egg' situation. Different ideological or philosophical orientations to mental health care will influence decisions to section and this will have resource implications. For example, the reluctance to section people requires a certain level of community resources if safe, tenable situations outside of hospital are to be created. At the same time, organisational pressures in busy inner-city areas can make certain treatment philosophies untenable, or at least harder to put into practice - even though individual practitioners might agree with them.

The main point is simple but important; namely, that the prevailing treatment ideology is likely to have an important influence on practitioners' orientation towards MHA assessments, and whether the deployment of 'social worker' and 'therapist' roles during their course is perceived as desirable.

9.6.3 Peer discussion and support

Peer group discussion and peer support is one way that such treatment ideologies or organisational cultures are both made visible (to practitioners and researchers alike) and sustained. Below, a psychiatrist describes the subtle way this may operate, and how the views of certain influential individuals can affect local practice. He explained how the 'last resort' norm was invoked:

> "I would routinely find myself having to justify why I had sectioned somebody. And he [the lead psychiatrist] could be so scathing about why somebody had been sectioned, like 'God, what's *she* in for?'" [Psychiatrist, inner London]

Peer support for ASWs can amount to a sharing of the decision-making in the build-up to an assessment (e.g. "What do you think I should do?"). ASWs may also be offered emotional support, particularly after a "difficult" assessment (e.g. "Are you okay?").

The level of peer support available to members of different professional groups varied considerably. ASWs in outer London, in particular, routinely discussed MHA assessments with their colleagues soon after they had been completed. This tended not to be the case for the S12 doctors involved, who typically turned up, signed the medical recommendation, and left without much ceremony. The peer group discussion appeared to be an important way through which the organisational culture of ASWs was communicated and sustained in the outer London teams.

Box 9.7: Communicating MHA assessment norms to new staff (events after Assessment 6, outer London)

The ASW had been with the social work team a few days before undertaking her first MHA assessment there. The assessment resulted in a Section 2 admission. She returned to the office and, over a coffee, was asked by the team leader and other colleagues how it had gone. On being told of the decision to detain the patient, the others asked the ASW whether she and the assessment team had considered other alternatives. She appeared mildly taken aback and defensive. In response, the team leader reassured the ASW; softly and matter-of-factly explaining that the team always discusses MHA assessments afterwards in order to consider what else might have been done. The

ASW later told me that they never did this in her previous social work team, so it had initially seemed as if her new colleagues were questioning her judgement.

On the face of it a redundant conversation – given that the assessment decision had already been made - discussing alternatives to compulsory admission with colleagues after the event is an important everyday method for communicating and sustaining the 'admission as last resort' norm. This is because it requires ASWs routinely to explain and *justify* to their colleagues the assessment decisions they have made. By communicating that such decisions are not taken lightly, it is also a very important method of invoking the *serious* nature of this work (discussed further in section 9.10 below). Such conversations were much less common in the busy inner London teams, who would probably argue that they simply did not have the time to reflect on such matters. This, in its own turn, reveals their pragmatic orientation to this work.

9.7 Tensions between ASW roles

There can sometimes be tensions between the multiple roles of the ASW. For example, ASWs described how they sometimes invoke a 'therapist' role through informing clients of their right to appeal. On the face of it a routine statutory obligation, this action was also seen by some ASWs to extend beyond their formal role as a legal advisor:

it was perceived to offer an opportunity to open up communication, facilitate client control and their involvement in the process, and to counter the damaging effects of compulsory admission ("This is a chance to exercise your right to be listened to"). However, role ambiguity may arise when the ASW signs the application, invoking their legal role as 'applicant', but immediately encourages the client to appeal against it. Unless handled skilfully, such an action may confuse the candidate patient and raise the question "Whose side is the ASW on?"

Such nuances of social interaction are not always obvious to participants at the time, though they may become evident later on. One example is the tensions between ASW's role as 'advocate' and 'policeman/jailer':

> "One person I'd sectioned said to me after: 'Well you're not one of those bastards who would section me, you're on my side'. And I had to say 'Well actually I'm the one who sectioned you!'" [ASW, inner London]

Such tensions can be particularly difficult for existing users of mental health services, where the involvement of "trusted" professionals, responsible for their ongoing care, can cause difficulties - at least at the time of the assessment:

> "Looking back I'm grateful to them [the ASW and my CPN-keyworker]. I think they're good guys. But at the time I rejected them." [Candidate patient, interviewee 2, outer London]

But, ultimately, trusted professionals may come to be seen to have been merely bureaucratically 'following the rules', and that it had indeed been 'nothing personal'. As one patient said of the ASW, his social worker of more than five years' standing:

> "Those are the rules that Brian [my social worker] is under, not the rules that he made. Brian has to follow those rules because he's employed by the company that deals with situations like that." [Candidate patient, interviewee 1, inner London]

I shall now turn to consider briefly the candidate patient's experience of assessment and compulsory admission, followed by an analysis of assessment teams' use of what I term 'veiled coercion'. Both of these issues have a bearing on whether undertaking MHA assessments might be viewed as the 'dirty work' of the mental health professions: the final issue to be considered in this chapter.

9.8 The candidate patient's experience

9.8.1 Breakdown

There is insufficient room in this chapter to do justice to the candidate patient's experience during the 'breakdown' stage of a compulsory admission (Lawson, 1966). Also, there is a limit to what can be reported on the basis of the four patient interviews and one relative/carer interview recorded for the study. That conceded, these few accounts are still able to show very clearly the huge gulf between their lifeworlds and the worlds of the professionals they were soon to meet in the assessment. The following interview extracts indicate what a truly horrific and frightening experience the 'breakdown' stage can be:

> "I thought the wrath of God was coming down from heaven and the crows, the birds in the park were getting more violent, sort of like 'Damien' [the movie] type of horror, devilish sort of feelings. They were really horrible... I kept thinking that outside there was this pink triangle, and it was trying to bring me to my knees so something out of the sky could bolt me in my body and my head and kill me." [Candidate patient, interviewee 1, inner London]

> "My husband took me to the police station, and I started hallucinating about bombs and seeing my husband's picture on

> the station walls. *{Like those 'Wanted' posters?}* Yeah. Then I got it into my head that there was a bomb in my stomach and my husband wanted to kill me… I thought he was kidnapping girls and taking them to work and torturing them, and drinking their blood, like a devil." [Candidate patient, interviewee 3, outer London]

It can also be a time of disturbed thoughts, confusion and sleeplessness:

> "It's mad to explain, but it's like you have certain doors in your brain innit, like all of them will open. 'Man, God!' you're thinking to yourself. Like one of the doors is open, then like you try to shut that door and the next door will open for you… I'm trying to shut these doors, but it's like trying to log off a computer which won't log off… I didn't really used to get to sleep." [Candidate patient, interviewee 4, inner London]

People may get up to some "pretty strange" activities:

> "Just prior to my assessment I was doing some pretty strange things… I was knocking at my parents' and friends' doors at four in the morning, phoning people in the middle of the night… It was part of a campaign on my behalf… I saw it as a kind of war between me and my family." [Candidate patient, interviewee 2, outer London]

This does not necessarily mean that, even in retrospect, they believed themselves to have been mentally ill and/or sectionable:

> "I didn't feel I was mentally ill… I wouldn't say there was nothing wrong with me, but I thought hospital treatment and medication was a bit excessive." [Candidate patient, interviewee 2, outer London]

> "I was not a threat… I've just been walking into restaurants and buying cold Coca Cola for 80, 90 pence when you could get them round the corner at Tesco's for 50p." [Candidate patient, interviewee 1, inner London]

For relatives and carers too, the build-up to a MHA assessment can be a time of considerable strain - especially when the safekeeping of their loved-one depends upon constant supervision:

> "She [my wife – interviewee 3] became paranoid, she started imagining so many things, hearing voices, thinking the place is being bombed, just in a minute it's going to explode. And she wanted to get through the [10th floor] balcony window and throw herself out, and go to the kitchen – I'd been hiding all the knives - to cut her throat. *{How long had that been going on?}* Almost a month or more… I couldn't sleep, I had to watch her 24 hours." [Carer, interviewee 5, outer London]

9.8.2 *Assessment and admission*

Interviews indicated that people's views on being sectioned are inextricably linked to their subsequent experience on the ward. In other words, they were not viewed as two separate processes, rather as part of the same thing: hospitalisation. This is indicated by responses to questions about how the assessment process might have been improved:

> *{Looking back, do you think things could have been handled differently, better?}* "You can't really say because of the state you's in… Because truthfully when I was in [hospital] they just left me how I was, didn't give me no medicine." [Candidate patient, interviewee 4, inner London]

> *{From your experience, can it be done in a way that isn't so horrible, the assessment?}* "I think it depends where you put the patient. I don't think it depends on the assessment, it depends on the hospital, and how the nurses keep the patient." [Candidate patient, interviewee 1, inner London]

For service users, a negative perception of the quality of the admission ward can have a direct bearing on whether they accept they need to be sectioned. For example, in one assessment I observed, the candidate patient was evidently horrified at the prospect of being admitted to a particular ward on which he had stayed before. From past experience, he told the assessment team that he would feel very threatened there. Searching for "security" and "rest", he asked the ASW and S12 doctor if he could be admitted elsewhere. In the absence of an alternative, the decision was made to section him.

In Chapter 3 I reviewed the large body of health service research literature showing that acute psychiatric wards in the UK can be unsafe and untherapeutic. Indeed the state of these wards was described as "Britain's Mental Health Scandal" in a recent television documentary.[53] ASWs in the present study shared this view, for example:

> "I wish as much attention was paid to the conditions on psychiatric wards as it is to how we get people onto them [under section]… The wards locally are appalling - they're the last place you'd want to send someone who has a depressive illness." [ASW, outer London]

Compulsory admission rates can be influenced by professional and client perceptions of conditions on acute psychiatric wards. With clients perceived by professionals to be at the "hard end", such perceptions are unlikely to affect the outcome of the assessment. But for "borderline" clients, where there is uncertainty about their need to be sectioned, such views may "influence [the assessment team's]

[53] *Dispatches: Britain's Mental Health Scandal.* Channel 4, 9 October 2006.

perceptions of options". The emergent picture is that professional perceptions of *what awaits* the person, should they be sectioned, typically has a subtle but pervasive influence on assessment decision-making:

> "I'm not one of those who thinks you shouldn't section people. But it does help if you know the ward you're sending them to is good." [ASW, inner London]

9.8.3 Long term consequences

Compulsory detention can also have negative consequences for the person's housing status or financial situation, particularly for those on housing benefit and income support. For example, people on income support who receive partial housing benefit may start building up rent arrears once their income support is replaced, at six weeks, by the lower-value allowance. This is because they might find it difficult to make up the shortfall between the benefit allowance and their actual rent. Social workers can play an important role in helping to re-schedule such arrears later on. But in some circumstances whether one's house is kept on can seem to come down to a mixture of "luck" and familial support:

> "I was lucky, my family kept my house on, but a lot of people can find themselves homeless after discharge… But then you

> get some families who really don't want the person to live on their own, so they let the house go." ['Survivor', informal interview]

Other disruptions to formal or informal social support structures include the possible loss of day centre or employment scheme places through non-attendance. There is also evidence of 'de-registration' of psychiatric patients with GPs (Buntwal *et al*, 1999).

The disruption to lifestyle and identity tends to be worse for first admissions, where people may for the first time experience the stigma of being labelled mentally ill. Such people may subsequently drop out of contact with services and avoid any attempts at follow-up. While a substantial number of involuntarily admitted patients do not retrospectively feel their admission was justified and beneficial (Katsakou & Priebe, 2006), some see it more positively. A few weeks after discharge, one interviewee told me how she was now much less socially-isolated:

> "It's really helped me a lot since going into hospital and having all this group therapy. At least I'm getting out doing things, because before I was just stuck in the flat, wasn't doing anything. And I've got a free bus pass so I'm out all the time… There's an [occupational therapy] sports group on Tuesday, mainly volleyball, rounders, swimming. Then a social sort of

> group on Friday… I think it's good, it's helped me a lot." [Candidate patient, interviewee 3, outer London]

9.9 Veiled coercion

Some people are well aware that they are being assessed under the MHA or perhaps that professionals are "building up files" on them, as one candidate patient subsequently put it to me. But others may be very unsure as to what is going on, particularly if they already have a tenuous grip on reality:

> "I thought the police station was some sort of cult, trying to take me away somewhere. I thought they were evil, even the police station didn't look at all real - like it had been quickly built, all plastic recording machines." [Candidate patient, interviewee 3, outer London]

Professionals may have good reasons to sustain ambiguity, and feel compelled to do so, for example in order to minimise client agitation and alarm. But the person may subsequently feel aggrieved about this and/or for not having been told what was going on and *why* they were being sectioned:

> "The doctor, he should have told me what was going on, or given me something to calm me down… and the police should

> have told me, not just left me in a room [a police cell] by myself." [Candidate patient, interviewee 3, outer London]

> "John [the ASW] could have said 'Listen, we're taking you to hospital, we don't want you upset, please bear with us. I hope you understand, you need to be put on a section'. In fact they didn't even tell me why they were sectioning me before they put me under section." [Candidate patient, interviewee 1, inner London]

Sectioned individuals may have deceptions played on them. I was told of certain mental health professionals who "lie through their teeth" to get the person into the ambulance or police vehicle (e.g. "Don't worry, you'll be back home later."). But the deception is typically more subtle and benign in intent than this. For example, compulsory admission in one case essentially involved transferring the patient from a general ward, where she had been assessed, to the psychiatric unit. Rather than presenting this as "compulsory detention under the Mental Health Act", the psychiatrist told the patient, who appeared highly confused and distressed, that she was being "transferred to a nicer ward" than the one she was currently in. There are parallels here with forms of deception in outpatient consultations that psychiatrists described in our interview study (Seale *et al*, 2006), and with disguised coercion on acute wards (see section 8.1 in the previous chapter). This suggests that deception of this type, which is typically rationalised by the psychiatrist and other mental health professionals as being in the best interests of the patient, occurs in various types of psychiatric encounter, ranging from the ostensibly voluntaristic (outpatient consultations) to the coercive (MHA assessments).

Such deliberate veiling of the coercive nature of the decision-making is typically aimed at facilitating a smoother assessment process, and may indeed pre-empt or minimise patient anxiety and non-cooperation (see Chapter 8). However, it may also cause patient resentment and mistrust in the future and obstruct professional endeavours to develop or maintain a future trusting relationship with the client. This analysis partially explains the blurring of the distinction between voluntary and legal status, as experienced by patients, discussed in Chapter 3. In other words, it is not surprising that a significant number of the compulsorily detained report not perceiving themselves to have been coerced (Hiday *et al*, 1997) given that the truth of this was deliberately fudged by the assessment team.[54]

9.10 Dirty work?

> "[MHA assessments] are a bit like funerals. No-one likes doing them but they've got to happen." [ASW, outer London]

[54] This adds support to the CA-derived claim, presented in the analysis of how pressure is applied in negotiations in outpatient consultations (Chapter 5), that things have to be *constituted* as pressure (or coercion) in interaction.

"AM: Visiting [a client] as a 'stormtrooper of the psychiatric system'!" [Entry made on the daily movement sheet by an ASW in outer London, relating to an S135 warrant about to be used to gain entry to the candidate patient's property]

In Chapter 3 I reviewed previous research undertaken in the USA (Emerson & Pollner, 1975) and the UK (Bean, 1980) which found mental health professionals to view compulsory admission as what Everett Hughes calls 'dirty work'. Hughes argues that 'dirty work' of some kind is found in all occupations and indeed that "it is hard to imagine an occupation in which one does not appear in certain repeated contingencies to be practically compelled to play a role of which he ought to be a little ashamed of morally" (Hughes, 1971). Emerson and Pollner (1975) investigated the process of compulsory detention by US psychiatric emergency teams, and found that in portraying such interventions as 'dirty work', to outsiders (e.g. researchers) and each other, practitioners invoke their organisational goals. In other words, displaying the morally dubious and *anomalous* nature of (in my terms) the 'policeman/jailer' role allows practitioners to communicate what they are *really* in the business of doing; that is, some kind of caring or social support role in which shared decision-making is the norm.

As the quotes at the head of this section indicate, such views and communication processes were prevalent. Indeed, it was quite common for ASWs to describe to me the constraints and moral difficulties they had experienced during assessments, for example:

> "I really hated doing it [MHA assessment followed by S3 admission] - even though it was done with humanity etc. At the time I was feeling 'I don't believe in doing this', even though it was legally okay." [ASW, outer London]

The fieldwork indicated that practitioners can find the compulsory admission of elderly people particularly difficult and "poignant". An elderly person with dementia may, for example, experience the process as both a 'humiliation' ("Don't let the neighbours see") and as part of the slide towards a complete loss of independence. An example of this is summarised below.

Box 9.8: Summary of Assessment 16 (inner London)

Elsie was sectioned in her flat, where she had been living with her husband. Up to this point, she and her husband had not spent a night apart for more than 40 years. The process of assessment was highly traumatic for all involved. The candidate patient's husband refused to let the assessment team in and barricaded the front door. Some hours later, after the assessment had finally been undertaken and both medical recommendations had been signed, the husband refused to let his wife be taken to hospital. The police had to be called in by the ASW to enforce the decision, and to make sure the candidate patient made it into the ambulance that was waiting outside. After a short stay on a psychiatric ward, Elsie was transferred to a nursing home. Her husband joined her there soon after.

Also problematic are cases involving people being admitted to hospital for the first time. Part of the problem with such admissions, and why it is "difficult [for ASWs] to feel good about them", emanates from the unpredictable outcome of their first spell of in-patient care. There tends to be less uncertainty for 'revolving door' clients.

Views on the nature and moral implications of MHA work were very mixed. When discussing the 'dirty work' hypothesis with an inner-London ASW, she commented:

> "This is something I feel very strongly about… I've never had a problem exercising my authority. The most authoritative things we can do as social workers are, one, taking children into care and, two, sectioning people under the Mental Health Act." [ASW, inner London]

Nonetheless, MHA assessments resulting in compulsory admission were certainly never portrayed by ASWs as their preferred type of work - they come a long way down that list. But is this because they perceive it to be 'dirty work', or are other factors now involved? In the busy inner-London teams, it seemed to be as much due to the extra work and voluminous paperwork generated by these assessments as it was to moral implications they have for the practitioner.

In my earlier discussion of the member validation techniques used in this study (see Chapter 4), I referred to the concern some ASWs expressed about how this discussion about 'dirty work' makes them appear in print. I should clarify a few points about this. First, no ASW or other practitioner actually used the term 'dirty work' to describe what they do. I use the term to convey the sense of it being 'dirty work... but somebody's got to do it'. Second, portraying assessments this way bears no reflection on the humane qualities of the ASW concerned. For example, the ASW who described himself on the daily movement sheet as a "stormtrooper of the psychiatric system" (see above) - with heavy irony, it must be stressed - was a palpably caring professional. But the key point is that it was the very seriousness and *solemnity* with which he and his colleagues conducted MHA assessments that made the extraordinary nature of this work clear. Indeed it would have been far more surprising, even shocking, to find such work undertaken or described in a matter-of-fact way, with no acknowledgement made of its morally dubious dimension. It certainly can be argued that arranging the detention of a person who does not wish to be detained, possibly on an unsafe ward and on medication with unpleasant side-effects, *should* cause the practitioners to occasionally pause for thought - even in situations where they feel the law compels them to act in a certain way. And third, despite such considerations, ASWs and other practitioners often see compulsory admission as a positive outcome, even though the process itself might be difficult. One example of this is where they can help a person 'ahead of time'.

9.10.1 The meaning of a "good piece of work"

While ASWs may derive some satisfaction from having done "a difficult job well" they rarely portray MHA assessments which end in a section as having been "a good piece of work" - regardless of how well they had been managed. This designation tends to be reserved for interventions involving the use of therapeutic and social work skills to create a tenable social situation for the candidate patient, such that hospitalisation is avoided. Particularly valued was work that "broke the cycle", or repeated pattern, of compulsory admission for 'revolving door' clients.

ASWs quite commonly presented compulsory admission as having been the "least-worst option", and the process as "the best we could [have done] under the circumstances":

> "[The night-time assessment followed by an S2 admission] was not ideal practice. First, the patient was seen separately by the two doctors [instead of at the same time, which is

preferred]. Second, the patient was disturbed by the assessment process. Third, I didn't escort the patient to hospital. And fourth there was no contact with the nearest relative [who lived abroad]... Objectively you could say it was bad practice, but subjectively I would say we did the best we could under the circumstances." [ASW, Emergency Duty Team in inner London]

Very occasionally, however, MHA assessments are portrayed by the co-ordinating ASW as having been a "good piece of work". The following example indicates how, in unplanned 'crisis' assessments, value is placed on deploying *social work* skills to help relatives of a person who is in crisis.

Box 9.9: MHA assessment thought by ASW to be a "good piece of work"

The case

An out-of-hours assessment where a woman, non-UK, turned up at a police station in central London, very confused, with two young children in tow. She asked the police to shoot her and take her children. She was unable to remember her name, address or any other identifying information. The ASW worked with another social worker on the case. The mother was admitted under Section 2 of the MHA.

Why 'good work'?

{Why do you see this as having been a good piece of work?}

"Because it was a good piece of social work. We helped her children and the police. The two doctors were sensitive with the mother. We involved the eldest child, letting him know what was happening, saying that they would be looked after tonight and taken to see their mother the next day." [ASW, inner London]

This indicates that perceptions of the nature of MHA assessments vary according to the institutional context in which they are undertaken. For instance, those undertaken with 'unknown' clients in crisis situations will have different perceived 'quality criteria' than those undertaken with existing service users. This is partly because Emergency Duty Team workers, for example, generally make "narrower" decisions out-of-hours than do community teams who have more resources at their disposal:

> "Don't forget, we only look at fairly extreme cases, emergencies, so people are more likely to get sectioned anyway. The decision for us is much narrower, we only have access to hospitals… You can't say, like community teams, 'Oh we'll send a CPN round'. The decision is essentially whether to section or not." [ASW, Emergency Duty Team in inner London]

In conclusion, it seems that the 'dirty work' view of MHA assessments has changed in certain institutional contexts. It remains prevalent, but the shorter hospital stays associated with developments in community-based mental health care mean that compulsory admissions are more likely to seen as part of a longer process of revolving door admissions - a cycle which good social work, as part of a multi-disciplinary team approach, might be able to help to break. Arguably there is less a sense of compulsory admission being an 'end-point' or failure than there was at the time when the earlier research was conducted (Emerson & Pollner, 1975; Bean, 1980). It seems plausible that the 'dirty work' view of MHA assessments has been diluted as a result of such developments, particularly in busy inner-city teams where concerns about workload are paramount. This analysis shows the importance of understanding MHA assessments in their specific institutional context - something which in any given situation is constituted of organisational resources and constraints (e.g. bed availability and levels of community resources) and the prevailing treatment ideology (e.g. pragmatism). Both of these factors may have a decisive influence on whether a tenable situation can be created for a candidate patient instead of an admission to hospital.

9.11 Discussion

People on the receiving end of a compulsory admission to hospital often experience it as a fateful moment in their lives. This is especially the case for first admissions where individuals may for the first time experience the stigma of being labelled mentally ill. Disruption to the person's lifestyle is exacerbated by some of the financial and other implications of being sectioned (e.g. rent arrears, loss of an employment scheme place). While some people ultimately come to view such disruption in a positive light, others may experience it far more negatively, for example as an escalation of their treatment career.

In this chapter I have attempted to describe how mental health legislation is applied in real-life situations, focusing on the experiences and multiple roles of a key participant: the Approved Social Worker. Conducted in a spirit of understanding rather than evaluation, the research has attempted to shed some light on how the world actually is in such assessments rather than how it ought to be (for example, as described in the Code of Practice). A key benefit of using observational methods, alongside interviews, comes from their capacity to identify the mundane but often crucially important improvisational skills of practitioners, who are operating in the face of multiple contingencies and in the context of organisational constraints. Observational studies such as this are well-suited to making these skills visible; not only to outsiders, but also to the practitioners themselves who may take them for granted.

The findings presented in this chapter indicate the time-consuming nature of MHA assessments, and the considerable skills required by

ASWs to pull them off. ASWs evidently have a significant stock of knowledge that extends well beyond their knowledge of the Act itself. Many roles can be adopted by, or cast upon, the ASW in any given MHA assessment. This research indicates that, in certain contexts, ASWs value moving outside of their legal-bureaucratic role through using social work or psycho-therapeutic skills. It also appeared that the social worker role was valued by the candidate patient, especially if it resulted in the creation of a tenable social situation as an alternative to hospital admission. Fieldwork observations suggested that the 'social worker' identity was generally more diluted among the extremely busy and 'stressed out' inner-London ASWs; it was certainly less commonly invoked in assessments. This is arguably because of their 'pragmatic' approach, arising in part from heavy caseloads and the perceived lack of realistic alternatives to in-patient care.

The multiple roles of the ASW, identified in the research, are a cause for some concern for social work practice. While there was much evidence of ASWs handling role-tensions skilfully and sensitively, the multiplicity of their roles clearly has the potential to (a) cause confusion in the minds of people being assessed, and (b) undermine trust, and damage the possibility of future therapeutic relationships. Tensions between the roles of 'advocate' for the patient and legal 'applicant' (where the ASW signs the papers to enact a decision the patient evidently does not want) has the potential to be particularly confusing. These findings support proposals for an advocate or representative of the candidate patient to be introduced into the assessment procedure, to the extent that this role cannot be plausibly performed by an ASW attached to the mental health team responsible for their care.

In conclusion, this chapter has focused on the exceptions to the rule (or at least the ideal) of shared decision-making in psychiatric practice. My argument is that these episodes of coercion represent, for service users, the *defining moments* in their relationships with psychiatrists and other mental health professionals. These contrast with the defining moments for psychiatrists, who perhaps view the moments when trust is achieved to be more significant (see Chapter 5). But there seems little doubt that the impact of a coercive episode on the patient can be profound, for three main reasons. First, the assessment process itself can be highly traumatic (see section 9.8 above). Second, the ward onto which the patient is admitted may be unsafe and untherapeutic (see Chapters 3 & 7). And third, methods of deception may have been used to pre-empt or overcome patient non-cooperation. Such deception is perhaps understandable from the team's point of view (the more benign forms of it, at least), but it can undermine trust, and jeopardise future relationships with mental health professionals. Indeed the patient may be inclined to conceal clinically relevant information from them during their hospital stay (see Chapter 8) and after discharge, for example in follow-up outpatient consultations (Chapters 5 & 6). It seems plausible that this will be most likely for the significant proportion of patients who retrospectively view their compulsory admission as having been neither beneficial nor justified (Katsakou & Priebe, 2006), including some for whom a tenable community situation could not be created as an alternative to hospital admission, because of a lack of community resources. At a time when NHS Trusts are cutting back on staffing levels in community mental health teams, due to a fiscal crisis, it is not difficult to envisage how this will create further obstacles to shared decision-making in psychiatric practice.

Chapter 10

Summary & conclusions

CONTENTS

10.1 Summary of findings

This book has brought together findings from three qualitative, observational studies to identify obstacles to the use of shared decision-making in modern psychiatric practice. Particular attention has been paid to how patients' choices about their treatment are facilitated or constrained by the actions of mental health professionals. Shared decision-making is characterised by the involvement of at least two participants (doctor and patient), information sharing by both parties, consensus-building about the preferred treatment, and the reaching of an explicit agreement on the treatment to be implemented (Charles *et al*, 1997). This book holds numerous examples of decision-making that fall outside of this model. Examples include where:

1. the patient walks out of a ward round, leaving the clinical team to make a unilateral treatment decision (see section 8.3.1)
2. relevant information is not shared, either by the doctor (who delivers the barest minimum of information on a drug's side effects - see 5.4), or the patient (who deliberately conceals clinically-relevant information – see 8.3.2)
3. pressure is applied by the psychiatrist such that an explicit agreement is reached (thus satisfying one criterion for shared decision-making), but not in a way that will have been experienced by participants as 'consensus building' (5.4).

There are two fundamental obstacles to the use of shared decision-making in everyday psychiatric practice. The first is that the unfolding doctor-patient relationship is constituted of a series of encounters, in some of which the patient's ability to make rational decisions is explicitly in question. In a crisis situation the psychiatrist may choose not to initiate shared decision-making, or may abort it, if the patient is considered to be too ill to make decisions that are in their own or others' best interests. This results in interactions that are fundamentally asymmetrical.

The second obstacle is that decision-making quite often occurs in contexts where the underlying threat of compulsion is difficult for participants to ignore. This 'elephant in the room' represents a problem for psychiatry as a profession, because it distances psychiatry from the rest of medicine. It is also presents a problem for individual practitioners, because it inhibits their ability to build therapeutic alliances with patients and distorts decision-making (see 3.4.2).

The analyses in Chapters 5 & 6 indicate that the outpatient consultation is a comparatively 'democratic' decision-making forum. Medication decisions were typically highly negotiated, with patients getting the outcome they wanted about as often as psychiatrists did. All decision sequences resulted in some sort of verbal contract, and there were no coerced decision outcomes, forced through against the patient's will. This may suggest that these were equally poised, balanced encounters. However, close inspection of a number of the decision sequences revealed a 'spectrum of pressure' in negotiated decision-making, with 'open' decisions at one end, 'pressure' decisions at the other, and 'directed' decisions in between. The analysis helps to explain why some shared decisions are experienced as considerably less 'shared' than others.

Communicating in outpatient consultations about the potentially difficult issue of adherence to long-term anti-psychotic prescribing poses risks to the immediate 'here and now' interaction, and the longer-term therapeutic relationship. The analysis in Chapter 6 revealed some of the ways in which psychiatrists and patients work together to make talking about non-compliance something that is less immediately threatening to 'face' (Goffman, 1959) and to the therapeutic alliance more generally.

Chapter 7 presented the argument that today's acute psychiatric wards are better understood as permeable institutions rather than closed or total institutions. While the total institution model remains valuable, my contention is that it fails to capture the highly permeable nature of the psychiatric institutions I studied. Future analysts may therefore find the permeable institution a more helpful ideal type against which to examine and compare empirical cases. Perhaps most helpful is to conceive of a continuum of institutional permeability with total and permeable institutions at each extreme.

The move from outpatient consultations to ward rounds produces a very different picture of psychiatric practice. Chapter 8 examined patients' methods of non-cooperation and resistance, which communicate that the patient is not cooperating with the decision-making process, or is resisting being guided or coerced into choosing the clinical team's preferred treatment option. This is discussed further below.

The move from the ward round to the MHA assessment transforms the picture of psychiatric practice further still. In Chapter 9 I argued that assessments for compulsory admission to hospital are the exceptions to the rule (or at least ideal) of shared decision-making in psychiatric practice, and that these encounters symbolise its breakdown. My contention is that that these episodes of coercion represent for service users their defining moments in their relationships with psychiatrists and other mental health professionals. These contrast with the defining moments of psychiatrists, who perhaps view the moments when trust is achieved to be more significant. This analysis helps to explain why psychiatrists are able to maintain a self image as being committed to a 'kind', empathetic approach in which shared decision-making is the ideal, while being experienced by a proportion of patients as providing a fundamentally controlling and sometimes 'cruel' treatment regime.

The following two sections combine, compare and contrast findings from the three studies. The typology of the pressures exerted on patients, presented in section 10.2 below, extends the earlier 'spectrum of pressure' (Chapter 5) by incorporating coercion. Section 10.3 presents a typology of patients' methods of non-cooperation and resistance in decision-making.

10.2 Pressures exerted on patients

Existing research literature, reviewed in Chapter 3, indicates that there are degrees of pressure and coercion exerted on patients in psychiatric encounters. Prior to the present study, there was little available for the use of more subtle forms of pressure and manipulation in *shared* decision-making.

The typology presented below encompasses decision-making in both routine encounters and crisis situations.

Table 10.1: Pressures exerted on patients in psychiatric practice

TYPE OF PRESSURE	EXAMPLES
Self-regulation by the service user, in the context of concordant healthcare relationships. The obligation for responsible self-monitoring is achieved through making the patient accountable for decisions made jointly with their doctor	• Psychiatrist and patient construct a situation of 'equipoise' (Gwyn & Elwyn, 1999) in which the patient is free to choose (see section 5.3) • Patients' reports of partial or non-adherence to prescribing are accepted/endorsed by the psychiatrist (6.4)
Tactful manipulation in decision-making, where the patient cooperates with being directed/ steered into choosing the psychiatrist's 'preferred'	• The patient is steered into choosing a different anti-psychotic to replace one that is causing him to experience seizures (5.4)

treatment option	
Pressured decision-making, where the patient actively resists the decision-making being steered toward a 'disprefered' treatment option. This can result in the psychiatrist 'backing off' or 'pressing on', or it may result in 'stalemate' (the adjacent column holds examples of each)	• In response to the patient's accusation that he is trying to "drug [her] up", the psychiatrist 'backs off' from attempting to persuade her to take anti-psychotic medication (5.5.1) • Despite patient resistance, the psychiatrist 'presses on' to elicit the patient's agreement to try a different anti-psychotic (5.5.2) • An inpatient successfully resists agreeing to have his anti-psychotic administered by injection before going on leave from hospital (8.3.3)
Veiled coercion, where the patient is deceived into believing that they are not being manipulated or coerced, although this may become apparent after the event	• A patient sectioned on a general ward is told by the psychiatrist she is being "moved to a nicer ward" (9.9) • To persuade a reluctant patient into the ambulance waiting outside to take her to hospital under section, the patient is told not to worry because she would be "home later" (9.9) • Nursing staff on an acute ward go to great lengths to 'persuade' a non-compliant patient to take her meds (8.1.1)

Overt coercion, where the patient is knowingly admitted into hospital against their will	• Compulsory admission to hospital under mental health legislation - see Chapter 9.

In the context of a therapeutic alliance, an episode of coercion can undermine trust and compromise shared decision-making in the future. Mental health professionals have three main opportunities to minimise such damage. The first is while the episode of coercion is in progress. For example, we have seen that an ASW may adopt a 'bureaucratic' role in the MHA assessment, thus conveying that they are 'following the rules' and that what they are doing is 'nothing personal' (see 9.5). In other words, coercion can be done such that a patient will understand (either at the time or later on) that the mental health professionals had *themselves* been compelled to act in the way that they did. Second, damage can be prevented or minimised by actions beforehand. Psychiatrists in our earlier interview study (Seale *et* al, 2006) spoke of how they sometimes discussed with patients in advance about when coercion might be necessary, agreeing a kind of informal 'advance directive'. And third, after the event and once the patient is considered to have regained competence, mental health professionals may attempt to reverse the damage done, by allowing the patient full participation in decision-making (ibid).

From the mental health professional's point of view, the deliberate veiling of the coercive nature of a MHA assessment may have short-term benefits, but it also carries risks for the longer term. Veiled coercion is typically aimed at facilitating a smoother assessment process, by pre-empting or minimising patient anxiety and resistance (see Chapter 9). While it may achieve these goals, it risks causing patient resentment and mistrust in the future and obstructing professional endeavours to develop or maintain a future trusting relationship with the client. Indeed, interviews with newly admitted patients (Bennett *et al*, 1993) found that deceit on the part of others was reported only rarely, but it evoked strong reactions when it was perceived to have occurred (for further discussion, see Chapter 3).

This underlines a recurrent theme; that the meaning of any contribution to interaction is dependent on more than just the local context of its production (the standard CA 'line'), it also needs to be considered in the context of the unfolding doctor-patient relationship.

10.3 Non-cooperation with decision-making

Chapter 8 described three techniques of non-cooperation and resistance used by patients in ward round decisions. The typology shown below has been expanded to include a method that is used more easily in community settings.

Table 10.2: Types of non-cooperation with treatment decision-making

TYPE OF NON-COOPERATION	EXAMPLES
Refusal to participate in decision-making, involving overt resistance by the patient	• Refusing to attend a ward round or walking out halfway through (see section 8.3.1) • Refusing to open the door to an MHA assessment team (9.2)
Avoidance of decision-making, involving covert resistance	• Deliberately 'forgetting' to attend an outpatient consultation (5.1) • Pretending to be asleep, or hiding away from surveillance space, to avoid attending a ward round (8.3.1) • Hiding in the local community or moving out of the area in order to avoid being assessed for compulsory admission to hospital (9.2)
Concealment of clinically-relevant information, in order to mislead the clinical team into thinking the patient is better than s/he	• Giving minimal responses to questions asked in a ward round, which is heard as concealment by the clinical team (8.3.2) • During an MHA assessment,

actually is	responding "That's a secret" when asked about use of medication (9.4.1)
Expressive discordance, where the patient explicitly rejects his/her diagnosis, psychiatric definitions of the problem, or specific proposals for treatment	• Staying within psychiatric discourse to argue against specific treatment proposals and suggestions by the clinical team (8.3.3)

The analysis of non-cooperation in Chapter 8 emphasised the importance of considering the institutional context in which treatment decisions are made. As noted, an acute ward is a place in which the patient's capacity to make rational decisions is in question, which means that expressive discordance is a risky manoeuvre because it is easily attributed to a lack of 'insight'.

Patients have two options for excluding themselves from ward rounds. They can either overtly refuse to take part, or avoid being called in. Once included, they have a further two options, either to give away as little about themselves as possible (concealment) or refuse to agree to what the clinical team evidently thinks is best (expressive discordance). In contrast, in MHA assessments the candidate patient's first line of defence is typically to try to keep the assessment team at arm's length (i.e. avoidance). Once 'caught up with', they can refuse to open the door to the team, or if they do they may try to 'hold it together' for the duration of the assessment (concealment). This underlines a second recurrent theme: the different types of non-cooperation described above are likely to be observed across psychiatric settings, although the specific form they take is constrained by the interactional circumstances in which they occur.

10.4 Implications

Psychiatric practice

Patients are likely to take medication effectively if they have been involved in discussions about treatment options, and understand and support the decision about what is prescribed (Drew *et al*, 2001). It is therefore important to understand how the communicative choices made by health professionals impact upon the quality of interactions in general and of patient participation in particular. Psychiatrists rarely get to see how their consultant colleagues attempt a shared approach to decision-making or how they communicate with patients about adherence. Observational studies such as the ones reported here offer a rare opportunity to examine practitioners' interactional skills, while also stressing the importance of the patient's contribution to the interaction. Such findings could fruitfully be fed into training and continuing professional development for psychiatrists, for example on how to deliver information on side effects or how to address treatment compliance.

The Mental Health Act (2007) removed the ASW role and replaced it with that of the 'Approved Mental Health Practitioner' (see Chapter 3). Findings from the MHA study are still relevant to these practitioners because they are likely to face similar challenges and role tensions to those experienced by ASWs. The inclusion of these research findings into training courses would be beneficial.

Research methodology

Two very different versions of qualitative research are reported in this book: ethnography and conversation analysis. 'Meaning' was central to the write-up of each set of findings, however while the analytic focus of the ethnographies was 'insider' knowledge and meanings, in the CA study it was on the activities that make those meanings possible in the first place. The methodological contribution of the book stems from its demonstration of how to produce a coherent, unified research account from different forms of qualitative inquiry. Despite the potential for analytic inconsistency, I believe that the book has far greater force and persuasiveness as a result of the attempt to combine, compare and contrast findings from three studies.

Sociological theory

I have argued that a sound theoretical base for sociological research may be created by combining Goffman's micro-sociology with Foucault's analyses of disciplinary power/knowledge. A Goffmanian 'home base' was adopted for this, with Foucauldian thinking applied to add a historical, 'macro' dimension. Foucault's work also provides the conceptual tools for examining the more subtle form of control through expertise that would be missed in a purely Goffmanian study. Other ways of combining their work were reviewed in Chapter 2.

10.5 Future research

There is much potential for extending the use of qualitative, observational research methods to shed further light into the 'black box' of de-institutionalised mental healthcare. Pragmatically, I see possibilities for undertaking further analyses of the enormous amount of data generated for the Prescribing Decisions Project. One option would be to examine the role of family carers in routine outpatient consultations, another to study how information about suicide risk is elicited, delivered and responded to. New CA research could be undertaken to investigate how psychological therapies are delivered in practice.

The MHA study was conducted 16 years after the enactment of the Mental Health Act 1983. The MHA study presented here could be repeated to evaluate the 2007 Act, quite feasibly with a similar methodology and in the same local authority areas. This would create a fascinating opportunity to compare how assessment decisions are made under different legal frameworks. Such work could inform the development of the code of practice.

10.6 Limitations

No real attempt has been made to analyse the many documents gathered during the course of the three studies, which included photographs of one of the acute wards, handwritten notes from service users, NHS leaflets describing the organisations where I did my research, administrative materials, and so on. This omission is partly due to the fact I already had plenty of data, in the form of field-notes and transcripts of consultations and interviews. But it is partly attributable to my lack of experience in analysing texts. Other researchers would have been able to make better use of these resources.

Unfortunately, most of my relationships with users/patients were all too fleeting. Some of the people I observed being sectioned I never saw again, and the short stays patients have on acute wards made it very difficult for me to get to know them and earn their trust (see

4.7). The result is an account in which the user's voice is less prominent than I would have liked, as compared with those of the ASW and psychiatrist.

Finally, the emphasis in much of the analysis has been on how pressure is applied on service users, which could give the misleading impression that the pressure applied is all one way. New analyses of the Prescribing Decisions Project data are required to identify the pressures exerted on psychiatrists in decision-making and how these are resisted. It would be fascinating to establish the degree of overlap between psychiatrists' and service users' methods for achieving their goals in these encounters.

Appendices

Appendix A

The following transcription conventions have been adapted from Heritage and Maynard (2007).

C, P: patient (P)	*Speaker identification*: Consultant psychiatrist (C);
[overlap]	*Brackets*: Onset and offset of overlapping talk
=	*Equal sign*: Utterances are latched or ran together, with no gap of silence
-	*Hyphen*: Preceding sound is cut off/self-interrupted
(0.4)	*Timed pause*: Silence measured in seconds and tenths of seconds
(.)	*Parentheses with a full-stop*: A micro-pause of less than 0.2 seconds
:	*Colon(s)*: Preceding sound is extended or stretched; the more the longer
£word£	*Pound sign:* Talk is produced while smiling
↑word↓	*Up arrow/down arrow*: Increased pitch relative to surrounding talk
↓word↑	*Down arrow/up arrow*: Decreased pitch relative to surrounding talk
.	*Full stop*: Falling or terminal intonation
,	*Comma*: Continuing or slightly rising intonation
?	Rising intonation
underline	*Underlining*: Increase volume relative to surrounding talk
°soft°	*Degree signs*: Decreased volume relative to surrounding talk
›fast‹	*Greater-than/less-than signs*: Increased pace relative to surrounding talk
‹slow›	*Less-than/greater-than signs*: Decreased pace relative to surrounding talk
˙h	*Superscripted full-stop preceding h's*: Inbreaths; the more the longer
h	*H's*: Outbreaths; the more the longer
hah/heh	*Laugh token*: Relative open or closed position of laughter

(doubt)	*Filled single parentheses*: Transcriptionist doubt about talk
((Cough))	*Filled double parentheses*: Scenic detail/event/sound not easily transcribed

Appendix B

INFORMATION SHEET FOR PATIENTS (OBSERVATION)

TITLE OF PROJECT:

Life on an acute psychiatric ward

INFORMATION:

The Royal College of Psychiatrists is currently investigating what life is like on acute psychiatric wards, focusing on what it feels like to be a patient. At the end of the study a report will be written which will include recommendations for improving psychiatric in-patient care. The focus will be on patients' views about this.

The research will involve Alan Quirk, the researcher, spending time on this ward in order to find out (a) what life here is like, and (b) people's views about the time they have spent here. He will be observing what goes on and chatting to, or occasionally interviewing, some patients and staff. The research is also being carried out in two other wards so that comparisons can be made between the treatment and care that is available.

You can, at any time, refuse consent to allow him to be present in a situation or refuse to be directly involved in the study. Basically, if you want to be left alone let Alan or a member of staff know, and he will respect your wishes. Anything you do say to him will be CONFIDENTIAL; the study is anonymous with no names ever being used, and nothing you say will be reported back to any professionals involved in your care. (The only exceptions to this are, obviously, if there are issues of self-harm or risk to others.)

Your agreement would be greatly appreciated but please note that if you refuse, your health care will not be affected in anyway. If you have any queries at any time about this study, please contact:

Alan Quirk
Royal College of Psychiatrists' Research Unit
83 Victoria Street
London SW1H OHW
Phone: (020) 7227 0831

Appendix C

MHA Study: Topics guide for follow-up interviews with candidate patients

Note: the guide was updated after 2 interviews. The square bullet points denote the five new topics that were added at this point.

Topics

- ▪ Talked about MHA assessment/hospital with anyone else (prof or social)?
- ▪ What's been happening since time in hospital/the assessment?
- What happened and how felt about it?
  - -Why brought into hospital back in [xxx month]?
  - -Did it feel like an 'assessment'?
- Lay beliefs/perceptions of 'illness'
  - -Did doctors say anything the matter with you? Views on that.
- Help-seeking
  - -What happened before assessment/hospital?
  - -Did you feel you needed help? If so, what?
  - -Active attempts to avoid being seen by profs?
  - *[Hypothesis on service use influences: (a) Is view of illness same as profs? (b) cohesive social group? (c) improved personal knowledge?]*
- Views on medication
  - -Being prescribed any medicine (before/after assessment)?
  - -Side effects? Views?
  - -Non-compliance in build up to assessment?
- Views on ward
  - -Any expectations? Previous experience?
  - -How was it actually?
  - *[Hypothesis: influence of perceived quality of care on sectioning]*
- Views of profs' role(s)
  - -Which profs were there? What for?

[Hypothesis: Whose side is the ASW on? Tensions between roles etc.]

- Involvement of relatives
  - -Views? Sense of betrayal? Grateful now?
- Lifestyle
  - -Before/after assessment?
  - -Has the assessment changed things? If so, how?
- Person-specific questions

Appendix D

Teams involved in the MHA Study

Local authority 1 (outer-London)

Social Work Team A

- SETTING: A stand-alone building in the grounds of an old psychiatric hospital.
- STAFF: A team of approximately nine social workers (mostly ASWs) plus administrative workers. Members of the 'crisis team' rotate on a daily basis (see below).
- REMIT: Includes the provision of MHA assessments as required.
- OPERATING HOURS: MHA assessments conducted via a 24-hour crisis service. Social workers and other crisis team personnel work 9 a.m. to 5 p.m. Out-of-hours work is conducted by the same staff, organised by a rota system.
- ASSESSMENT PROCEDURES/TEAMS: The majority of MHA assessments are preceded by a visit from the crisis team. The crisis team is comprised of a social worker (usually an ASW), CPN and a doctor (generally not S12 approved). A crisis assessment is not an MHA assessment: the aim is often to explore whether this is actually necessary. When an MHA assessment is indicated, the ASW stays on to finish the task while appropriate personnel are brought in. Telephone referrals are taken by a full-time, office-based crisis co-ordinator (weekdays only). His or her responsibility includes co-ordinating the crisis visit, for example arranging when staff can attend, gathering and passing on information and liasing with the candidate patient.

Social Work Team B

- SETTING: Offices in the psychiatric unit of a general hospital.
- STAFF: A team of approximately 14 social workers (mostly ASWs) plus administrative workers. Members of the 'crisis team' rotate on a daily basis.
- REMIT: Includes the provision of MHA assessments as required.

- OPERATING HOURS: As in Social Work Team A.
- ASSESSMENT PROCEDURES/TEAMS: As is Social Work Team A.

Local authority 2 (inner-London)

Community Mental Health Team A

- SETTING: A stand-alone building in the community which houses care managers/social workers, health workers (psychiatrists, CPNs, psychologists) and administrative staff
- STAFF: A team which includes a total of approximately 18 care managers (mostly ASWs) covering two health localities, plus health personnel. An integrated social services/health duty team processes and allocates urgent referrals. It is typically staffed by a full-time supervisor and full-time S12 doctor, plus three Care Managers and two CPNs on weekly rotation. Calls for statutory assessments are passed to ASWs to arrange.
- REMIT: Includes the provision of MHA assessments as required.
- OPERATING HOURS: From 9 a.m. to 5p.m. weekdays. Out-of-hours assessments are covered by a separate team and the Emergency Duty Team (discussed below).
- ASSESSMENT PROCEDURES/TEAMS: Each morning the duty team meets to discuss referrals and share out tasks. Individual ASWs initially co-ordinate statutory assessments from their duty office base, e.g. organising attendance of doctors and the police. Where possible, MHA assessments involving allocated cases are organised by the person's care manager.

Community Mental Health Team B

- SETTING: A stand-alone community building which houses care managers/social workers, health workers and administrative staff.
- STAFF: A team which includes approximately six care managers (mostly ASWs) plus health personnel. Calls to the duty team are shared, with a care manager taking them in the morning and a CPN taking them in the afternoon. An ASW is always available for statutory assessments.
- REMIT: Includes the provision of MHA assessments as required.

- OPERATING HOURS: From 9 a.m. to 5 p.m. weekdays. Out-of-hours assessments are covered by a separate team and the Emergency Duty Team (described below).
- ASSESSMENT PROCEDURES/TEAMS: The duty worker will initiate the build-up to a statutory assessment when it is indicated. This may entail passing the referral straight away to an ASW, e.g. when the care manager on duty is not an ASW. The ASW typically organises the assessment from the office. As in CMHT A, allocated cases are co-ordinated by the person's care manager where possible.

Emergency Duty Team

- SETTING: Staff tend to work from home until they receive the first referral. They typically use the team's office in a local authority building during part of their shift, e.g. to type up reports.
- STAFF: One social worker (ASW) per shift, drawn from a team of approximately five. Each shift lasts either 16 hours (weekdays) or 24 hours (weekends)
- REMIT: Unlike in the teams above, the ASW also deals with other emergency social work referrals (e.g. Children and Families) and not just mental health. The EDT shares out-of-hours work in LA 2 with the local Out of Hours team (not directly involved in the research). Its workers provide back-up when the other team is operating (i.e. up to late-evening and limited hours at the weekend) and full cover when it is not.
- OPERATING HOURS: From 5 p.m. to 9 a.m. weekdays, plus weekends.
- ASSESSMENT TEAM/PROCEDURE: Referrals are taken by a 'night duty operator' who pages the social worker. The latter phones though at the earliest opportunity for further information. The ASW then co-ordinates and undertakes any necessary assessment.

Appendix E

NUD*IST index tree: coding frame for MHA Study qualitative data

(1)	/FACTS
(1 1)	/FACTS/Area
(1 1 1)	/FACTS/Area/Hosp SW team A (LA 1)
(1 1 2)	/FACTS/Area/Hosp SW team B (LA 1)
(1 1 3)	/FACTS/Area/CMHT A (LA 2)
(1 1 4)	/FACTS/Area/CMHT B (LA 2)
(1 1 5)	/FACTS/Area/EDT (LA 2)
(1 2)	/FACTS/Setting
(1 2 1)	/FACTS/Setting/Police statn
(1 2 2)	/FACTS/Setting/Psych hosp
(1 2 3)	/FACTS/Setting/Community
(1 2 4)	/FACTS/Setting/Other (S'tng)
(1 3)	/FACTS/Outcome
(1 3 1)	/FACTS/Outcome/s2
(1 3 2)	/FACTS/Outcome/s3
(1 3 3)	/FACTS/Outcome/s4
(1 3 4)	/FACTS/Outcome/Inf admissn
(1 3 5)	/FACTS/Outcome/Other (Otcm)
(1 4)	/FACTS/Gender
(1 4 1)	/FACTS/Gender/Male
(1 4 2)	/FACTS/Gender/Female
(1 5)	/FACTS/Ethnicity
(1 5 1)	/FACTS/Ethnicity/White Brit
(1 5 2)	/FACTS/Ethnicity/Other (Ethy)
(1 6)	/FACTS/Age
(1 6 1)	/FACTS/Age/16 - 34 yrs
(1 6 2)	/FACTS/Age/35 - 64 yrs
(1 6 3)	/FACTS/Age/65+ yrs
(1 7)	/FACTS/Type data
(1 7 1)	/FACTS/Type data/Field note (assessment)
(1 7 2)	/FACTS/Type data/Field note (other)
(1 7 3)	/FACTS/Type data/Interview (taped)
(2)	/SECTIONS

(2 1)	/SECTIONS/Setting
(2 2)	/SECTIONS/Field relns
(2 3)	/SECTIONS/Documents
(2 4)	/SECTIONS/Methodology
(2 5)	/SECTIONS/Services & procedures
(2 6)	/SECTIONS/Lingo
(2 7)	/SECTIONS/Analysis
(3)	/METHODOLOGY
(3 1)	/METHODOLOGY/Access
(3 1 1)	/METHODOLOGY/Access/Access - LA 1
(3 1 2)	/METHODOLOGY/Access/Access - LA 2
(3 1 3)	/METHODOLOGY/Access/Access - Case spec
(3 2)	/METHODOLOGY/Sampling
(3 3)	/METHODOLOGY/Data collection
(3 4)	/METHODOLOGY/Analysis
(3 5)	/METHODOLOGY/Field relations
(4)	/ISSUES
(4 1)	/ISSUES/Rich,poor
(4 2)	/ISSUES/Ward cond
(4 3)	/ISSUES/Team support
(4 4)	/ISSUES/ASW roles
(4 5)	/ISSUES/Prof roles
(4 6)	/ISSUES/Prof relations
(4 7)	/ISSUES/ASW accountable
(4 8)	/ISSUES/Rights balancing
(4 9)	/ISSUES/Ideology
(4 10)	/ISSUES/Peer support
(4 11)	/ISSUES/Good work
(4 12)	/ISSUES/Coercion
(4 13)	/ISSUES/Relative
(4 14)	/ISSUES/Identity
(4 15)	/ISSUES/Resources
(4 16)	/ISSUES/Section 25
(4 17)	/ISSUES/Section 135
(4 18)	/ISSUES/Section 136
(4 19)	/ISSUES/Misc
(5)	/SERVICES
(5 1)	/SERVICES/Hosp SW team A (LA 1)

(5 1 1) /SERVICES/Hosp SW team A (LA1)/Personnel, roles
(5 1 2) /SERVICES/Hosp SW team A (LA 1)/Serv context
(5 2) /SERVICES/Hosp SW team B (LA 1)
(5 2 1) /SERVICES/Hosp SW team B (LA 1)/Personnel, roles
(5 2 2) /SERVICES/Hosp SW team B (LA 1)/Serv context
(5 3) /SERVICES/CMHT A (LA 2)
(5 3 1) /SERVICES/CMHT A (LA 2)/Personnel, roles
(5 3 2) /SERVICES/CMHT A (LA 2)/Serv context
(5 4) /SERVICES/CMHT B (LA 2)
(5 4 1) /SERVICES/CMHT B (LA 2)/Personnel, roles
(5 4 2) /SERVICES/CMHT B (LA 2)/Serv context
(5 5) /SERVICES/EDT (LA 2)
(5 5 1) /SERVICES/EDT (LA 2)/Personnel, roles
(5 5 2) /SERVICES/EDT (LA 2)/Serv context
(5 6) /SERVICES/Team meetings (all teams)
(6) /ASSESS PROCESS
(6 1) /ASSESS PROCESS/General,overview,misc
(6 2) /ASSESS PROCESS/Build up
(6 3) /ASSESS PROCESS/Assessment
(6 4) /ASSESS PROCESS/Aftermath
(6 5) /ASSESS PROCESS/Threats
(6 6) /ASSESS PROCESS/Aborted,partial
(6 7) /ASSESS PROCESS/Post-'aftermath'
(7) /PATIENT & CARER
(7 1) /PATIENT & CARER /Illness experience
(7 2) /PATIENT & CARER /Lay beliefs
(7 3) /PATIENT & CARER /Help-seeking
(7 4) /PATIENT & CARER /Section experience
(7 5) /PATIENT & CARER /Section views
(7 6) /PATIENT & CARER /Hospital experience
(7 7) /PATIENT & CARER /Hospital views
(7 8) /PATIENT & CARER /Prof relations
(7 9) /PATIENT & CARER /Social relations
(7 10) /PATIENT & CARER /MHA knowledge
(7 11) /PATIENT & CARER /Medicine
(7 12) /PATIENT & CARER /Lifestyle
(7 13) /PATIENT & CARER /Follow-up

References

Abas, M., Vanderpyl, J., Le Prou, T., *et al.* (2003) Psychiatric hospitalisation: reasons for admission and alternatives to admission in South Auckland, New Zealand. *Australian and New Zealand Journal of Psychiatry*, 37: 620-625.

Alaszewski, A., Alaszewski, H., Ayer, S. & Manthorpe, J. (2000) *Managing Risk in Community Practice: Nursing, Risk and Decision Making.* London: Balliere Tindall.

Anderson, T.F. & Mooney, G. (1990) Medical practice variations: where are we? In T.F. Anderson & G. Mooney (Eds.), *The Challenges of Medical Practice Variations,* pp. 1-15. MacMillan, London.

Armstrong, D. (1983) *Political Anatomy of the Body: medical knowledge in Britain in the twentieth century.* London: Cambridge University Press.

Armstrong, D. (1984) The patient's view. *Social Science and Medicine*, 18 (9): 737-744.

Armstrong, D., Reyburn, H. & Jones, R. (1996) A study of general practitioners' reasons for changing their prescribing behaviour. *British Medical Journal*, 312: 949-52.

Arney, W.R. & Bergen, B.J. (1984) *Medicine and the Management of Living: taming the last great beast.* London: University of Chicago Press.

Atkinson, J.M. & Heritage, J. (1984) Introduction. In, Atkinson JM & Heritage J (eds) *Structures of Social Action: Studies in conversation analysis.* Cambridge: University Press.

Audini, B., Duffet R., Lelliott, P., Pearce, A. & Ayers, C. (1999) Over-occupancy in London's acute psychiatric units - fact or fiction? Psychiatric Bulletin, 23: 590-594.

Babiker, I.E. (1986) Noncompliance in schizophrenia. *Psychiatric Developments,* 4, 329-337.

Barker, S. (2000) *Environmentally Unfriendly: Patients' views of conditions on psychiatric wards.* London: Mind.

Barker, P., Campbell, P., Davidson, B. (eds) (1999) *From the Ashes of Experience: Reflections on Madness, Survival and Growth.* London: Whurr.

Barnham, P. & Hayward, R. (1991) *From the Mental Patient to the Person.* London: Routledge.

Baron, C. (1987) *Asylum to Anarchy.* London: Free Association.

Barret, R.J. (1996). *The Psychiatric Team and the Social Definition of Schizophrenia: An Anthropological Study of Person and Illness.* Cambridge: Cambridge University Press.

Baruch, G. & Treacher, A. (1978) *Psychiatry Observed.* London: Routledge & Kegan Paul.

Basaglia, F. (1987) *Psychiatry Inside Out.* Edited by N. Scheper-Hughes, N. & A.M. Lovell. New York: Columbia University Press.

Baszanger, I., & Dodier, N. (1997) Ethnography: relating the part to the whole. In D. Silverman (ed) *Qualitative Research: theory, method and practice.* London: Sage.

Bean, P. (1980) Compulsory Admissions to Mental Hospitals. Chichester: John Wiley and Sons.

Becker, H.S. (1967) Whose side are we on? *Social Problems*, 14: 239-247.

Becker, H.S. (1970a) Problems of inference and proof in participant observation. In Becker, H. S. (ed) *Sociological Work: method and substance.* Chicago: Aldine, pp. 25-38.

Becker, H.S. (1970b) Fieldwork evidence. In Becker, H. S. (ed) *Sociological Work: method and substance*. Chicago: Aldine, pp. 25-38.

Becker, T., Hulsmann, S., Knudsen, H.C., *et al*. (2002) Provision of services for people with schizophrenia in five European regions. *Social Psychiatry and Psychiatric Epidemiology*, 37: 465-474.

Beech, P. & Norman, I.J. (1995) Patients' perceptions of the quality of psychiatric nursing care: findings from a small-scale descriptive study. Journal of Clinical Nursing, 4: 117-23.

Bennett, N.S., Lidz, C.W., Monahan, J. *et al*. (1993) Inclusion, motivation, and good faith: the morality of coercion in mental health admission. *Behavioural Science and the Law*, 11 (3): 295-306.

Bergmann, J.R. (1992). Veiled morality: notes on discretion in psychiatry. In: P. Drew, J. Heritage. *Talk at Work: Interaction in Institutional Settings*. Cambridge: Cambridge University Press.

Bhugra, D. & Holsgrove, G. (2005). Patient-centred psychiatry, training and assessment: the way forward. *Psychiatric Bulletin*, 29: 49-52.

Bindman, J. (2000) Why is there variation in the use of the Mental Health Act at the local level: a study in eight Trusts. Abstract. Presentation at *'Shaping the New Mental Health Act: Key Messages from the Department of Health Research Programme'*, 6th March 2000, Church House Conference Centre, Westminster. Royal College of Psychiatrists Research Unit, London.

Bissell, P., May, C.R. & Noyce, P.R. (2004). From compliance to concordance: barriers to accomplishing a re-framed model of health care interactions. *Social Science & Medicine,* 58: 851-862.

Bittner, E. (1967) Police discretion in emergency apprehension of mentally ill persons. *Social Problems*, 14: 278-292.

Black, N. & Thompson, E. (1993) Obstacles to medical audit: British doctors speak out. *Social Science and Medicine*, 36: 849-56

Bloor, M. (1997a) Addressing social problems through qualitative research. In D. Silverman (ed) *Qualitative Research: theory, method and practice.* London: Sage.

Bloor, M. (1997b) Techniques and validation in qualitative research: a critical commentary. In G. Miller & R. Dingwall (eds) *Context and Method in Qualitative Research*. London: Sage.

Bloor, M. & McIntosh, J. (1990) Surveillance and concealment: a comparison of techniques of client resistance in therapeutic communities and health visiting. In S. Cunningham-Burley & N. McKeganey (eds) *Readings in Medical Sociology.* London: Routledge.

Borkan, J.M. (1993) Conducting qualitative research in the practice setting. In Bass, M.J. et al (eds) Conducting Qualitative Research in the Practice Setting, pp 69-84, Newbury Park, CA: Sage.

Bowers, L., Jarrett, M., Clark, N. Kiyimba, F. & McFarlane, L. (1999) Absconding: why patients leave. *Journal of Psychiatric and Mental Health Nursing*, 6: 199-205.

Bowers, L., Jarrett, M., Clark, N. Kiyimba, F. & McFarlane, L. (1999a) Absconding: why patients leave. *Journal of Psychiatric and Mental Health Nursing*, 6: 199-205.

Bowers, L., Jarrett, M., Clark, N. Kiyimba, F. & McFarlane, L. (1999b) Absconding: how and when patients leave. *Journal of Psychiatric and Mental Health Nursing*, 6: 207-211.

Bowers, L., Crowhurst, N., Alexander J., *et al.* (2002) Safety and security policies on psychiatric acute admission wards: results from a London-wide survey. *Journal of Psychiatric and Mental Health Nursing,* 9: 427-433.

Bowers, L., Clark, N. & Callaghan, P. (2003) Multidisciplinary reflections on assessment for compulsory admission: the views of approved social workers, general practitioners, ambulance crews, police, community psychiatric nurses and psychiatrists. *British Journal of Social Work*, 33: 961-968.

Bowers, L., Simpson, A. & Alexander J. (2003a) Patient-staff conflict: results of a survey on acute psychiatric wards. *Social Psychiatry and Psychiatric Epidemiology,* 38: 402-408.

Bowers, L., Crowhurst, N., Alexander, J, *et al*. (2003b) Psychiatric nurses' views on criteria for psychiatric intensive care: acute and intensive care compared. *International Journal of Nursing Studies,* 40:145-152.

Bowers, L., Chaplin, R., Quirk, A. & Lelliott, P. (2007) A conceptual model of the aims and functions of acute inpatient psychiatry. *Journal of Mental Health* (in press).

Boyd, E. & Heritage, J. (2007) Taking the history: questioning during comprehensive history taking. In J. Heritage, D.W. Maynard (eds). *Communication in Medical Care*, Cambridge: Cambridge University Press.

Bradley, C.P. (1992a) Factors which influence the decision whether or not to prescribe: the dilemma facing general practitioners. *British Journal of General Practice*, 42: 454-458.

Bradley, C.P. (1992b) Uncomfortable prescribing decisions: a critical incident study. *British Medical Journal*, 304: 294-296.

Brewer, J.D. (2000) *Ethnography*. Buckingham: Open University Press.

Britten, N. & Ukoumunne, O. (1997) The influence of patients' hopes of receiving a prescription on doctors' perceptions and the decision to prescribe: a questionnaire survey. *British Medical Journal*, 315: 1506-1510.

Britten, N., Stevenson, F.A., Barry, C.A. *et al.* (2000) Misunderstandings in prescribing decisions in general practice. *British Medical Journal*, 320: 484-488.

Britten, N., Stevenson, F.A., Gafaranga, J. (2004) The expression of aversion to medicines in general practice consultations. *Social Science and Medicine*, 320: 484-488.

Britten, N., Stevenson, F., Gafaranga, J., Barry, C. & Bradley, C. (2005) The expression of aversion to medicines in general practice consultations. *Social Science and Medicine*, 59 (7): 1495-1503.

Bulmer, M. (1982) *Social Research Ethics: the merits and demerits of participant observation.* London: Macmillan.

Buntwal, N., Hare, J. & King, M. (1999) The struck-off mystery. *Journal of the Royal Society of Medicine*, 91 (9): 443-45.

Burns, T., Priebe, S. (1999). Mental health care failure in England. *British Journal of Psychiatry*, 174: 191-192.

Busfield, J. (2005) Mental health problems, psychotropic drug technologies and risk. *Health, Risk & Society*, 6 (4): 361-375.

Butler, C.C., Rollnick, S., Pill, R., Maggs-Rapport, F. & Stott, N. (1998) Understanding the culture of prescribing: qualitative study of general practitioners' and patients' perceptions of antibiotics for sore throats. *British Medical Journal*, 317: 637-642.

Cahill, S.E. (1998) Toward a Sociology of the Person. *Sociological Theory*, 16 (2): 131-148.

Carpenter, M. (2000) 'It's a small world': mental health policy under welfare capitalism since 1945. *Sociology of Health and Illness*, 22 (5): 621-639.

Castel, R. (1991) From dangerousness to risk. In G. Burchell, C. Gordon & P. Miller (eds). *The Foucault Effect.* Hemel Hempstead: Harvester Wheatsheaf, pp. 281-298.

Castel, R., Castel, F. & Lovell, A. (1982) *The Psychiatric Society*. New York: Columbia University Press.

Caudhill, W. (1958) *The Psychiatric Hospital as a Small Society*. London: Harvard University Press.

Chaplin, R. & Kent, A. (1998) Informing patients about tardive dyskinesia: controlled trial of patient education. *British Journal of Psychiatry*, 172: 78-81.

Chamberlain, J. (2005) Confessions of a non-compliant patient. *Newsletter Articles by NEC Staff and Affiliates*. Electronic version: www.power2u.org/bobby/recovery/confessions.html.

Chaplin, R. & Kent, A. (1998). Informing patients about tardive dyskinesia: controlled trial of patient education. *British Journal of Psychiatry*, 172: 78-81.

Charles, C., Gafni, A. & Whelan, T. (1997). Shared-decision-making in the medical ancounter: what does it mean? (or it takes at least two to tango). *Social Science & Medicine,* 44: 681-692

Charmaz, K. (1990) Discovering chronic illness: using grounded theory. Social Science and Medicine, 30: 1161-72.

Clarke J. Mad, bad and dangerous: the media and mental illness. *Mental Health Practice* 2004, 7 (10): 16-19.

Cohen, S. (1985) *Visions of Social Control: crime punishment and classification.* Cambridge: Polity.

Cohen S., & Taylor, L. (1972) *Psychological Survival: The experience of long-term imprisonment.* Harmondsworth: Penguin.

Collins, S., Drew, P., Watt, I. & Entwistle, V. (2005) 'Unilateral' and 'bilateral' practitioner approaches in decision-making about treatment. *Social Science and Medicine*, 61: 2611-2627.

Commander, M., Odell, S. (1998). Admission of the homeless mentally ill in the UK. *Psychiatric Bulletin*, 22: 207-210.

Cope, N. (2000) Drug use in prison: the experience of young offenders. *Drugs-Education Prevention and Policy*, 7 (4): 355-366.

Cormack, D. (1976) Psychiatric Nursing Observed: A Descriptive Study of the Work of the Charge Nurse in Acute Admission Wards of Psychiatric Hospitals. London: Royal College of Nursing.

Cornwall, P.L., Hassanyeh, F. & Horn, C. (1996) High-dose antipsychotic medication: improving clinical practice in a psychiatric (intensive) care unit. *Psychiatric Bulletin*, 20: 676-680.

Coupland, N., Coupland, J., Giles, H. (1991) *Language, Society and the Elderly*. Oxford: Blackwell.

Crabtree, B.J. & Miller, W.L. (1992) *Doing Qualitative Research*. Newbury Park, CA: Sage.

Cruz, M. & Pincus, H.A. (2002). Research on the influence that communication in psychiatric encounters has on treatment. *Psychiatric Services,* 53(10): 1253-1265.

Crosby, C., Barry, M.M. (eds) (1995). *Community Care: Evaluation of the Provision of Mental Health Services.* Aldershot: Avebury.

Cuff, E.C., Sharrock, W.W. & Francis, D.W. (1990) *Perspectives in Sociology*. Third Edition. London: Routledge.

Daly, J. (1989) Innocent murmurs: echocardiography and the diagnosis of cardiac normality. *Sociology of Health and Illness*, 11: 99-116.

Davidson, J. (1984) Subsequent versions of invitations, offers, requests and proposals dealing with potential or actual rejection. In, Atkinson S & Heritage (1984) *Structures of Social Action: Studies in conversation analysis*. Cambridge: University Press.

Davies, S., Thornicroft, G., Leese, M., *et al.* (1996) Ethic differences in risk of compulsory psychiatric admission among representative cases of psychosis in London. British Medical Journal, 312: 533-37.

Davis, A. (1996) Risk work and mental health. In H. Kemshall & J. Pritchard (eds) *Good Practice in Risk Assessment and Risk Management.* London: Jessica Kingsley.

Day, J.C. & Bentall, R. (1996) Neuroleptic medication and psychosocial treatment of psychotic symptoms: some neglected issues. In G. Haddock & P.D. Slade (eds) *Cognitive-behavioural interventions with psychotic disorders* (pp.235-264). Hove, New York: Brunner-Routledge.

Deacon, M. (2003) Caring for people in the 'virtual ward': the practical ramifications for acute nursing work. *Journal of Psychiatric and Mental Health Nursing*, 10: 465-471.

Department of Health (1989). *Caring for People: Community Care in the Next Decade and Beyond.* London: HMSO.

Department of Health & Welsh Office (1999) Code of Practice: Mental Health Act 1983. Published March 1999, pursuant to Section 118 of the Act. London: The Stationery Office.

Department of Health (2000a) *Shaping the New Mental Health Act: key messages from the Department of Health research programme.* London: Department of Health.

Department of Health (2000b) *Safety, Privacy and Dignity in Mental Health Units.* London: Department of Health.

Department of Health. (2001) *The Expert Patient: a new approach to chronic disease management in the 21st Century.* London: HMSO. PDF available online at http://www.dh.gov.uk.

Dimsdale, J.E., Klerman. G., Shershow, J.C. (1979). Goals in treatment between patients and staff. *Social Psychiatry*, 14, 1-4.

Dingwall, R. (1997) Accounts, interviews and observations. In G. Miller & R. Dingwall (eds) *Context and Method in Qualitative Research*. London: Sage.

Dolan, M. & Kirwan, H. (2001) Survey of staff perceptions of illegal drug use among patients in a medium secure unit. *Psychiatric Bulletin*, 25: 14-17.

Drew, P., Chatwin, J. & Collins, S. (2001) Conversation analysis: a method for research into interactions between patients and health-care professionals. *Health Expectations*, 4: 58-70.

Drew P & Heritage J. (1992) Analyzing talk at work: an introduction. In Drew P & Heritage J. (eds) *Talk at Work: Interaction in institutional settings*. Cambridge: Cambridge University Press.

Emerson, R.M. (1989) Tenabilities and troubles: the construction of accommodative relations by psychiatric emergency teams. *Perspectives on Social Problems*, 1: 215-237.

Emerson, R.M. & Pollner, M. (1975) Dirty work designations: their features and consequences in a psychiatric setting. *Social Problems*, 23: 243-55.

Emerson, R.M. & Pollner, M. (1978) Policies and practices of psychiatric case selection. *Sociology of Work and Occupations*, 5 (1): 75-96.

Estroff S. (1981) *Making it Crazy: An Ethnography of Psychiatric Clients in an American Community*. London: University of California Press.

Fakhoury, W. & Priebe, S. (2002) The process of deinstitutionalization: an international overview. *Current Opinion in Psychiatry*, 15:187-192.

Fisher, W.A. (1994) Restraint and seclusion: a review of the literature. *American Journal of Psychiatry*, 151: 1584-1591.

Fitzpatrick, R., & Hopkins, A. (1993) Patient satisfaction in relation to clinical care: a neglected consideration. In Fitzpatrick, R. & Hopkins, A. (eds) *Measurement of Patients' Satisfaction with their Care*, pp 77-86, London: Royal College of Physicians of London.

Fleischmann, H. (2003) What expectations do mental disordered people have about the treatment in a psychiatric hospital? *Psychiatric Praxis*, 30 (Supplement 2): S136-S139.

Ford, R., Durcan, G., Warner, L. *et al.* (1998) One day survey by the Mental Health Act Commission of acute adult psychiatrist in-patient wards in England and Wales. *British Medical Journal*, 317: 1279-1283.

Forrester-Jones, R.V.E., Grant, G. (1997). *Resettlement from Large Psychaitric Hospital to Small Community Residence.* Aldershot: Avebury.

Foucault, M. (1967) *Madness and Civilisation: A History of Insanity in the Age of Reason*. London: Routledge.

Foucault, M. (1977) *Discipline and Punish: the birth of the prison.* London: Penguin.

Foucault, M. (1981) *The History of Sexuality: an introduction*. London: Penguin.

Foucault, M. (1982) The subject and power. In Dreyfus, H. & Rabinow, P. (eds) *Michel Foucault: beyond structuralism and hermeneutics.* Chicago: University of Chicago Press.

Foulks, E.F., Persons, J.B. & Merkel, R.L. (1986) The effect of patients' beliefs about their illnesses and compliance in psychotherapy. *American Journal of Psychiatry*, 143, 340-344.

Freidson, E. (1983) Celebrating Erving Goffman, 1983. *Contemporary Sociology*, 12 (4): 359-362.

Fulop, N., Koffman, J. & Carson, S. (1994) One-day census of acute, low-level secure and elderly mentally ill acute and assessment psychiatric patients across North and South Thames Regions. Report. KCW Health Commissioning Agency.

Giddens, A. (1988) Goffman as a systematic social theorist. In Drew, P. & Wootton, A. (eds) *Erving Goffman: exploring the interaction order.* Oxford: Polity.

Gilbody, S. & House, A. (1999) Variations in psychiatric practice: neither unacceptable nor unavoidable, only under-researched. *British Journal of Psychiatry*, 175: 303-305.

Glaser, B., & Strauss, A. (1967) *The Discovery of Grounded Theory.* Chicago: Aldine.

Goffman, E. (1959) *The Presentation of Self in Everyday Life.* London: Penguin.

Goffman, E. (1961) Asylums: Essays on the Social Situation of Mental Patients and Other Inmates. London: Penguin.

Goffman, E. (1969) The insanity of place. *Psychiatry Journal of Interpersonal Relations*, 32 (4): 357-386. (Reprinted in Davey, B. *et al. Health and Disease: A Reader.* Milton Keynes: Open University Press.

Goffman, E. (1976) *Frame Analysis: An Essay on the Organization of Experience.* Boston: Northeastern University Press.

Goffman, E. (1981) *Forms of Talk.* Oxford: Basil Blackwell.

Goffman, E. (1983) The Interaction Order. American Sociological Association, 1982 Presidential Address. *American Sociological Review*, 48: 1-17.

Goffman, E. (1989) On fieldwork. Transcribed and edited by L.H. Lofland. *Journal of Contemporary Ethnography*, 18 (2): 123-132.

Gold, R. (1958) Roles in sociological field observation. *Social Forces*, 36: 217-23.

Goldbeck, R., Tomlinson, S. & Bouch, J. (1999) Patients' knowledge and views of their depot neuroleptic medication. *Psychiatric Bulletin,* 23: 467-470.

Goldie, N. (1976) Psychiatry and the medical mandate. In Wadsworth, M. & Robinson, D. (eds) *Studies in Everyday Medical Life*, pp. 177-193, London: Martin Robertson & Co.

Goodwin, C. & Heritage, J. (1990) Conversation analysis. *Annual Review of Anthropology*, 19: 283-307.

Gordon, D., Alexander, D.A., Dietzan, J. (1979). The psychiatric patient: a voice to be heard. *British Journal of Psychiatry*, 135: 115-21.

Greer, A.N. (1988) The state of the art versus the state of science: the diffusion of new medical technologies into practice. *International Journal of Technology Assessment in Health Care*, 4: 5-26.

Gwyn, R. & Elwyn, G. (1999) When is a shared decision not (quite) a shared decision? Negotiating preferences in a general practice encounter. *Social Science and Medicine*, 49: 437-447.

Hacking, I. (2002a) *Historical Ontology*. London: Harvard.

Hacking, I. (2002b) *Mad Travelers: reflections on the reality of transient mental illness.* London: Harvard.

Hacking, I. (2005) Between Michel Foucault and Erving Goffman: between discourse in the abstract and face-to-face interaction. *Economy and Society*, 33 (3): 277–302.

Hall, A.D., Puri, A.K., Stewart, T. & Graheme, P.S. (1995) Doctors holding power in practice - section 5 (2) of the Mental Health Act 1983. Medicine, Science and the Law, 35: 231-36.

Ham, C. (1999) *Health Policy in Britain: The Politics and Organisation of the National Health Service.* Fourth Edition. London: MacMillan

Hamilton, B. (2007) Open doors: invitations to self-govern in acute psychiatric units. Draft abstract for presentation at *World Psychiatry International Congress 2007.*

Hamilton, B. & Manias, E. (2006) 'She's manipulative and he's right off': a critical analysis of psychiatric nurses' oral and written language in the acute inpatient setting. *International Journal of Mental Health Nursing,* 15: 84-92.

Hammersley, M. (1992) *What's Wrong with Ethnography: methodological explorations.* London: Routledge.

Hammersley, M. & Atkinson, P. (1982) *Ethnography: principles in practice*. London: Tavistock.

Haney, C.A. & Michielute, R. (1968) Selective factors operating in the adjudication of incompetency. *Journal of Health and Social Behaviour*, 9: 233-242.

Harre, R. (1984) *Personal Being*. Cambridge, MA: Harvard.

Harrington, M., Lelliott, P., Paton C. *et al.* (2002a) Variation between services in the prescribing of high doses and polypharmacy of antipsychotic drugs to in-patients. *Psychiatric Bulletin*, (in press).

Harrington, M., Lelliott, P., Paton, C. *et al.*(2002b) The results of a multi-centre audit of the prescribing of antipsychotic medication for in-patients in the United Kingdom. *Psychiatric Bulletin*, (in press).

Harrison, J., Barrow, S. & Creed, F. (1995) Social deprivation and psychiatric admission rates among different diagnostic groups. *British Journal of Psychiatry*, 167: 456-462.

Healy, D. (2002) *Psychiatric Drugs Explained*. 3rd Edition. London: Churchill Livingstone.

Health Select Committee. (1998). *Public Expenditure Inquiry.* London: The Stationary Office.

Hem, M.H. & Heggen, K. (2003) Being professional and being human: one nurse's relationship with a psychiatric patient. *Journal of Advanced Nursing*, 43:101-108.

Henriksen, K. & Hansen, E.H. (2004). The threatened self: general practitioners' self-perception in relation to prescribing medicine. *Social Science and Medicine,* 59: 47-55.

Heritage, J. (1984) *Garfinkel and Ethnomethodology*. Cambridge: Polity Press.

Heritage, J. (1997) Conversation analysis and institutional talk. In, Silverman, D. (ed) *Qualitative Research: Theory, method and practice*. London: Sage.

Heritage, J. & Sefi, S. (1992) Dilemmas of advice: aspects of the delivery and reception of advice in interactions between health visitors and first-time mothers. In P. Drew & J. Heritage (eds) *Talk at Work: Interaction in Institutional Settings*. Cambridge: Cambridge University Press.

Heritage, J. & Maynard, D.W. (2007) Introduction: analyzing interaction between doctors and patients in primary care encounters. In J. Heritage, D.W. Maynard (eds). *Communication in Medical Care*, Cambridge: Cambridge University Press.

Heritage, J. & Maynard, D.W. (2007) Introduction: analyzing interaction between doctors and patients in primary care encounters. In J. Heritage, D.W. Maynard (eds). *Communication in Medical Care*, Cambridge: Cambridge University Press.

Higgins, R., Hurst, K. & Wistow, G. (1999) *Psychiatric Nursing Revisited: The Care Provided for Acute Psychiatric Patients*. London: Whurr.

Hillam, J. & Evans, C. (1996) Neuroleptic drug use in psychiatric intensive therapy units: problems with complying with the consensus statement. *Psychiatric Bulletin*, 20: 82-84.

Hinsliff, G. (2003) Crack 'creating fear on mental wards'. *The Observer*, November 16th, p.7

Hoge, S.K., Lidz, C., Mulvery, E. *et al.* (1993) Patient, family and staff perceptions of coercion in mental hospital admission: an exploratory study. *Behavioural Sciences and the Law*, 93 (11): 281-293.

Holloway, J. (1999) The other world. In, Barker, P., Campbell, P., Davidson, B. (eds) (1999) *From the Ashes of Experience: Reflections on Madness, Survival and Growth.* London: Whurr.

Holstein, J.A. (1993) *Court-Ordered Insanity: Interpretive practice and involuntary commitment.* New York: Aldine de Gruyter.

Hughes, E.C.(1971) *The Sociological Eye: Selected Papers*. New York: Aldine.

Hummelvoll, J.K. & Severinsson, I.E. (2001a) Imperative ideals and the strenuous reality: focusing on acute psychiatry. *Journal of Psychiatric and Mental Health Nursing*, 8: 17-24.

Hummelvoll, J.K. & Severinsson, E. (2001b) Coping with everyday reality: mental health professionals' reflections on the care provided in an acute psychiatric ward. *Australian and New Zealand Journal of Mental Health Nursing*, 10: 156-166.

Hummelvoll, J.K. & Severinsson, E. (2002) Nursing staffs' perceptions of persons suffering from mania in acute psychiatric care. *Journal of Advanced Nursing*, 38:416-424.

Hutchby I & Wooffitt R. (1998) *Conversation Analysis: Principles, Practices & Applications*. Cambridge: Polity.

Hutchby I. (2002) Resisting the incitement to talk in child counselling: aspects of the utterance "I don't know". *Discourse Studies*, 4 (2): 147-168.

Hutchby I. (2005) Active listening: formulations and the elicitation of feelings-talk in child counselling. *Research on Language and Social Interaction*, 38 (3): 303-329.

Huxley, P. & Kerfoot, M. (1993) Variation in requests to social services departments for assessment for compulsory admission. *Social Psychiatry and Psychiatric Epidemiology*, 28: 71-76.

Johansson, I.M. & Lundman, B. (2002) Patients' experiences of involuntary psychiatric care: good opportunities and great losses. *Journal of Psychiatric and Mental Health Nursing*, 9: 639-647.

Jones, J., Ward, M., Wellman, N., *et al* (2000) Psychiatric inpatients' experience of nursing observation. *Journal of Psychiatric Nursing*, 38 (12): 10-20.

Jones, R. (1999) *The Mental Health Act Manual*. 6th Edition. London: Sweet and Maxwell.

Kaplan, R.M. (2004) Shared medical decision making: a new tool for preventive medicine. *American Journal of Preventive Medicine*, 26 (1): 81-83.

Katsakou, C. & Priebe, S. (2006) Outcomes of involuntary hospital admission – a review. Acta Psychiatrica Scandinavica, 114 (4): 232–241.

Kesey, K. (1962). *One Flew Over the Cuckoo's Nest.* New York: Viking.

Kumar, S., Little, P. & Britten N. (2003). Why do general practitioners prescribe antibiotics for sore throat? Grounded theory interview study. *British Medical Journal,* 326: 138-143.

Lacro, J.P., Dunn, L.B., Dolder, C.R., Leckband, S.G. & Jeste, D.V. (2002). Prevalence of and risk factors for medication nonadherence in patients with schizophrenia: a comprehensive review of recent literature. *Journal of Clinical Psychiatry,* 63(1): 892-909.

Lamb, H.R. & Bachrach, L.L. (2001) Some perspectives on deinstitutionalization. *Psychiatric Services*, 52: 1039-1045.

Lareau, A. (1996) Common problems in fieldwork: a personal essay. In A. Lareau & J. Shultz (eds) *Journeys Through Ethography: realistic accounts of fieldwork*. Oxford: Westview.

Lawson, A. (1966) *The Recognition of Mental Illness in London: A Study of the Social Processes Determining Compulsory Admission to an Observation Unit in a London Hospital*. London: Oxford University Press.

Lazarus, J.A. & Sharfstein, S.S. (eds) (1998) *New Roles for Psychiatrists in Organized Systems of Care.* Washington D.C.: American Psychiatric Press.

Leavey, G., King, M., Cole, E., *et al*. (1997) First-onset psychotic illness: patients' and relatives' satisfaction with services. *British Journal of Psychiatry,* 170: 53-57.

Lelliott, P. (1996) Meeting the accommodation needs of the most severely mentally ill. *Journal of Interprofessional Care*, 10 (3): 241-247.

Lelliott, P., Audini, B. & Darroch, N. (1995) Resolving London's bed crisis: there might be a way, is there the will? Editorial. *Psychiatric Bulletin*, 19: 273-275.

Lelliott, P., Audini, B., Johnson, S. & Guite, H. (1997) London in the context of mental health policy. In Johnson S *et al* (eds) *London's Mental Health: The Report to the King's Fund London Commission.* London: King's Fund.

Lelliott, P. & Quirk, A. (2004) What is life like on acute psychiatric wards? *Current Opinion in Psychiatry*, 17: 297-301.

Lelliott, P. & Wing, J. (1994) A national audit of new long-stay psychiatric patients II: impact on services. *British Journal of Psychiatry*, 165: 170-178.

Lelliott, P., Paton, C., Harrington, M. *et al.* (2002) Antipsychotic drugs prescribed to in-patients: the influence of patient variables on polypharmacy and dose. *Psychiatric Bulletin*, (in press).

Levinson, D.J. & Gallagher, E.B. (1964) *Patienthood in the Mental Hospital.* Houghton-Muffin.

Levinson, S.C. (1983) *Pragmatics*. Cambridge: University Press.

Leyser, O. (2003) The body as a resource: doing masculinity in a mental hospital. *Journal of Contemporary Ethnography*, 32 (3): 336-59.

Lidz, C.W. & Hoge, S.K. (1993) Coercion: theoretical and empirical understanding. *Behavioural Science and the Law*, 11 (3): 237-238.

Lin, L.S. (1968) The mental hospital from the patient perspective. *Psychiatry*, 31: 213-23.

Lilly, R., Quirk, A., Rhodes, T. & Stimson, G.V. (1999) Juggling multiple roles: staff and client perceptions of keyworker roles and constraints on delivering counseling and support services in methadone treatment. *Addiction Research*, 7 (4): 267-289.

Lilly, R., Quirk, A., Rhodes, T. & Stimson, G.V. (2000) Sociality in methadone treatment: understanding methadone treatment and service delivery as a social process. *Drugs: Education, Prevention and Policy*, 7 (2): 163-178.

Lyall, M. & Tiller, J. (2001) Concordance or collusion. *Psychiatric Bulletin,* 25: 33.

Marcus, G.E. (1998) *Ethnography Through Thick and Thin.* Chichester: Princeton.

Marder, S.R. (2003). Overview of partial compliance. *Journal of Clinical Psychiatry,* 64, 3-9.

Mays, N., & Pope, C. (1996) *Qualitative Research in Health Care.* London: BMJ Publishing.

McCabe, R., Heath, C., Burns, T. & Priebe, S. (2002) Engagement of patients with psychosis in the consultation. *British Medical Journal*, 325: 1148-1151.

McCourt Perring, C. (1993). *The Experience of Psychiatric Hospital Closure: An Anthropological Study*. Aldershot: Avebury.

McDonagh, M.S., Smith, D.H. & Goddard, M. (2000) Measuring appropriate use of acute beds: a systematic review of methods and results. *Health Policy*, 53: 157-184.

McHugh, P. (1970) A commonsense conception of deviance. In, J. Douglas (ed.) *Deviance and Respectability: the social construction of moral meanings.* New York: Basic Books.

McGeorge, M., Lelliott, P. (2000). *Managing Violence in Psychiatric Wards: Preliminary Findings of a Multi-Centre Audit.* Report. London: Royal College of Psychiatrists' Research Unit.

McIntyre, K., Farrell, M., David, A.S. (1989). What do psychiatric patients really want? *British Medical Journal*, 298: 159-60.

McKorkell, J.A. (1998) Going to the crackhouse: critical space as a form of resistance in total institutions and everyday life. *Symbolic Interaction, 21* (3): 227-252.

McPherson, K. (1990) Why do variations occur? In T.F. Anderson & G. Mooney (Eds.), *The Challenges of Medical Practice Variations* (pp.16-35). London: MacMillan.

Mead, N. & Bower, P. (2002) Patient-centred consultations and outcomes in primary care: a review of the literature. *Patient Education and Counselling,* 48: 51-61.

Mehan, H. (1990) Oracular reasoning in a psychiatric exam: the resolution of conflict in language. In A.D. Grimshaw (ed) *Conflict Talk: Sociolinguistic investigations of arguments in conversations*. Cambridge: Cambridge University Press.

Mellesdal, L. (2003) Aggression on a psychiatric acute ward: a three-year prospective study. *Psychological Report*, 92: 1229-1248.

Mental Health Act Commission. (2003) *Placed Amongst Strangers.* TSO: London, 2003.

Miller, D. & Schwartz, M. (1966) Observations of commitments to a state mental hospital. *Social Problems*, 14: 26-35.

Miller G. (1997) Building bridges: The possibility of analytic dialogue between ethnography, conversation analysis and Foucault. In, Silverman, D. (ed) *Qualitative Research: Theory, method and practice*. London: Sage.

Mills, C.W. (1959) *The Sociological Imagination*. Oxford: Oxford University Press.

MILMIS Project Group (1995) Monitoring inner London mental illness services. Psychiatric Bulletin, 19: 276-280.

Mind (2005) *Ward Watch: Mind's report on hospital conditions for mental health patients.* Electronic version available from www.mind.org.uk.

Morgan, D.L. (1992) Doctor-caregiver relationships: an exploration using focus groups. In Crabtree, B.J. & Miller, W.L. (eds) Doing Qualitative Research, pp. 205-227, Newbury Park, CA: Sage.

Morrall, P.A. (1999) Social exclusion and madness. The complicity of psychiatric medicine and nursing. In M. Purdy & D. Banks (eds). *Health and Exclusion*. London: Routledge.

Morrall, P., Hazelton M. (2000) Architecture signifying social control: the restoration of asylumdon in mental health care? *Australian and New Zealand Journal of Mental Health Nursing*, 9: 89-96.

Muijen, M. (1999) Acute hospital care: ineffective, inefficient and poorly organised. Editorial. *Psychiatric Bulletin*, 23: 257-259.

NACRO Mental Health Advisory Committee. (1995) *The Resettlement of Mentally Disturbed Offenders.* London: NACRO.

NACRO Policy Committee on Homelessness and Crime. (1993) *Evidence of the Links Between Homelessness, Crime and the Criminal Justice System*. London: NACRO.

National Health Service. (1999). *National Service Framework for Mental Health: Modern Standards and Service Models*. National Health Service. London: HMSO.

National Schizophrenia Fellowship (2000) *A Question of Choice*. London: NSF.

Nettleton, S. (1995) *The Sociology of Health and Illness.* Cambridge: Polity.

Nijman, H., Merkelbach, H., Evers, C., *et al*. (2002) Prediction of aggression on a locked psychiatric admissions ward. *Acta Psychiatria Scandanavia*, 105: 390-395.

NSCSHA. (2003) *Independent Inquiry into the Death of David Bennett*. Cambridge: Norfolk, Suffolk & Cambridgeshire Strategic Health Authority.

O'Brien, L. & Cole, R. (2003) Close-observation areas in acute psychiatric units: a literature review. *International Journal of Mental Health Nursing*, 12: 165-176.

O'Brien, A.J. & Godling, C.G. (2003) Coercion in mental healthcare: the principle of least coercive care. *Journal of Psychiatric and Mental Health Nursing*, 10 (2): 167-173.

Olofsson, B. & Norberg, A. (2001) Experiences of coercion in psychiatric care as narrated by patients, nurses and physicians. *Journal of Advanced Nursing*, 33(1): 89-97.

Olusina, K.O., Oheari, J.U. & Olatawura, M.O. (2002) Patient and staff satisfaction with the quality in in-patient psychiatric care in a Nigerian general hospital. *Social Psychiatry and Psychiatric Epidemiology*, 37: 283-288.

Palmer, D. (2000) Identifying delusional discourse: issues of rationality, reality and power. *Sociology of Health and Illness*, 22 (5): 661-678.

Peay, J., Eastman, N. & Roberts, C. (2000) Attitudes, knowledge and decision processes of professionals operating the Mental Health Act 1983. Abstract. Presentation at *'Shaping the New Mental Health Act: Key Messages from the Department of Health Research Programme'*, 6th March 2000, Church House Conference Centre, Westminster. Royal College of Psychiatrists Research Unit, London.

Peckover, S. (2002) Supporting and policing mothers: an analysis of the disciplinary practices of health visiting. *Journal of Advanced Nursing,* 38 (4): 369-377.

Perakyla, A. (1989) Appealing to the 'experience' of the patient in the care of the dying. *Sociology of Health and Illness*, 11 (2): 118-134.

Perakyla, A. (2004) Two traditions of interaction research. *British Journal of Social Psychology*, 43: 1-20.

Phillips, P., & Johnson, S. (2003) Drug and alcohol misuse among in-patients with psychotic illnesses in three inner-London psychiatric units. *Psychiatric Bulletin*, 27: 217-220.

Pilgrim, D. (1990). Competing histories of madness: some implications for modern psychiatry. In R.P. Bentall (ed) *Reconstructing Schizophrenia.* pp. 211-233. London: Routledge.

Pilgrim, D. & Rogers, A. (1999) *A Sociology of Mental Health and Illness.* 2nd Edition. Buckingham: Open University Press.

Porter, R. (1990) Foucault's Great Confinement. *History of the Human Sciences*, 3: 51.

Porter, R. (2002) *Madness: A Brief History.* Oxford: Oxford University Press.

Potter, J. (1997). Discourse analysis as a way of analysing naturally occurring talk. In D. Silverman. *Qualitative Research: Theory, Method and Practice.* London: Sage.

Priebe, S. & Turner, T. (2003) Reinstitutionalisation in mental health care. Editorial. *British Medical Journal*, 326: 175-176.

Prior, L. (1991) Community versus hospital care: the crisis in psychiatric provision. *Social Science and Medicine*, 32 (4): 483-489.

Prior, L. (1993) *The Social Organization of Mental Illness*. London and Newbury Park; CA.

Prior, P.M. (1995) Surviving psychiatric institutionalisation: a case study. *Sociology of Health and Illness,* 17 (5): 651-657.

Quirk, A. (1997) *How are Methadone Decisions Made?: combining conversation analytic and ethnographic approaches.* Unpublished thesis for MA in Sociology (with Special Reference to Qualitative Research). Goldsmiths' College, London.

Quirk, A. & Lelliott P. (2001) What do we know about life on acute psychiatric wards in the UK?: a review of the research evidence. *Social Science and Medicine,* 53 (12): 1-10.

Quirk, A. & Lelliott, P. (2004) Users' experiences of inpatient services. P Campling, S Davies & G Farquharson (eds) *From Toxic Institutions to Therapeutic Environments.* London: Gaskell.

Quirk, A. Rhodes, T. & Stimson, G,V. (1998) 'Unsafe protected sex': qualitative insights on measures of sexual risk. *AIDS Care*, 10 (1): 105-114.

Quirk, A., Lelliott, P., Audini, B., Buston, K. (2000). *Performing the Act: A Qualitative Study of the Process of Mental Health Act Assessments.* Final report to the Department of Health. London: The Royal College of Psychiatrist' Research Unit.

Quirk, A., Lilly, R., Rhodes, T. & Stimson, G.V. (2003a) Negotiating a script: the dynamics of staff/client relationships. In, G. Tober & J. Strang (eds) *Methadone Matters: Evolving UK Practice of Community Methadone Treatment of Opiate Addiction.* Harwood Academic Press.

Quirk, A., Lelliott, P., Audini, B. & Buston, K. (2003b) Non-clinical and extra-legal influences on decisions about compulsory admission to psychiatric hospital. *Journal of Mental Health*: 12 (2): 119-130.

Quirk, A., Rhodes, T., Lilly, R. & Stimson, G.V. (2004) Negotiating a script: the dynamics of staff/client relationships. In G. Tober & J. Strang (eds) *Methadone Matters: Evolving Community Treatment of Opiate Addiction.* London: Martin Dunitz (Taylor Francis Group)

Quirk, A., Lelliott, P. & Seale, C. (2004) Service users strategies' for managing risk in the volatile environment of an acute psychiatric ward. *Social Science and Medicine*, 59: 2573-2583.

Quirk, A., Lelliott, P. & Seale, C. (2005) Risk management by patients on psychiatric wards in London: an ethnographic study. *Health, Risk & Society*, 7 (1): 85-91.

Quirk, A., Lelliott, P. & Seale, C. (2006) The permeable institution: an ethnographic study of three acute psychiatric wards in London. *Social Science & Medicine*, 63: 2105-2117.

Rabinow, P. (1984) Introduction. In P. Rabinow (ed) *The Foucault Reader*. London: Penguin.

Rain, S.D., Williams, V.F., Robbins, P.C. *et al.* (2003) Perceived coercion at hospital admission and adherence to mental health treatment after discharge. *Psychiatric Services,* 54 (1): 103-105.

Ramon, S. (ed) (1992). *Psychiatric Hospital Closure: Myths and Realities.* London: Chapman Hall.

Rethink (2003) *Just One Per Cent: The experiences of people using mental health services*. Rethink: Kingston upon Thames.

Rethink (2003) *Just One Per Cent: The experiences of people using mental health services*. Rethink: Kingston upon Thames.

Rethink (2006) *Side Effects: mental health service users' experiences of the side effects of anti-psychotic mediciation.* Rethink: Kingston upon Thames.

Rhodes, L.A. (1991). *Emptying Beds: The Work of an Emergency Psychiatric Unit*. Oxford: University of Californian Press.

Rhodes, T. & Quirk, A. (1998) Drug users' sexual relationships and the social organisation of risk: the sexual relationship as a site of risk management. *Social Science and Medicine*, 46 (2): 157-169.

Richards, L. (2002) *Using N6 in Qualitative Research.* Victoria: QSR International.

Riggall, M. (1929) *Reminiscences of a Stay in a Mental Hospital.* London: A.H. Stockwell.

Robinson, J.D. (2001) Closing medical encounters: two physician practices and their implications for the expression of patients' unstated concerns. *Social Science and Medicine*, 53: 639-656.

Rogers, A. (1993) Coercion and "voluntary" admission: an examination of psychiatric patient views. *Behavioural Sciences and the Law*, 93 (11): 259-267.

Rogers, A., Pilgrim, D. (1994). Service users' views of psychiatric nurses. *British Journal of Nursing*, 3 (1): 16-18.

Rogers, A., Day, J.C., Williams, B., Randall, F., Wood, P., Healy, D. & Bentall, R.P. (1998). The meaning and management of neuroleptic medication: a study of patients with a diagnosis of schizophrenia. *Social Science and Medicine,* 47(9): 1313-1323.

Rogers, A. & Pilgrim, D. (2001) *Mental Health Policy in Britain*. Second Edition. Basingstoke: Palgrave.

Rollnick, S., Seale, C., Rees, M. & Butler, C. (2000) Inside the routine general practice consultation: an observational study of consultations for sore throats. *Family Practice*, 18 (5): 506- 510.

Rose, N. (1986) Psychiatry: the discipline of mental health. In, P. Miller & N. Rose. *The Power of Psychiatry*. Cambridge: Polity.

Rose, N. (1998) *Inventing Our Selves.* Cambridge: Cambridge University Press.

Rose, N. (1999) *Governing the Soul.* Second Edition. London: Free Association.

Rose, D. (2001) *Users' Voices: The perspectives of mental health service users on community and hospital care.* London: Sainsbury Centre for Mental Health.

Rosenhan, D.L. (1973) On being sane in insane places. *Science,* 179: 250-258.

Rothbard, A.B. & Kuno, E. (2000) The success of deinstitutionalization: empirical findings from case studies on hospital closures. *International Journal of Law and Psychiatry*, 23: 329-344.

Royal College of Psychiatrists (2004) *Good Psychiatric Practice*. 2nd Edition. CR125. London: Royal College of Psychiatrists.

Royal College of Psychiatrists (2004) *Draft Mental Health Bill: Royal College of Psychiatrists Anxious about Civil Liberties, Ethics, practicality and Effectiveness: Unfair, stigmatising and dangerous.* Press Release, 8-9-2004. Royal College of Psychiatrists, London.

Ryan, C. & Bowers, L. (2005) Coercive manoeuvres in a psychiatric intensive care unit. *Journal of Psychiatric and Mental Health Nursing*, 12: 695-702.

Sacks H. (1992) *Lectures on Conversation: Volumes 1 & 2*. Oxford: Blackwell.

Sacks H, Schegloff EA & Jefferson G. (1974) A simplest systematics for the organization of turn-taking for conversation. *Language*, 50(4): 696-735.

Sainsbury Centre for Mental Health. (1998) *Acute Problems: A Survey of the Quality of Care in Acute Psychiatric Wards.* London: Sainsbury Centre for Mental Health.

Salib, E. & Iparragirre, B. (1998) Detention of in-patients under section 5 (2) of the Mental Health Act. *Medicine, Science and the Law*, 38: 10-16.

Schegloff EA. (1988) Goffman and the analysis of conversation. In Drew P and Wootton A (eds). *Erving Goffman: Exploring the Interaction Order.* Oxford: Polity.

Schutz, A. (1967) *The Phenomenology of the Social World.* Evanston, IL: Northwestern University Press.

Schwartz, R.K., Soumerai, S.B. & Avorn, J. (1989) Physician motivations for non-scientific drug prescribing. *Social Science and Medicine*, 28 (6): 577-582.

Scott, J.C. (1987) *Weapons of the Weak.* London: Yale University Press.

Scull, A. (1993) *The Most Solitary of Afflictions: madness and society in Britain 1700-1900.* London: Yale University Press.

Seale, C. (1999) *The Quality of Qualitative Research.* London: Sage.

Seale, C., Chaplin, R., Lelliott, P. & Quirk, A. (2006) Sharing decisions in consultations involving anti-psychotic medication: a qualitative study of psychiatrists' experiences. *Social Science & Medicine.* 62: 2861-2873.

Sedgewick, P. (1981) *Psychopolitics.* London: Pluto.

Shepherd, G., Beardsmore, A., Moore, C., et al. (1997). Relation between bed use, social deprivation and overall bed availability in acute adult psychiatric units, and alternative residential units. *British Medical Journal*, 314, 262-266.

Sheppard, M. (1990) Mental Health: the role of the Approved Social Worker. Sheffield: Joint Unit for Social Services Research, Sheffield Univesity, in collaboration with Community Care.

Silverman, D. (1981) The child as a social object: Down's Syndrome children in a Paediatric Cardiology Clinic. *Sociology of Health and Illness*, 3: 254-74.

Silverman, D. (1987) *Communication and Medical Practice: social relations in the clinic*. London: Sage.

Silverman, D. (1997) *Discourses of Counselling: HIV counselling as social interaction.* London: Sage.

Silverman, D. (ed) (1997) *Qualitative Research: theory, method and practice.* London: Sage

Silverman, D. (1998) *Harvey Sacks: Social Science and Conversation Analysis.* Cambridge: Polity.

Smart, B. (1989) *Michel Foucault.* London: Routledge.

Smith, J.A., Hughes, I.C.T. & Budd, R.J. (1999) Non-compliance with anti-psychotic medication: users' views on advantages and disadvantages. *Journal of Mental Health*, 8 (3): 287-296.

Smith, S., Henderson, M. (2000) What you don't know won't hurt you: information given to patients about the side-effects of anti-psychotic drugs. *Psychiatric Bulletin*, 24: 172-174.

Stevenson, F.A., Britten, N., Barry, C.A. *et al.* (2002) Perceptions of legitimacy: the influence on medicine taking and prescribing. *Health*, 6 (1): 85-104.

Stimson, G.V. & Webb, B. (1975) *Going to See the Doctor: the consultation process in general practice.* London: Routledge & Kegan Paul.

Strauss, A., Schatzman, L., Bucher, R., *et al.* (1964). *Psychiatric Ideologies and Institutions*. London: Collier-MacMillan.

Strauss, A.L. & Corbin, J. (1990) *Basics of Qualitative Research: grounded theory procedures and techniques.* Newbury Park, CA: Sage.

Strong, P. (1979) *The Ceremonial Order of the Clinic*. London: Routledge.

Sutherland, S. (1977) *Breakdown: A Personal Crisis and a Medical Dilemma.* London: Granada.

Swartz, M.S. Swanson, J.W. & Hannon, M.J. (2003) Does fear of coercion keep people away from mental health treatment? Evidence from a survey of persons with schizophrenia and mental health professionals. *Behavioural Sciences and the Law*, 21 (4): 459-472.

Szasz, T.S. & Hollender, M.H. (1955) A contribution to the philosophy of medicine: the basic models of the doctor-patient relationship. *A.M.A. Archives of Internal Medicine*, 97: 585-592.

Szmukler, G. & Applebaum, P. (2001) Treatment pressures, coercion and compulsion. In G. Thornicroft & G. Szmukler (eds) *Textbook of Community Psychiatry* (pp.529-543). Oxford: Oxford University Press.

Taylor, I. (1992). *Discharged With Care: A Report on Practical Arrangements for People Leaving Psychiatric Hospital and the Prevention of Homelessness.* Edinburgh: Edinburgh University (Mental Health Unit) in collaboration with Scottish Council for Single Homeless.

Ten Have, P. (1999) *Doing Conversation Analysis: A Practical Guide.* London: Sage.

Thomas, S.P., Shattell, M. & Martin, T. (2002) What's therapeutic about the therapeutic milieu? *Archive of Psychiatric Nursing*, 16: 99-107.

Thompson, A., Shaw, M., Harrison, G., *et al* (2004) Patterns of hospital admission for adult psychiatric illness in England. *British Journal of Psychiatry*, 185: 334-341.

Thompson, A.G.H. (2007) The meaning of patient involvement and participation in health care consultations: A taxonomy. *Social Science & Medicine*, 64 (6): 1297-1310

Thornton, J. (ed). (1996). *Out of Sight, Out of Mind.* Castleford: Yorkshire Art Circus.

Towell, D. (1975) Understanding Psychiatric Nursing: A Sociological Study of Modern Psychiatric Nursing Practice. London: Royal College of Nursing.

Tuckett, D., Boulton, M., Olosn, C. & Williams, A. (1985) *Meetings Between Experts*. London: Tavistock.

Vittengl, J.R. (2002) Temporal regularities in physical control at a state psychiatric hospital. *Archive of Psychiatric Nursing,* 16: 80-85.

Wall, S., Churchill, R., Hotopf, M., Buchanan, A., & Wessely, S. (1999*) A Systematic Review of Research Relating to the Mental Health Act (1983).* London: Department of Health.

Ward, M., Gournay, K. & Thornicroft G. *et al.* (1998) *In-patient Mental Health Services in Inner-London.* Report no. 16. London: Royal College of Nursing.

Ward. M.J. (1947) *The Snake Pit*. London: Cassell.

Warren, J. & Beardsmore, A. (1997) Preventing violence on mental health wards. *Nursing Times,* 8 August 1997, 93: 34.

Watts, J. & Priebe, S. (2002) A phenomenological account of users' experiences of assertive community treatment. *Bioethics,* 16 (5): 439-454.

Weijts, W., Houtkoop, H. & Mullen, P. (1993) Talking delicacy: speaking about sexuality during gynaecological consultations. *Sociology of Health and Illness*, 15 (3): 295-314.

Weinstein, R.M. (1994) Goffman's *Asylums* and the Total Institution Model of Mental Hospitals. *Psychiatry,* 57: 348-367.

Weston, W.W. (2001) Informed and shared decision-making: the crux of the patient-centred dilemma. *Canadian Medical Association Journal*, 165: 4.

WHO. (2001) *Atlas: country profiles on mental health resources*. Geneva: World Health Organization.

White, C. (2003) Doctors fail to grasp concept of concordance. *British Medical Journal*, 327: 642.

Wilde, W.A. (1968) Decision-making in a psychiatric screening agency. *Journal of Health and Social Behaviour*, 9: 215-221.

Williams, R. (1988) Understandings Goffman's methods. In Drew, P. & Wootton, A. (eds) *Erving Goffman: exploring the interaction order*. Oxford: Polity.

Williams, R., & Cohen, J. (2000) Substance use and misuse in psychiatric wards. *Psychiatric Bulletin*, 24: 43-46.

Wing, J. (1962) Institutionalism in mental hospitals. *British Journal of Social and Clinical Psychology*, 1: 38-51.

Working Party. (1997) *From Compliance to Concordance: achieving shared goals in medicine taking*. Report of the Working Party. London: Pharmaceutical Society of Great Britain/Merck, Sharp & Dome.

World Health Organization (2003) *Adherence to Long-Term Therapies: evidence for action.* Geneva: World Health Organization.

Wyn R. (2002) Medicate, restrain or seclude? Strategies for dealing with violent and threatening behaviour in a Norwegian university psychiatric hospital. *Scandanavian Journal of the Caring Sciences*, 16: 287-291.

Wynaden, D., Chapman, R., McGowan, S., *et al*. (2002) Through the eye of the beholder: to seclude or not to seclude. *International Journal of Mental Health Nursing,* 11: 260-268.

Vuokila-Oikkonen. P., Janhonen, S., Saarento, O. & Harri, M. (2002) Storytelling of co-operative team meetings in acute psychiatric care. *Journal of Advanced Psychiatric Nursing,* 40: 189-198.